# GREAT

*Mary-Anne Boermans*

# BRITISH

## FORGOTTEN TREASURES FOR MODERN BAKERS

# BAKES

◨ SQUARE PEG

Published by Square Peg 2013

10 9 8 7 6 5 4 3 2 1

Copyright © Square Peg 2013
Text and photography © Mary-Anne Boermans 2013

Extract from *Maskerade* © Terry and Lyn Pratchett, 1995, reproduced by kind permission of
The Orion Publishing Group Ltd, London. Handwritten original manuscripts
courtesy of The Wellcome Library. Hogarth engraving of David Loudon's bun house reproduced
with kind permission of Look and Learn History Picture Gallery. John Roque's 1746 map
and Richard Horwood's 1799 map courtesy of Motco Enterprises Limited www.motco.com.
Richard Hand business card courtesy of The Yale Center for British Art, Paul Mellon Collection.

First published in Great Britain in 2013 by
Square Peg
Random House, 20 Vauxhall Bridge Road,
London SW1V 2SA
*www.vintage-books.co.uk*

Addresses for companies within The Random House Group Limited can be found at:
*www.randomhouse.co.uk/offices.htm*
The Random House Group Limited Reg. No. 954009

A CIP catalogue record for this book is available from the British Library

ISBN 978 0 22 409556 3

Typeset and designed by Anna Green at *www.siulendesign.com*

Printed and bound in India by Replika Press Pvt. Ltd.

# CONTENTS

# FOREWORD

Mary-Anne Boermans remains one of the most original and exceptional bakers I have encountered during my time on *The Great British Bake Off*, and this impeccably researched and fabulously eclectic cookbook, years in the making, is her masterpiece.

Much of our current British culinary obsession appears to be focused on modernity; the latest thing, the shock of the new—be it molecular gastronomy, foraging, seasonality, or nose to tail eating. What Mary Anne's book reminds us, is that there is no such is as a new idea, and that all these fashionable culinary conceits are simply reworkings of those things our forebears considered to be basic, prudent home economics.

What excites me most, however, is the way that Mary Anne's recipes bring British history to life through the prism of the palate. Thanks to her baking, I've been transported from 17th century England to 18th century Wales, 19th century Scotland and beyond. Now it's your turn.

For food historians, for seasoned bakers looking for pastures new (yet old) and for curious novices alike—this is YOUR chance to taste-bud time travel.

Enjoy.

*Sue Perkins*

# PREFACE

I believe that being able to prepare food, whether for yourself or
for others, is such a fundamental skill, it is as important as knowing
how to swim. I also love a bargain—whatever the context (auction,
car boot sale, supermarket)—because getting a bargain means
that I've won! It's a great feeling, and you can win so often in the
kitchen. Food you make yourself is cheaper, better tasting and
better for you than anything made commercially. You can dodge
all the additives and preservatives. Most of all, it is the simplest,
easiest and quickest way to job satisfaction: an architect might wait
a decade before seeing a project constructed, but give me a store-
cupboard and a hot oven and I can have a batch of amazing scones
baked in just over 20 minutes. It can make you feel proud when
others enjoy your food but you can also feel excited just looking at
a batch of baking and thinking 'I made that!'. I also love the sheer
alchemy of baking: mix basic ingredients this way and get cake, vary
them slightly and get pastry. Magic.

I have always had an interest in cooking because I was surrounded
by it as a child. In those days, which are only as far back as the
1970s, meals weren't bought from a shop; they were lovingly
created from scratch at home. In our pantry, the tins for home-
made biscuits and cakes were never empty. I don't remember seeing
either my mother or my grandmother use a recipe book. The need
for self-reliance imposed during the Second World War had, for
them, become habit, and now everything was carried in their heads
and adapted to the ingredients available. I am lucky enough, and
old enough, to have had cookery lessons in school, during which I
learned how to make pastry, cakes and the basics of meal-making.
Later, when I travelled the world and then lived and worked
overseas in Kuwait, Singapore and Australia, I was always interested
in the local foods and eager to try making the dishes for myself.

When I started a family, I was keen for my daughter to eat
traditional, home-made food, unadulterated with artificial additives

and preservatives, and so I turned to the recipes of the past, when preservatives, colouring and flavourings weren't so much a part of daily food. I began picking up old cookery books in charity and second-hand bookshops, others I found on online auction sites. My collection steadily grew and is rapidly heading towards a thousand publications, but with it I discovered a whole variety of baking and cooking ideas that, over the years, had somehow fallen by the culinary wayside: books devoted solely to cakes and biscuits; hundreds of local and regional specialities now long forgotten; traditional pie and tart recipes based on local, fresh ingredients and home-made breads. Then I discovered whole books online, either painstakingly transcribed by hand, or digitally reproduced through scanned images of their pages. The Wellcome Institute Library has made available online its archive of 17th-century manuscript books, containing almost ten thousand handwritten recipes; these have proved an absolute goldmine of fascinating recipes and household tips.

In 2011 I entered the BBC's *Great British Bake Off* and was successful enough to reach the final of the competition. In developing recipes for the weekly challenges, I was able to draw on the many resources I had collected and was surprised and delighted by the sheer number of unusual, quirky and tasty baking recipes I found. This book represents the merest tip of a gigantic baking iceberg or treasure trove to be found in the recipes of the past.

The more I read and experiment, the more I learn from these old, but not forgotten, recipe collections. My approach to each recipe has developed something of a pattern. Out of respect to the original author, I initially bake each recipe, to the best of my ability, exactly as it was written, however many centuries ago that was. Depending on the result, I then tweak it, or not, as required. When I'm happy with the taste, I take a photograph of it. Each recipe in this book has been baked by myself at least three times, and some of them many more times, until they are perfect.

My aim with this book is to highlight and, hopefully revive, the range and surprising sophistication of our baking ancestors. No need for expensive ingredients either: the simplest of cupboard contents can be drawn on to create delicious bakes dating back over 400 years. I also learned a great deal from the recipe writers, many of them anonymous and unknown, including how to test a brick oven is at the right temperature, the size of a Restoration spoonful (25ml) and how to hot ice a fruit cake.

I hope you enjoy discovering these recipes and their stories and also that you find delight in the traditional baking of the British Isles.

# INTRODUCTION

Everyone likes something new and exciting, and I'm no exception. When it comes to food, however, for me, 'old' is the new 'new'. I'm both intrigued and enchanted by the long-forgotten recipes of our past and have long wondered why they have fallen by the culinary wayside.

We've come a long way from open fires in the kitchen and laboriously preparing all of our food by hand. Modern kitchens and gadgets allow us to spend the majority of our leisure time as we would wish, and not, as our grandmothers and their mothers before them did, in the preparation of food.

Looking at the ingredients listed in just a few of the many industrially manufactured and processed foods available in our shops, some might say we've come a bit too far, with preservatives, artificial flavours, colourings and suchlike present in nearly everything we buy. I wanted to see if it were possible to combine the convenience we enjoy in our modern kitchens with the purity of the recipes of the past, and to revive and rescue some of the recipes we used to enjoy baking long ago, to enjoy again today.

These recipes aren't brand new, they're not the latest fashionable item and they don't involve complicated techniques or rare ingredients. They are the kinds of recipes that fill me with confidence because they are tried and tested and have proven their long-term worth. They have been prepared and refined by experience and without reliance on manufactured, pre-packaged, processed or adulterated ingredients.

The selection of recipes to include in this book has proved challenging because there were so many to choose from. They offer a tantalising glimpse into the range of treats that comprise the fantastic baking tradition in the UK. In general, I've scaled them down to make quantities suitable for modern bakers, and adjusted the methods only to take advantage of the equipment we have available to us nowadays.

In the past, we were time-rich but gadget-poor, and so it was deemed perfectly acceptable to have as an instruction in a cake recipe to 'beat the batter for eight hours' because there would have been an unlucky kitchen maid to do just that. Today we might be time-poor, but we are gadget-rich. The average 21st-century kitchen is streets ahead of its Jacobean or Georgian forebear.

But if Jacobean bakers could make biscuits, cakes, pies and meringues with what few gadgets they had, I reasoned that, with all the conveniences of a modern kitchen to hand, to follow a recipe should be fairly straightforward. I have concentrated on a modern approach, making extensive use of gadgets such as the food processor and stand mixer. There are other means of achieving success without resort to gadgetry, such as rubbing in fats for pastry by hand, or whisking egg whites with a balloon whisk, but I wanted to take full advantage of the technology available to us today to emphasise that a good recipe is a good recipe, no matter how old, and that these recipes deserve to be in our repertoire today because they are now so easy, and quick, to make.

In centuries past the work of a baker was tough. As an example, in addition to our time-saving gadgets, nowadays we are spoiled in the quality and easy availability of ingredients. Three hundred years ago, if the recipe called for ground almonds, those almonds first had to be blanched to remove their skins, then dried, chopped, and finally pounded with a mortar and pestle. To stop the almonds releasing their oil during the pounding, they had to be moistened with either rosewater or orange-flower water. It could be a rather tricky juggling act to determine the right quantity of liquid to add, because too little and the almonds would become oily, too much and the liquid would overpower their flavour. Similarly, all flour had to be dried in the oven and then sifted, while sugar came in giant cones that had to be chopped, grated, ground and then sieved to the required quality. Literally hours of work went into the mere preparation of ingredients, let alone the combining of them into recipes.

In this day and age, we all now have the luxury of an oven that can be precisely set to a specific temperature at the turn of a button. The modern oven is an appliance that we take very much for granted. Our baking ancestors had to put in a tremendous amount of time and effort just to get the oven to a suitable temperature, something we now almost absent-mindedly achieve with the flick of a wrist.

Baking ovens used to be built of brick, similar to some pizza ovens in use today, but with a metal door at the front that could be opened or shut to help control the heat. On baking days, the oven would be filled with wood and set alight. As the wood was consumed, more would be added, including, towards the end, large logs. After about two hours, any fire and ashes remaining would be scraped out and the floor of the oven mopped with hot water to both clean it and to introduce a little steam. Then the oven door would be shut and the oven left for 15–20 minutes to 'set' the heat. This was because the fire would not have burned evenly throughout the oven, and so there would be hot spots that might cause the bread and cakes to cook unevenly. Once the heat in the oven had stabilised, the baking could commence, and here is where my admiration for these bakers soars, because baking in a brick oven meant baking in a perpetually cooling oven.

The order of baking had to be rigidly organised and items lined up in serried ranks so that, as the oven cooled, each item went into it at the right time. First to be baked was the white bread, then the coarser wholemeal bread and big fruit cakes. Pies and tarts were next, followed by small cakes and biscuits, bottles of fruit for preserving, and small cakes of fruit paste. Lastly, flour would be dried for the next baking day, alongside any meringue-like confections. Not only did it take great skill to know when the oven was at the right temperature for each item, but baking times had to be calculated by a sand-timer and, in the kitchen, the cook needed to know when to begin making each item so that it was ready to go into the oven at the correct time. Many sponge-cake recipes from before the time of baking powder include instructions for the cake mix to be beaten until it went into the oven. With whipped eggs relied upon to provide aeration, any delay in getting the cake to the oven would cause the cake to sink and become heavy.

Bread was usually baked free-form: that is, without a tin. Other baked goods needed careful preparation, even construction, of equipment. Large cakes were baked in hoops on sheets of paper; wooden hoops were recommended for fruit cakes to prevent the fruit at the edges burning; something we would do well to adopt today. If you didn't have a hoop, you could always sew yourself something from thick paper or cardboard, buttering it well to keep your cake from sticking, just as we do today. Smaller cakes were cooked in shaped tins, sometimes of fancy design, and with these too, little paper 'coffins', as they were called, could be substituted if circumstances dictated. Elsewhere, the gadget-poor baker used what was to hand, such as mussel and scallop shells for cakes and biscuits, and sycamore leaves to slip underneath buns. It was almost taken for granted that there would be no specialised cutters in the kitchen, and so recipes recommend using plates, glasses and even thimbles to achieve the shapes required.

I am in awe of the determination and effort put in: our ancestors must have really wanted some cake! And this is another reason why these old recipes fascinate me: so much preparation and mixing work was needed, in addition to the stoking, heating and monitoring of the oven. Surely all this effort wasn't expended for just mediocre recipes? How good must these recipes be for the mistresses of the house and their bakers to be prepared to go to all this trouble?

In discovering the answer, I have not been disappointed and I have learned a lot as I have baked my way through these recipes. I've learned not to judge a recipe until I have baked it as written. Out of respect for the original author, or the person who faithfully copied out the instructions, I think each recipe deserves its time in the spotlight. After this initial baking, I have occasionally tweaked the method to take advantage of modern utensils and gadgets but, wherever possible, I've tried to stay true to the original flavours.

The rediscovery of the spice mixes has been a delight: their flavours refreshingly different from that of the sometimes overbearing vanilla and chocolate which seem to dominate today's baking. The generous use of dried fruit, especially the underrated currant, has meant that the fruited cakes and loaves require just a token quantity of sugar. Using yeast as a raising agent has produced cakes that are light and delicate, and a far cry from the dark, soggy and dense fruit cakes that haunt my dreams and were the bane of my childhood.

I think we do ourselves a great disservice if we dismiss the recipes of the past. The sheer sophistication of the baking over the last 400 years is something we should celebrate. It is my hope that readers of this book will be inspired by my discoveries to try some of these glories of our baking heritage.

# INGREDIENTS

I love history programmes that include the food of the era, but I am both frustrated and exasperated that the recipes shown invariably have something of a freak show about them. Quite apart from the difficulty in sourcing ingredients, I can't think of any occasion where I might need to roast a calf's head or make a pie of lamb's tails, but it is just these kinds of recipes that seem to populate historical documentaries. It's pretty obvious that knowing the Georgians enjoyed rather nice fruit cakes isn't going to provide much in the way of ghoulish fascination, but for the sake of balance at least, it would be nice if it were mentioned.

This section is intended to reassure readers that the recipes in this book can, for the most part, be made with ordinary ingredients found in cupboards and fridges. The numbers in the brackets show the total number of recipes that use each ingredient. Simply put:

if you have everything on this list, you can make every recipe in this book. Some ingredients are only used once or twice, but I have tried to limit these to items that could be used in other recipes. The ingredients in italics might be less easy to locate, and online sources for them are listed at the end.

### FLOURS
Plain flour (51)
Strong white flour (16)
Cornflour (10)
Self-raising flour (3)
Rice flour (3)
Stone-ground wholemeal flour(1)
Rye flour (1)

### GRAINS
Medium oatmeal (1)
Ground rice (3)
Semolina (1)

### SUGARS
Caster sugar (87)
Icing sugar (17)
Treacle (5)
Dark muscovado sugar (4)
Demerara sugar (3)
Honey (2)
Soft brown sugar (3)
*Nibbed sugar (2)*
Lump sugar (1)

### FATS AND OILS
Butter (71)
Lard (2)
Oil (1)

### RAISING AGENTS
Yeast (21)
Baking powder (13)
Bicarbonate of soda (6)
Cream of tartar (1)

### FRESH FRUIT
Lemons (31)
Oranges (6)
Raspberries (5)
Bramley apples (4)
Damsons (2)
Coconut (2)
Fruit purée (1)
Eating apples (1)
Citrus peels (1)
Seville orange (1)
Redcurrants (1)
Blackcurrants (1)
Gooseberries (1)
Rhubarb (1)

### DRIED FRUIT AND NUTS
Currants (14)
Ground almonds (9)
Raisins (5)
Sultanas (3)
*Slivered almonds (3)*
*Crimson raisins (2)*
Desiccated coconut (2)
Prunes (1)

Dates (1)
Dried cranberries (1)
Flaked almonds (1)
Whole blanched almonds (1)
Chopped almonds (1)
Chopped roasted hazelnuts (1)

EGGS AND DAIRY
Eggs (59)
Egg whites (18)
Milk (26)
Double cream (20)
Cream cheese (3)
*Curd cheese (2)*
Clotted cream (2)
Natural yoghurt (1)

SPICES AND FLAVOURINGS
Salt (24)
Nutmeg (21)
Cinnamon (sticks or ground) (21)
Ground ginger (12)
Ground mace (11)
Cloves (whole or ground) (9)
Caraway seeds (9)
*Rosewater (8)*
*Aniseed (5)*
*Orange-flower water (5)*
Vanilla extract (5)
Allspice (4)
Ground coriander (2)
Saffron (2)
Cocoa powder (1)
White peppercorns (1)
Mixed spice (1)
Ground cardamom (1)

Fresh rosemary (1)
*Dried ginger (1)*

PRESERVES
Apricot glaze (1)
*Candied orange peel (10)*
*Candied citron peel (9)*
*Candied lemon peel (7)*
Apple jelly (2)
Seedless raspberry jam (1)
*Candied apple pieces (1)*

ALCOHOL
Cream sherry (8)
Brandy (4)
Madeira (2)
*Mead (2)*
Sweet dessert wine (1)
Red wine (1)
Beer (1)

EVERYTHING ELSE
Puff pastry (9)
Food colouring (2)
Cake crumbs (2)
Mashed potato (1)
White bread (1)
Breadcrumbs (1)
Gelatine leaves (1)
Apple juice (1)
*Gum tragacanth (1)*
Almond paste (1)
Elderflower cordial (1)

*Nibbed sugar*

This is a compressed form of pearl sugar used mainly in the decoration of baked goods. Available from:

*www.bakerybits.co.uk*
*www.melburyandappleton.co.uk*
*www.amazon.co.uk*

*Slivered almonds*

Matchstick almonds. Fabulous for adding crunch and texture. Available from:

*www.amazon.co.uk*

*Curd cheese*

Available in delicatessens and some supermarkets. Be sure to drain it well before use by wrapping it in muslin and putting a weight on top to squeeze out the excess liquid. Alternatively, you can easily make your own by adding vegetarian rennet to whole milk. Vegetarian rennet is available from:

*www.thehealthbay.com*
*www.vit-shop.co.uk*

*Rosewater and orange-flower water*

Rosewater can be a tricky, because everyone has their own preference: from light and floral to dark and musky. Also, being a little too heavy-handed while baking and it's just a hop and a skip into unpleasant soapiness. For a traditional English flavouring the aroma should be light and delicately floral, as opposed to the more boldly perfumed rosewaters popular in Arabic and Indian cuisines. I've tried many brands over the years, and my current recommendation is Nielsen-Massey Rosewater (available from: *www.amazon.co.uk*); similarly for orange-flower water, although the strength and variation of flavour is less than that of rosewater.

*Aniseed*

An unusual flavouring in 21st-century cookery, aniseed is wonderfully delicate and I thoroughly recommend trying to acquire some if possible. You can substitute with star anise if preferred,

although it is rather more robust, and so you should refrain from using a straight 1:1 substitution. I prefer to bake with whole aniseed. Ground aniseed is insipid and I prefer to bite into a little zing of flavour every now and then.
Available from:
*www.healthysupplies.co.uk*
*www.melburyandappleton.co.uk*
*www.amazon.co.uk*
*www.souschef.co.uk*

*Dried ginger*
Readily available in the high stree, however, I've found the intensity of flavour is quick to fade. I now prefer to buy dried ginger and grind it as and when I require. It looks a little like bark chippings, but the flavour once ground is astonishingly rich and complex. If you have a spice grinder, dried ginger chips are available from:
*www.buywholefoodsonline.co.uk*

*Candied peel*
I have included a recipe for making your own candied peel towards the end of the book (see page 319). Unfortunately, not all citrus fruits are available to us in the UK. Citron is a large, green citrus fruit that, going by the manuscript books of the 17th and 18th centuries, used to be almost commonplace on these shores. Nowadays, alas, the fresh fruit is exceedingly rarely seen and the candied peel usually limited to just a couple of slivers in packets of whole peel. Luckily, I've found an online supplier from whom you can buy packs of bright green candied citron all by itself.
Available from:
*www.buywholefoodsonline.co.uk*

*Mead*
Mead is becoming increasingly popular as more and more artisan producers spring up, however, unless you're familiar with a farmers' market or farm shop that stocks it, you will have to order online.
Available from:
*www.lindisfarne-mead.co.uk*

*www.cornishmead.co.uk*
*www.lurgashall.co.uk*
*www.monkhide.com*

*Gum tragacanth*
Gum tragacanth, or Gum Dragon as it used to be called, is still in use today in the workshops of artisan cake decorators. Happily, this means it is readily available in specialist cake decorating shops as well as online at:
*www.goodcookshop.com*
*www.craftcompany.co.uk*
*www.cakesforyou.biz*

# BAKER'S NOTES

I have tried not to be too prescriptive when it comes to ingredients and utensils, but to avoid confusion, here are some notes about the instructions given within this book.

Butter is unsalted.

Milk is whole fat.

Eggs, yolks and whites are large and preferably free-range.

In some cases I have specified the type of sugar to use in a particular recipe. Caster is generally ideal for white sugar, but granulated is a perfectly good alternative. The texture might be a little coarser, but this would only be noticeable, if at all, in items of a delicate texture. Soft brown sugar can be light or dark to suit personal preference. If in doubt, go for soft dark brown.

*Tins and trays*
Again, I have tried not to be too prescriptive; descriptions such as 'deep' and 'shallow' aren't particularly helpful as they are

subjective terms. Please do use whatever you have to hand, but if you are concerned that you aren't using the right tin, here are the dimensions of my own, for reference. You can bake everything in the book with the following tins and trays:

Standard loaf tin (22 x 12 x 7cm)
Loaf tin (24 x 14 x 8cm)
20cm sandwich tin (4cm deep)
20cm loose-based cake/tart tin (4cm deep)
24cm springform cake tin (6cm deep)
Rectangular tart tin (35 x 12 x 2.5–3cm deep—can be substituted with a 24cm spring-form cake tin)
12-hole jam–tart tins (2.5–3cm deep)
12-hole fairy-cake tin (4cm deep)
24-hole mini-muffin tin (3cm deep)
Tray-bake tin (20 x 25 x 4cm deep)
4-hole Yorkshire-pudding tin (2–2.5cm deep)
1.2-litre silicone or metal decorative cake mould

*Cooling and storage*
Once baked, items should be removed from the heat source as soon as possible (this includes tins/baking sheets). However, most hot things are also quite delicate, so a balance needs to be created between length of time something cools in/on a tin and when it can safely be moved or transferred to a cooling rack. The general rules are:

*Large cakes* —the heavier the cake, the longer it stays in the tin. Fruit cakes should be cooled in the tin completely, whereas sponge-type cakes should cool for only 10 minutes before being removed from their tins and allowed to cool completely on a wire rack. Large cakes should be wrapped in parchment and/or foil, and stored at room temperature in a tin.

*Small cakes* (usually baked in paper cases)—should be allowed to cool for just 5 minutes before being moved to a wire rack to cool completely. Store in an airtight tin, box or zip-lock bag at room temperature.

*Biscuits* —need an initial cooling time to make moving them easier, but this can be achieved by sliding the parchment on which they are baked off the hot baking sheet and on to a worktop. Some biscuits (Naples Biscuits, Pearl Biscuits) cool completely on the parchment before being removed, and some (e.g. shortbread) need to cool in the tin because they are too fragile to move when warm. Store in an airtight tin, box or zip-lock bag at room temperature.

*Pastry* —small tarts or pies should be removed from their tins after 5 minutes cooling; large tarts usually cool in the tin. Pastry should be stored in an airtight box at room temperature; it can be warmed gently to 'refresh' it before serving. Only chill pastry if the filling requires refrigeration, because the cold will make the pastry tough.

*Bread and yeast items* —can be removed from tins once cooked, apart from Lardy Cake which should cool in the tin. Some (e.g. Butter Buns and Wiggs, but others also, according to preference) are wrapped in cloth to cool in order to keep the crust soft. Bread and yeast items should be stored at room temperature in boxes, crocks, paper bags or zip-lock bags. Clean crumbs away daily and make sure storage is dry to keep items fresh. Items to be frozen should be well protected with plastic, to avoid freezer burn.

*Puddings* —most are either warm, and therefore served immediately, or chilled before serving. Chilled puddings should be covered when in the fridge, either in a box or with cling film, to prevent them becoming tainted with other strong flavours that might be in there.

# 1

# *LARGE CAKES*

Cakes have traditionally been associated with special occasions, and were often integral and symbolic components of ceremonies: think of Bride Cake and Twelfth Night Cake. For Harvest Festival, cakes were baked with the bounty of the earth—the grains, fruits and nuts—and offered in thanks. We maintain this tradition today with cakes for baptisms, birthdays, weddings, funerals and holidays such as Easter and Christmas but, thankfully, we no longer need to limit our enjoyment of cake to special occasions, and can take pleasure in the remarkable variety and range of cakes from times past whenever we like.

# *APPLE CAKE*

*20th century*

I love cakes made with fresh fruit: they can really make the taste buds tingle, especially if care is taken not to over-sweeten them. Apple cake is both very traditional and very varied. Each part of the UK seems to have its own particular version, each fiercely defensive that theirs is the definitive recipe. There are cakes with big or small chunks of fruit, with apple slices or apple purée, pudding cakes, caramelised toffee-apple cakes and more.

Of course, everyone's idea of the perfect apple cake is different, and I searched for my own personal ultimate apple cake recipe for years. Each time I thought I'd found 'The One', only to be disappointed with the end result: it was either too wet, too heavy, too chewy or the cake-to-apple ratio was all wrong. However, my search eventually came to an end and all those woeful apple cakes are behind me now, because I did finally find 'The One' and this is it. It comes with two added bonuses: it's a proportional cake, which means you can scale it up or down depending on the resources you have; and it's eggless, which is an advantage if you have dietary concerns, and it also makes it a great store-cupboard standby for when you feel the need to bake something tasty but find you are all out of eggs.

This cake is gorgeous eaten warm, straight from the oven. It also makes a scrumptious pudding with some cream or custard drizzled over it. Cold, it is sturdy enough to be packed into picnics and lunch boxes. You can make it in a traditional round cake tin if you like, though my personal preference is for a tray bake.

The size and shape of the tin you choose to bake this cake in will determine the number of portions, but as a rough guide, this will produce 8–10 generous servings.

The proportions by weight are: 1-part apple; 1-part plain flour; ½-part sugar; ½-part butter; 1 teaspoon of baking powder for each 150g flour; milk, to mix.

As a more conventional recipe:

*380g plain flour*
*190g butter, plus extra for greasing*
*190g caster sugar, plus extra for sprinkling*
*2½ tsp baking powder*

*380g peeled and chopped Bramley apples (from 450g whole apples)*
*milk, to mix*

*1 x baking tin (20 x 25cm)*

SERVES 8–10 (GENEROUSLY)

Preheat the oven to 180°C/160°C fan/gas 4. Grease and line the baking tin with baking parchment.

Put the flour, butter, sugar and baking powder into the bowl of a food processor and blitz until the mixture resembles breadcrumbs. Alternatively, rub the butter in by hand.

Tip the mixture into a large bowl. Add the peeled and chopped apples and stir to combine. Add just enough milk to make a firm dough: the fruit will release juice as it cooks, so you don't want the mixture to be too moist initially.

Spread the mixture evenly into the tin and bake for 45–50 minutes, turning the tin around after 30 minutes to ensure even colouring. The cake is done when a skewer inserted into the middle comes out clean. (Don't mistake fruit purée for uncooked batter—this is a very moist cake.)

Remove from the oven and sprinkle the top of the warm cake with caster sugar. If you're not eating it straight away, allow it to cool in the tin for 10 minutes then carefully transfer to a wire rack to cool completely.

## VARIATIONS

*Apple Cake variations*

You can adjust the overall flavour of this cake simply by varying
the apples you choose: I chose Bramley apples because I like sharp
flavours and they also tend to break down into a fluff when cooked.
Rough-coated Russet apples would hold their shape and lend an
almost nutty flavour to the finished cake—why not throw in a
handful of chopped walnuts with them as well? Experiment!

*Pear Cake*

I've also used this same recipe to bake a pear cake. Choose
slightly under-ripe fruit that will hold its shape and won't add
too much liquid to the mix in the form of juice. Add the zest
of 1 lemon to bring out the flavour, and the juice of the lemon,
too, if you like the sharpness. The nashi (Asian) pear is readily
available in supermarkets and would make another deliciously
different variation. It is crunchier than our home-grown pears and
wonderfully refreshing.

*Gooseberry Cake*

This variation was suggested by the recipe's original author. Using a
sharp knife, prepare the gooseberries by cutting them into quarters
if small, and eighths if large. This might seem tedious, especially if
you have a food processor glinting at you from the worktop, but I
have tried blitzing the gooseberries and the resulting mush makes
a heavy and far too sweet; I ended up throwing out the result.
After adding the fruit to the dry ingredients, add 60ml elderflower
cordial. Elderflower and gooseberry is a combination made in
heaven and it's no coincidence that the two are in season at the
same time. Continue as above, adding enough milk to make a firm
dough. Bake a little longer than for apple cake, about 60 minutes,
and sprinkle with caster sugar while warm.

# BEER CAKE
*1820s*

This is an antique recipe rescued by Miss Florence White. She featured it in her book *Good Things in England,* published in 1932, which attempted to 'capture the charm of England's cookery before it is completely crushed out of existence.' The contributor, a Miss Heath from Tonbridge, confirmed that although the recipe was more than 100 years old, she had recently baked it herself and vouched for its flavour. The use of beer in a cake is a nod to times before sanitation, when a barrel of home-made beer might be the healthiest liquid available to drink. It's also a reminder of the great yeast-raised cakes of long ago.

Made with a traditional British bitter beer, the cake retains the distinctive aroma of hops. However, if that is not to your taste, there's a huge range of other options available. With the rise in popularity of both artisan and microbreweries, even supermarkets now offer bottled-beer selections with flavours that include honey, banana bread, chocolate and ginger. By selecting a different beer each time you make this cake, from the palest of pale ales to the most chocolatey of dark stouts via refreshing fruit-flavoured Belgian beers, you can achieve almost limitless flavour variations from this single recipe. Pair the sugar with your chosen beer—white caster with the palest ale, for example, through to dark muscovado with a thick, rich stout.

SERVES 6–8

*85g butter, softened, plus extra for greasing*
*85g soft brown sugar*
*1 egg*
*225g plain flour*

*½ tsp bicarbonate of soda*
*150ml beer*
*85g sultanas or raisins or currants*

*1 x 20cm cake tin*

Preheat the oven to 180°C/160°C fan/gas 4. Grease and line the cake tin with baking parchment.

Cream the butter until thoroughly soft. Add the sugar and continue to beat until light and fluffy. Add the egg and mix thoroughly to combine. Gradually add the flour until well mixed.

Dissolve the bicarbonate of soda in the beer and stir this into the mix. When thoroughly combined, fold in the dried fruit.

Pour the mixture into the prepared cake tin and spread evenly. Bake for 30–40 minutes until the cake is well risen, has slightly shrunk away from the sides of the tin, and an inserted skewer comes out clean.

Rest in the tin for 10 minutes then transfer to a wire rack to cool.

# BIG BISCUIT CAKE
*1675*

This is a cake from the handwritten manuscript books I discovered via the Wellcome Library. I was searching for a plain cake that would suit a number of occasions, from picnics and packed lunches to afternoon tea. This recipe seemed to fit the bill perfectly. Initially I was drawn to its name, which is always something of a lucky dip because in recipes this old, 'cake' could mean anything from a biscuit to a cake and all points in-between.

Having tried the recipe, I found that it was a firm sponge and, if made with the original quantities, would deserve the title 'pound cake'. Further experimentation resulted in the discovery that, with just a few little tweaks, it could be transformed into a number of equally delicious variations. I firmly believe that in the genealogy of cakes (should such a thing exist) this recipe could be a strong contender for the 'mother recipe' from which a whole slew of classic teatime treats are descended.

Delicately flavoured with lemon zest and nutmeg, the original recipe is most enjoyable and far more flavourful than its somewhat ordinary name might suggest. A small tweak transforms it into a seed cake, that staple of a bygone era, equally enjoyed by city ladies who spent their mornings visiting in town, and burly farm workers in the countryside in celebration of the spring sowing. It also makes a fine Madeira cake, so called because it was usually enjoyed with a glass of the liqueur. When past its delicious best, it can be sliced and drizzled with sherry and brandy to make trifle, or crumbled into the fillings of tarts.

When I first tested this recipe, I baked it exactly as per the original, without using artificial raising agents. The eggs must be thoroughly whisked into the mixture—at least 5 minutes per egg on high speed—in order to maximise the air and lightness in the mixture. It turned out beautifully, but I must admit that it did help greatly to have a stand mixer to save straining my arm. If you prefer a less rigorous approach, either replace the plain flour with self-raising, or add ½ teaspoon of baking powder.

SERVES 10–12

*225g plain or self-raising flour,*     *225g butter, softened,*
*or 225g plain flour plus ½ tsp*     *plus extra for greasing*
*baking powder*                     *225g caster sugar*
*zest of 1 lemon*                 *4 eggs*
*⅓ nutmeg, grated, or 2 tsp*
*ground nutmeg*                  *1 x 24cm cake tin*

Preheat the oven to 180°C/160°C fan/gas 4. Grease and line the base and sides of the cake tin with baking parchment.

Sift the flour into a bowl. Add the lemon zest and nutmeg and stir to combine. Set aside.

In a separate bowl, beat the butter until light and fluffy—at least 5 minutes, provided the butter is very soft. Add the sugar and beat on high speed for 5–10 minutes. Scrape the sides of the bowl down to ensure that the mixture is fully incorporated. It will become almost white in colour and very light in texture.

Add the eggs, one at a time, beating each one for 5 full minutes before adding the next. Gently and gradually add the flour mixture until fully combined, and continue to mix on high speed until ready for the oven.

Pour the mixture into the prepared tin. Do not spread the batter out as this will flatten all the air you spent so long getting into the mixture and cause the cake to be flat and heavy. Just shake the tin gently to encourage the batter towards the sides of the tin. Don't worry if it isn't completely even, it will sort itself out in the oven.

Bake for 60–80 minutes until the sponge has shrunk away slightly from the sides of the tin and a skewer inserted into the middle

of the cake comes out clean. Rest in the tin for 10 minutes then turn out on to a wire rack to cool.

## VARIATIONS

*Seed Cake*
Omit the nutmeg and add 1 tablespoon of seeds—caraway are traditional, but you can also use aniseed or cumin.

*Madeira Cake*
Omit the nutmeg and lay 2 strips of candied citron peel on top of the cake just as it goes into the oven. Cover the cake with baking parchment if, after 50 minutes, the peel looks to be in danger of burning.

*Lemon Drizzle Cake*
Omit the nutmeg and add the zest of another lemon to the mix. Just before the cake has finished cooking, make the drizzle by squeezing the juice from both lemons and mixing it with 100g granulated sugar. Stir well then pour the mixture over the hot cake and leave to cool. The larger grains of the granulated sugar won't dissolve fully, and this is deliberate: they will form a wonderfully crunchy topping for the cake.

*Orange Cake*
Omit the lemon and nutmeg and add the zest of 2 oranges to the cake batter. If you'd like a hint of spice, add ½ teaspoon of ground cardamom. Make orange drizzle as above, with the juice of just 1 orange and the juice of 1 lemon for a bit of zing. Alternatively, mix 1 tablespoon of orange juice, 1 tablespoon of lemon juice and 1 tablespoon of egg white with enough icing sugar to make a soft icing, and spread over the cooled cake.

*Cherry Cake*
Cherry cakes are notoriously difficult to get right in baking competitions since the most important criterion is usually the even dispersal of cherries throughout the mix when the cake is cut, and

glacé cherries display an almost lemming-like tendency to hurl themselves to the bottom of the cake tin. Follow these few tips, however, and success should be yours. For a cake of this size, 200g glacé cherries gives a generous, but not overly dense distribution of fruit, but you can use more or less as you desire. To achieve an even distribution of fruit, three changes to the recipe are required. First, you need to thicken the mixture a little to make it less easy for the cherries to slip down to the bottom, so add 112g ground almonds to the flour and omit the nutmeg. Second, rinse all the sugar syrup from the cherries and dry them carefully; the sugar syrup on the outside acts almost like a lubricant and will practically guarantee cherry-drop. Third, cut the cherries in half and toss them in plain flour: this removes all traces of moisture and provides some traction against them slipping through the cake mixture. The final secret to success is in the method. Just before you stir through your dusted cherries, add half of the cake mixture to the prepared tin. Fold the cherries through the remaining half before adding to the tin. The 24cm tin makes for a relatively shallow cake, but this has the advantage that the glacé cherries don't have very far to fall. If you'd like to show off your cherry cake expertise, choose a smaller diameter tin such as a tall 20cm tin, which will make a deeper cake; however, the deeper the cake, the more care is needed in the baking, to ensure it is thoroughly cooked through.

# COCONUT CAKE

*1880*

This is a deliciously moist and textured cake that I found in a handwritten Victorian recipe book. Freshly grated coconut in a cake not only gives it a great texture, it also keeps it moist. Having the coconut on the outside as well turns this cake into a real showstopper of dazzling whiteness.

SERVES 8–10

*For the cake*
*½ fresh coconut, peeled and grated*
*85g butter, softened, plus*
  *extra for greasing*
*150g caster sugar*
*150ml egg white, lightly beaten*
*zest of 1 lemon*
*2 tbsp milk*
*1 tsp baking powder*
*200g plain flour, plus extra for*
  *mixing*

*For the icing*
*300g cream cheese*
*zest and juice of 1 lemon*
*2–3 tbsp icing sugar, to taste*

*To decorate*
*fresh coconut, or a mixture of fresh*
  *and toasted desiccated coconut*

*2 x 20cm sandwich tins*

Preheat the oven to 200°C/180°C fan/gas 6. Grease and line the sandwich tins.

First prepare the fresh coconut. With a sharp-pointed implement, poke a hole through one of the three 'eyes' located at one end of the coconut. (There is always one that is weaker than the other two, so if the one you try first seems too hard, try one of the others.) Shake out the coconut water—it makes a refreshing drink!

Put the empty coconut in the oven for 20 minutes. This will crack the coconut shell and also help loosen the flesh from the shell.

Wrap the coconut in a clean hand towel and strike it against a hard surface to break the shell into pieces.

Ease out the white flesh from the hard shell and remove the dark skin with a sharp knife or vegetable peeler. Grate the white flesh either by hand or using a food processor.

Cream the butter in a large bowl then add the caster sugar and beat until light and fluffy. Add the egg white, lemon zest, grated coconut and milk, and stir well.

In a separate bowl, mix the baking powder and flour together and stir this into the mixture. Add more flour if necessary until you have a 'dropping' consistency (i.e. it should fall off the spoon easily).

Divide the mixture between the prepared tins and smooth the surfaces. Bake for 20–25 minutes until risen and golden and a skewer inserted into the sponges comes out clean. Transfer to a wire rack to cool.

To make the icing, beat the cream cheese with the lemon zest and juice until smooth. Add icing sugar to taste.

Use half the icing to sandwich the cooled cake. Pour the other half over the top of the cake, or on both the top and sides. Sprinkle the top with fresh coconut and either use more fresh coconut on the sides or, for contrast, use toasted desiccated coconut.

# A (CURRANT) CAKE
## 1685

One of the reasons I love looking through old manuscript cookery books is that I find it fascinating to see the recipe choices made by anonymous hands so many decades, and occasionally centuries, ago. Often these recipe books also contained recipes for medicinal cures, which were also the province of the lady of the house. Sometimes this led to unintentional humour, such as the recipe I found for 'yellow macaroons', which appeared opposite a cure for jaundice. Among the many other quirky and amusing gems I have discovered in my hours of browsing, the main thing that struck me has been the occasionally curious choices made regarding the selection of recipe names.

Some are named after the person from whom the recipe was obtained; one such recipe I found in an 18th-century manuscript was entitled 'Lady Frances Sanderson's Cake'. Despite extensive searching, the only snippet of information I could find was the following comment in a letter from Lady Marlborough to Lady Huntingdon:

*'Now there is Lady Frances Sanderson's great rout to-morrow night; all the world will be there, and I must go. I do hate that woman as much as I hate a physician; but I must go, if for no other purpose but to mortify and spite her.'* [1]

Baker of fine cakes she might have been, but it would appear that this alone did not guarantee Lady Sanderson's universal popularity.

In contrast, many recipes lack even the gloss of a distinguished author's name. I found over 60 recipes entitled simply 'A Cake'. Ordinarily, I might skip over anything with such a lacklustre title but, considering that these were written in a day and age where writing implements were expensive, someone had thought it worth their while to record these recipes and so I was curious to see whether their efforts were justified. With so many to choose from, I literally closed my eyes and stuck a pin in the list, and I was rewarded with an absolutely stellar recipe. As a yeast-raised cake, it is light and crumbly, kept tender by the double cream. The generous helping of currants means that only the tiniest amount of sugar is needed and just a fraction of butter compared with regular cakes. The spice mix is unusual to our 21st-century taste buds, but delicious nonetheless. Contrary to modern practice, the cake is iced hot with a delicately perfumed early form of royal icing.

SERVES 8–10

*For the cake*
200ml double cream
115g butter
450g plain flour
35g caster sugar
1 tsp ground cinnamon
1 tsp grated nutmeg
1 tsp ground mace
450g currants
2 sachets (14g) fast-action yeast

2 eggs
1 egg yolk
150ml milk

*For the icing*
225g icing sugar
1 egg white
1 tsp rosewater

1 x 24cm spring-form cake tin

Preheat the oven to 200°C/180°C fan/gas 6. Line the base and sides of the tin with baking parchment. The parchment for the sides needs to be double thickness.

Put the cream and butter into a pan over a low heat and warm gently until the butter is melted. Remove from the heat and allow the mixture to cool to body temperature, which you can check by dipping a finger into the liquid.

Sift the flour, caster sugar and spices into a large bowl and stir in the currants and the yeast.

In a separate bowl, whisk the eggs, yolk and milk together. Add this mixture to the dry ingredients along with the cooled cream and butter. Mix thoroughly and pour into the prepared tin, spreading the mixture out to an even layer. Cover with a clean cloth and set in a warm place to rise for 20 minutes. (If you have a double oven, you could put the tin on a shelf in the top oven. Do not put the cake tin directly on the bottom of the oven as it will be too hot.)

Once the cake has risen, make a cover out of foil to prevent the top scorching. Bake for 45 minutes, turning the tin halfway through to ensure an even bake. The cake is done when it has risen and shrunk away from the sides of the tin. If in doubt, insert a cake tester or skewer: it should come out clean.

While the cake is baking, whisk all the icing ingredients together for 10 minutes until you have the consistency of double cream. The cake is iced hot, so when you're happy with the state of 'done-ness', remove the cake from the tin and set it on to a wire rack. Leave the oven on for now. Put the rack on to a baking tray with sides, to stop it sliding around too much.

Using a pastry brush (traditional or silicone), cover the whole of the cake with the icing mixture. When the top and sides of the cake are iced, return the cake to the oven, turn it off and leave the cake for 15 minutes, until the icing has set. The icing will start to brown if left too long, so keep an eye on it.

Remove the cake from the oven and leave to cool completely.

# SCOTS SEED CAKE
*1736*

As a nation, the Scots have a legendary sweet tooth as well as an impressive tradition in baking. If there's one cake that would seem to embody both these traditions, it is the Dundee Cake. It was first made by the Dundee-based Keiller company, as an off-season sideline to their marmalade manufacturing business. By gentleman's agreement, no other bakers in the city made the cake and Keiller's popularised their creation under the name Dundee Cake.

However modern recipes for Dundee Cake rarely produce a cake bearing any resemblance to the light, buttery delicacy stuffed with sultanas, almonds and candied peel described in *The Oxford Companion to Food*. Additionally, as a symbol of the great tradition of Scottish baking, I don't believe it to be a particularly good ambassador: it's very geographically specific, relatively modern and, originally, factory-made.

I'd like to propose instead the Scots Seed Cake of Mrs McLintock, authoress of Scotland's first recipe book published in 1736. Do not be put off by the name; this cake is so much more than just a seed cake. It's packed with the sweet sharpness of candied orange and citron and enriched with almonds. The aroma of the caraway is delicate and not at all overpowering. It's perfect with a glass of sherry or Madeira, as ladies in polite society would have enjoyed it, or with a refreshing cup of tea. Well wrapped it will keep for several days and is a great treat to have on hand in the kitchen cupboard or pantry.

SERVES 8–10

250g plain flour
250g butter, softened, plus
  extra for greasing
250g caster sugar
5 eggs

2 tsp baking powder
⅓ nutmeg, or 2 tsp grated
  nutmeg
½ tsp ground caraway seeds
60g ground almonds

*120g candied orange peel, thinly*
*  sliced*  .
*75g candied citron peel, thinly*
*  sliced*
*60ml brandy*

*a little milk, as required*
*nibbed sugar and caraway seeds,*
*  for sprinkling, optional*

*1 x 24cm spring-form cake tin*

Preheat the oven to 110°C/90°C fan/gas ¼.

Sift the flour on to a baking tray and dry in the oven for 20 minutes.

Remove the flour and increase the oven temperature to 170°C/150°C fan/gas 3. Grease and line the cake tin with baking parchment.

When the flour has cooled, sift it into a bowl to remove any lumps.

Cream the butter until pale and fluffy. Add the sugar and mix for a further 5 minutes. Add the eggs, one at a time, making sure each one is thoroughly mixed in before adding the next.

In a separate bowl, sift together the flour, baking powder and spices then add this to the creamed butter mix, a spoonful at a time, until thoroughly combined. Fold in the ground almonds and the candied peel, then loosen the mix with the brandy. If it still seems rather stiff, add a little milk, but not too much as a sloppy mix will allow the peel to sink.

Pour the mixture into the prepared tin and smooth the surface. Sprinkle with nibbed sugar and caraway seeds, if liked.

Bake for 60–90 minutes until well risen and golden on top. The cake is ready when an inserted skewer comes out clean.

Let the cake rest in the tin for 10 minutes then remove and set on to a wire rack to cool.

# MEAD CAKE

*Based on a traditional recipe*

This cake started out as quite a different one altogether. Growing up in Herefordshire, I was always aware of cider being a local product. Both the Bulmer plant in Hereford and the smaller, more local, Westons cider plant in Much Marcle, have traditions stretching back generations to the 1880s. Numerous small artisan producers have also flourished in the county. I wanted to include a cider cake for my home county that was also an example of a cake baked with regional produce.

I chose an old recipe from a little booklet of farmhouse recipes from the 1940s, because the author lived in Little Burch, just outside Hereford. I am always drawn to personal recipes because, even without knowing the author, I believe a tried and tested family recipe is always going to be preferable to an anonymous printed one. It was simple and straightforward, letting the generous quantity of cider be the star. As with the Beer Cake (see page 26), there is a whole range of different cider varieties that can be used to tweak the flavour of this cake in gentle and subtle ways so that you can vary the flavour each time you bake it. As a guide, the better the quality of the cider you use, the better the resulting flavour of the cake. While you *can* make this cake with the absolute cheapest unbranded cider you can find, the flavour of the cake will reflect it. I know this because I tried it myself. The result was not special.

After substituting other liquids to try to broaden the range of variations even further, I can also recommend two slightly more unusual drinks. Perry is a drink similar to cider, but it is made from perry pears. Even more specifically regional than cider, it is traditional to the Three Counties—Gloucestershire, Herefordshire and Worcestershire—and the best-quality perry is akin to champagne. As with cider, the quality you choose will affect the flavour of the cake: look in farm shops and at farmers' markets rather than on supermarket shelves.

The final and most unusual suggestion, and the one to which I have awarded the title of this recipe, is mead. One of the oldest alcoholic beverages, it is also known as honey wine. There are artisan producers all around the UK reviving this most ancient beverage. Unless you know of a local producer, it is probably easiest to obtain some online. Recipes are also available online for those adventurous enough to try making their own. As with cider, perry and beer, there are many variations that can subtly tweak your cake flavourings. Try to match the sugar in the recipe with your mixing liquid: keep it light with caster sugar, or darker and richer with soft brown or muscovado. I've added some mead-flavoured cream cheese icing and a dusting of cinnamon to make my recipe extra special, but you can also enjoy it plain.

Savour a slice of your cake with a glass of whatever you have chosen to put into it, or simply with a cup of tea or coffee.

SERVES 8–10

_For the cake_
113g butter, softened, plus extra
 for greasing
113g sugar
2 eggs
225g plain flour
⅕ nutmeg, grated
1 tsp bicarbonate of soda
200ml mead

_For the icing_
300g cream cheese
2–3 tbsp icing sugar, to taste
2 tbsp mead
ground cinnamon, for dusting

1 x 24cm spring-form cake tin

Preheat the oven to 180°C/160°C fan/gas 4. Grease and line the tin with baking parchment.

Cream the butter until soft, then add the sugar and beat until the mixture is light and fluffy, about 10 minutes. Add the eggs, one at a time, making sure the first egg is thoroughly incorporated before adding the second.

In a separate bowl, sift the flour, nutmeg and bicarbonate of soda together. Gradually add half the flour to the butter and egg mixture, keeping it light and fluffy. Stir in the mead, then gradually beat in the rest of the flour.

Pour into the prepared tin and bake for 40–45 minutes until the cake has shrunk away from the sides of the tin and an inserted skewer comes out clean. Set aside for 10 minutes to cool a little before removing from the tin and leaving to cool completely on a wire rack.

To make the icing, beat the cream cheese until smooth and add icing sugar to taste. Add the mead and beat again.

Spread the icing over the cooled cake and dust the top with a little cinnamon.

## VARIATIONS

As mentioned in the introduction to this recipe, you can use a whole range of ciders, perry or mead in this recipe: always remembering that the better the quality, the better your cake will taste.

# ORANGE CAKE

*19th century*

The recipe for this cake comes from a little handwritten book
I bought at auction. As with many such collections, it is anonymous,
but the recipes appear to have been chosen with care and several are
enthusiastically spattered with ancient liquids. Some people might
prefer their cookery books to remain pristine, but I'm a huge fan
of bespattered books that show how much their recipes were used
and enjoyed.

I was drawn to this recipe mostly because of the filling, which is an
unusual but delicious departure from jam or buttercream. It lifts
the whole cake with its tang and freshness and turns what might at
first appear a somewhat ordinary cake into something rather special.
The method is a little out of the ordinary too, with the whipped egg
white being folded in just before baking, but I'm always curious to
test new approaches, because you never know when you might hit
on that one thing that just works effortlessly for you. To complete
the whole festival of orange for this cake, it is topped with a soft
icing, flavoured with orange and garnished with candied orange
peel. Personally I love the orange explosion of tastes and textures,
but I can also appreciate that it might be a bit much for some,
so if you're feeling unsure, try it with either icing or filling, rather
than both.

SERVES 8–10

*For the cake*
85g butter, plus extra for
  greasing
85g caster sugar
3 eggs, separated
zest of 1 orange
85g plain flour
½ tsp baking powder

*For the filling*
zest and juice of 1 lemon
zest and juice of 2 oranges
112g caster sugar
30g cornflour mixed with 250ml
  cold water

### For the icing
200g icing sugar
a little orange juice
a little egg white, lightly beaten

### To finish
50g candied orange peel, cut into
 small cubes

1 x 20cm spring-form cake tin

Preheat the oven to 180°C/160°C fan/gas 4. Grease and line the cake tin with baking parchment.

Cream the butter and sugar together until light and fluffy then whisk in the egg yolks, one at a time, followed by the orange zest.

Sift the flour and baking powder together and stir into the mix.

In a separate bowl, whisk the egg whites to stiff peaks and fold this into the creamed mixture.

Pour into the prepared tin and bake for 25–30 minutes until well risen and firm to the touch, and a skewer inserted into the middle comes out clean. Cool for 10 minutes in the tin then turn out on to a wire rack to cool completely.

*To make the filling*
Put the zest and juice of the lemon and oranges into a small pan over a low heat. Add the caster sugar and cornflour mixture. Stir gently until thickened then remove from the heat and pour into a dish. Cover with cling film and set aside to cool.

*To assemble the cake*
Cut the cake in half horizontally. Spread the filling on the bottom half of the cake. (The filling is quite zesty, so don't feel obliged to use it all.) Replace the top half of the cake.

Mix the icing ingredients together to a smooth, spreadable paste.

Dip a knife, or palette knife, into hot water (to make spreading the icing easier), pour the icing over the top of the cake and use the warmed knife to spread it.

Sprinkle the chopped peel around the top edge of the cake, to finish.

# RICE CAKE
*1854*

This cake was a pleasant surprise to find in a 19th-century Scottish recipe book. I've always thought the availability of rice flour to be a modern luxury, but apparently not. If you need to avoid wheat for whatever reason, then this recipe means you can still rustle up a delicious baked treat without having to resort to the various powders and potions that many modern gluten-free recipes seem to require. If you're not sure whether your baking powder is gluten-free (and it usually is), replace it with ½ teaspoon cream of tartar and ¼ teaspoon bicarbonate of soda. The sponge itself is very light and flavourful and I particularly like the crisp crust that forms around the edges. It can also be used as a basis for desserts such as Trifle and Chantilly Cake (see pages 213 and 50).

SERVES 6–8

*112g butter, plus extra
  for greasing
112g caster sugar
3 eggs
1 tsp baking powder
112g rice flour*

*zest of 1 lemon
jam and fresh whipped cream,
  to serve
icing sugar, for dusting*

*1 x 20cm cake tin*

Preheat the oven to 180°C/160°C fan/gas 4. Grease and line the cake tin with baking parchment.

Cream the butter and sugar together until light and fluffy.

Add the eggs, one at a time, and mix thoroughly to combine each one before adding the next.

Sift the baking powder and rice flour together and gradually add to the creamed mixture, a spoonful at a time. Stir in the lemon zest.

Pour the cake batter into the prepared tin and smooth the top.

Bake for 30–40 minutes until well risen and firm to the touch. If the cake seems to be browning too fast, cover with a sheet of baking parchment.

Let the cake rest in the tin for 10 minutes then remove and transfer to a wire rack to cool.

To serve, cut in half horizontally and spread with jam and fresh whipped cream. Dust the top with icing sugar.

## VARIATION

*Chantilly Cake*
This is a fabulous mix of cake and dessert. It's also known as Trifle Cake. Cut the centre out of the cooled rice cake, being careful not to cut too close to the sides or through the bottom of the cake: essentially, you're making a bowl out of it. Alternatively, if you have a tin 8cm smaller than your rice cake tin, grease the outsides and rest it on the cake mix before baking. When cooked, lift the smaller tin from the cake to leave a ready-made hollow for the cake filling.

Transfer the cake to your serving platter and drizzle with sweet or cream sherry. Spread seedless raspberry jam around the hollow of the cake and spoon in a rich, thick, cold custard. Top with sweetened, whipped cream and decorate with nuts, mixed raisins and candied peel.

# *SAVOY CAKE*
## 1806

A Savoy Cake is a fantastic dessert cake, originally from the Savoy region of France, which can be as simple or as elaborate as you wish. It is a fatless sponge baked in a moulded cake tin then filled and decorated with whipped cream and fresh fruit and topped off with a dusting of icing sugar. As long as you are careful with the preparation of your mould, there's remarkably little work required to create something with real wow-factor.

Savoy Cake is just one of a variety of fatless sponge confections, including Naples Biscuit and Spanish Biscuit, which made their way to Britain during the 17th century. The original recipe was used to make sponge-finger biscuits; baking the mixture in larger, more ornate moulds only became popular in the early 18th century.

The original moulds were made of copper, and preparing them to ensure the cakes turned out without breaking must have been a stressful undertaking. The advice of John Simpson, the original author of this recipe, is just as relevant today as it was then: *'Be very particular with the moulds, for there is as much art in preparing the mould, as in mixing the batter for the cake.'*

Nowadays, of course, we have the advantage of non-stick tins and silicone moulds to make things a little easier. Careful preparation is still the key, though: clarified butter, caster sugar and cornflour making up the three ingredients that form the distinctive, biscuit-like crust on the outside. I prefer to use clarified butter because it easily coats all the little nooks and crannies in the mould and contains no milk solids, which might cook a little darker and blemish the outside of the cake.

This dessert cake is best enjoyed fresh, but even when it is past its best it can form the basis of other delicious desserts, such as Tipsy Cake and Trifle (see pages 56 and 213).

SERVES 6–8

*For the mould*
75g butter or clarified butter
  (see page 329)
2–3 tbsp caster sugar
2–3 tbsp cornflour

1 x decorative metal or silicone
  cake mould

*For the cake*
225g caster sugar
4 eggs, separated
zest of 1 lemon
1 sachet (7g) powdered egg white
  (optional)
175g plain flour

Preheat the oven to 120°C/100°C fan/gas ½.

First prepare the mould. If you need to clarify your butter, melt slightly more than the recipe requires (100g) in a small pan over a low heat. Skim the surface and pour off the clear butter, leaving the milk solids in the bottom of the pan. Generously coat the inside of your cake mould with the clarified butter, leaving no area uncovered. The central funnel is as important as the ornate sides. Tip out any excess and let the mould drain thoroughly. Add the caster sugar to the mould and shake it around, making sure the whole of the inside is coated. Tip out any excess.

Finally, add the cornflour and repeat as with the caster sugar. Set aside.

For the cake, add 200g of the sugar to the egg yolks and whisk until light and creamy. Stir in the lemon zest.

In a separate bowl, stir the remaining 25g sugar and the powdered egg white together. The powdered egg white is optional, but it gives the meringue a slightly firmer consistency, which of course leads to an airier sponge.

In another bowl, start whisking the egg whites with an electric whisk on a low speed.

When they reach the frothy, bubbly stage, increase the speed slightly and gradually add the sugar mix, a spoonful at a time, waiting a few moments before adding the next to give the sugar a chance to dissolve. Increase the speed of the whisk slightly after each addition. When all the sugar is added, increase the speed to maximum and whip to stiff peaks.

Briskly mix one-third of the whipped egg whites with the creamed sugar and egg yolks to lighten the mixture. Don't worry about being gentle at this stage, in effect you 'sacrifice' this portion of the egg whites so that it is easier to fold in the remainder. Gently fold in the remaining egg whites.

Gradually sift in the flour in 3 or 4 batches, gently folding it into the mixture.

Pour the batter into the prepared tin. Don't fill the mould completely as the mixture will rise during cooking. Having said this, don't worry too much, as any excess can easily be trimmed before serving.

Tap the filled tin on the work surface 2 or 3 times to ensure the mixture gets into all the nooks and crannies and to dispel large air bubbles. Transfer to the oven and bake until well risen and an inserted skewer comes out clean. This will take quite a long time, probably longer than expected: my (silicone) cake mould holds just over 1.2 litres, and takes 1¼ hours to bake. Wait at least 40 minutes before checking on the cake, and try not to keep opening the oven door as this may cause the cake to sink and become heavy.

Once cooked, let the cake sit in the tin for 5 minutes then turn out on to a wire rack to cool. If you have been diligent with your preparation, it should just slip out of the mould.

## SERVING SUGGESTIONS

*Simple*
Fill the middle of the cake with sweetened whipped cream, dust
with icing sugar and drape with fresh berries.

*Boozy*
Keep the cake for 3–4 days then use as a basis for a Tipsy Cake
as follows: put the cake on to a serving dish and drizzle it with the
alcohol of your choice (sweet wine, sweet or cream sherry, rum,
brandy or a mixture of all four!) until the cake is soaked and the
liquid has begun to run out. Decorate the outside of the cake with
flaked almonds, pushing them into the softened sponge. Fill the
centre of the cake with a rich, thick, cold custard, pouring any extra
around the base. Finally, add whipped cream on the top.

*Traditional*
See recipe for Chantilly Cake (page 50).

# SPICE CAKE
*Gervase Markham, 17th century*

Gervase Markham was a chatty man. He had a lot to say and did his level best to say it in poetry, discourse and instruction. Multilingual, a poet, a soldier of fortune, notable agriculturalist, forestry expert and horse breeder, he wrote extensively on a whole range of topics. His enthusiasm for sharing his knowledge led him to regularly reprint his works under different titles, and repeat himself often. At one point his exasperated booksellers actually petitioned him to stop issuing books on certain subjects. Not content with holding forth on his range of manly interests, he even found time to lecture on domestic matters in his most famous publication, *The English Hus-wife* (1615):

> *'Contayning, the inward and outward vertues which ought to be in a complete woman. As, her skill in Physick, Cookery, Banqueting stuffe, Distillation, Perfumes, Wool Hemp, Flax, Dayries, Brewing, Baking and all other things belonging to a household. A worke very profitable and necessarie, gathered for the general good of this kingdom.'*

I love how he sees his work as being for the benefit of the realm, not just a few friends and acquaintances. I'm also very curious as to how his advice was received by the women for whom it was intended. I'm not sure how appreciative I would be for someone who wasn't even an expert in the field, to tell me what I should be doing and how.

The irritating thing is, Gervase Markham's recipes really are rather good. His instructions for the best way to make pancakes (see Lace Pancakes, page 194) were recognised and printed (plagiarised?)[2] in The Netherlands, and if there is a nation that knows about pancakes and the like, it is the Dutch.

This recipe for Spice Cake makes a delicious loaf of what we would term a tea loaf. Rich with butter, studded with fruit and bursting with exotic spices, it is extraordinarily tasty. The richness of the crust, golden with saffron, resembles shortbread in its crispness and crumb, and the spices are flavoursome without being overpowering. It is tasty on its own or spread with fresh butter for an even richer treat. As a yeast cake it is wonderfully light and moist, lacking the heaviness of our modern fruit cakes. If you needed any more convincing, of all the possible recipes at his disposal, this is the only large cake recipe Gervase saw fit to include in *The English Hus-wife*. So if Gervase thought it delicious enough to warrant pride of place in his book, I'm not going to disagree.

SERVES 8–10

| | |
|---|---|
| *150ml double cream* | *¼ tsp salt* |
| *150ml whole milk* | *1 tsp aniseed* |
| *55g butter* | *½ tsp ground cloves* |
| *55g caster sugar* | *1 tsp ground mace* |
| *¼ tsp saffron strands* | *1½ tsp ground cinnamon* |
| *450g plain flour* | *1 egg* |
| *2 sachets (14g total) fast-action* | *1 egg yolk* |
| *yeast* | *450g currants* |

Put the cream, milk, butter, sugar and saffron into a saucepan and heat gently until the butter has melted. Set aside to allow the saffron to infuse and release its colour and flavour.

Mix the flour and yeast in a large bowl. Add the salt and spices.

When the saffron cream has cooled to below body temperature (test by dipping your finger into it), whisk the egg and yolk together. Slowly pour the cooled saffron mixture on to the beaten eggs, while whisking, and then mix the liquids into the flour and spices.

Knead the mixture into a soft dough and set aside to rise for 1 hour. After the dough has been rising for 30 minutes, preheat the oven to 110°C/90°C fan/gas ¼ and put the currants in to warm.

When the dough has proved, tip it out of the bowl and pat it down to release the air bubbles. Pull the dough into pieces and knead in the currants. Increase the oven temperature to 180°C/160°C fan/gas 4.

Shape the fruited dough into a round, cover and set it aside to rise a second time for about 20 minutes. You can leave it in a free-form shape on a baking sheet, or place it in a greased and lined cake tin, if preferred.

Bake for 40–60 minutes, covering with baking parchment after 30 minutes to prevent the currants from scorching. Don't worry if they still burn; once cooled they can easily be brushed off the outside of the loaf. Remove from the oven once well risen and golden brown. Transfer to a wire rack to cool.

# WELSH HONEY CAKE
*1796*

This recipe comes from a rather unusual book called *The Diary of a Farmer's Wife, 1796–1797*. Anne Hughes lived in the borderlands of England and Wales at the close of the 18th century. For a little over a year she kept a diary of daily life at her husband's farm, of local celebrations and festivities, and of the recipes she cooked in her kitchen. Serialised by Jeanne Preston in 1937 in *Farmers Weekly*, there is some dispute as to its authenticity since the original sources from which it was created, including Anne's 'Boke', have been lost. Some of the anecdotes are thought to have been told to Jeanne as a child by Anne Hughes's daughter, while some of the recipes came from a book belonging to Jeanne's mother. Nevertheless, it is a charming, believable, if somewhat erratically-spelled, glimpse into rural life over 200 years ago.

I completely agree with Anne when she declares *This be a verrie prettie cake*'. The honey brings such a gorgeous amber colour to it that I prefer to enjoy it plain, so I've chosen to ignore Anne's instruction to add 'swete plums' (raisins). I also use the plainest, runniest honey I can find, because it makes for a light, delicate flavour that is not at all sickly or overpowering. There is another version of Welsh Honey Cake where the cake is topped with a meringue and then returned to the oven until set, and this is a great way to embellish this cake for a special occasion.

**SERVES 8–10**

170g honey
170g butter, softened, plus
  extra for greasing
170g caster sugar
3 eggs

340g self-raising flour
milk, if required

1 x 1kg/23cm loaf tin, or similar
  capacity

Preheat the oven to 170°C/150°C fan/gas 3. Grease and line the loaf tin with baking parchment.

If necessary, warm the honey until runny, but not too hot. Set aside to cool a little if required.

In a bowl, beat the butter and sugar together until pale and fluffy. Add the honey and mix thoroughly. Add the eggs, one at a time, making sure each is thoroughly mixed in before adding the next. Fold in the flour. The mixture should be of a 'dropping' consistency (it should drop freely off a spoon). Add a little milk if necessary until the correct consistency is reached.

Pour the mixture into the prepared tin. Bake for 40 minutes–1¼ hours until risen and firm to the touch and a skewer inserted into the middle comes out clean. The cooking time will vary, depending on the size and shape of your tin, and the moisture content of your honey.

Leave to cool in the tin for 10–15 minutes then transfer to a wire rack to cool completely.

# WOOD STREET CAKE
*1675*

This recipe caught my eye because, although it originated in an era when cakes were usually named after the person who had passed on the recipe, or from the town where they originated, 'Wood Street' seemed an oddly specific location for a recipe title. But I kept coming across recipes for this rich fruited cake in the handwritten manuscripts of the Wellcome Library and it turned out to have an excellent and fascinating tradition.

Wood Street is located in London, between Cheapside and Cripplegate. In 1720 it is recorded as follows:

> *'Great Woodstreet is a Street well built and inhabited, and noted for the good Cakes here made; which are wont to be bought here for Weddings, Christnings, and Twelfthnights.'*

However, this was not a recent fame, and the reputation of the quality of the cakes produced here extends even further back, to the turbulent times of the English Civil War in the previous century.

In 1648, Lady Anne Murray (later Halkett) and her lover, the Royalist Colonel Joseph Bampfield, succeeded in rescuing the 14-year-old James, Duke of York (the future James II) from captivity in St James' Palace and smuggling him to the Continent dressed in women's clothing. In later years, Lady Anne would write in her uniquely spelled autobiography (1677):

> *'I dresed him in the women's habitt that was prepared, which fitted his Highnese very well, and was very pretty in itt. Affter hee had eaten something I made ready while I was idle lest his Highnese should bee hungry, and having sentt for a Woodstreet cake (which I knew hee loved) to take in the barge, with as much hast as could bee his Highnese wentt crose the bridge to the staires where the barge lay, C. B. [Colonel Bampfield] leading him; and imediately the boatemen plied the oare so well that they were soone outt of sight, having both wind and tide with them.'*

A remarkable woman for her time, it was the extent and
thoroughness of her planning that really inspires admiration.
Not only was she daring enough to take up with a married man
(although, in her defence, he had been presenting himself as a
widower), she was crucial to the success of the Prince's rescue.

While some accounts claim James was disguised in Lady Anne's
own clothing, her memoirs reveal that she had the costume tailor-
made to James' exact measurements, which she had secured through
cunning use of a length of ribbon on the occasions that she visited
him. Unwilling merely to sit patiently while the rescue was in
progress, she rustled up some dinner for the Prince in case he was
feeling a mite peckish, and if this weren't resourceful enough, she
also sent out for his favourite cake.

Now, this diligence impressed me enough to make me consult a
map: from St James' Palace to Wood Street and back again on foot
is the best part of 5 miles. Maybe it was Lady Anne's motherly
instinct that warranted the lengthy trip at such a risky moment—
or perhaps a Wood Street Cake really was that good. I must admit
that, were I to be intimately involved in the rescue of royalty in a
time of civil unrest, the provision of snacks might be pretty low
on my checklist of important tasks:

Escape route? *Check.*
Guards bribed? *Check.*
Disguise? *Check.*
Boatmen in place? *Check.*
Hold everything—have we got CAKE??

The cake itself is light and delicately spiced. The high fruit content
means that only a relatively small amount of sugar is needed, and
like most of the fruited cakes of this era, it is iced hot. And so,
without further ado, please enjoy a cake fit for a king.

SERVES 10–12

*For the cake*
600g plain flour
2 sachets (14g) fast-action yeast
112g caster sugar
1 tsp ground mace
½ tsp ground cloves
1 tsp ground nutmeg
2 tsp ground cinnamon
450g currants
150g raisins
150g butter

200ml double cream
2 egg yolks
1 egg
1–3 tbsp rosewater, to taste

*For the icing*
2 egg whites
1–2 tbsp rosewater, to taste
225g icing sugar

1 x 24cm spring-form cake tin

In a large bowl, mix together the flour, yeast, caster sugar, spices, currants and raisins.

Put the butter and cream into a saucepan over a low heat and warm gently until the butter is melted. Set aside to cool slightly.

In a separate bowl whisk the yolks and egg with the rosewater, then continue to whisk while slowly adding the cooled cream mixture.

Stir the liquids into the dry ingredients. The texture should be rather wet and similar to a modern fruit cake mix—too wet to knead. When thoroughly mixed, cover and set aside to rise in a warm place for 1 hour.

Preheat the oven to 200°C/180°C fan/gas 6 and grease and line the base of a the cake tin with baking parchment. Line the sides with a double layer of parchment and make sure it stands above the level of the tin itself by several centimetres. This will help keep the top of the cake from scorching, and also prevent the icing from colouring too much.

When the cake mix has risen, pour it into the prepared cake tin. Smooth the mixture but don't press down or you'll squash out all the air bubbles. Bake for 45–50 minutes.

While the cake is baking, prepare the icing by whisking the egg white to soft peaks and then adding the rosewater. Gradually add the icing sugar and whisk to stiff peaks. Set aside.

When the cake is fully baked, remove it from the oven and, while it's still in the tin, spoon the icing over the top. Return the iced cake to the oven and turn off the heat. Let the icing set for 15 minutes then remove the cake from the oven and leave to cool in the tin.

When it's completely cold, remove the cake from the tin. Run a knife around the edge of the icing to loosen the baking parchment and slowly peel away the paper.

# 2

# BISCUITS

Biscuits have a history almost as long as that of bread—the cooling bread ovens proving ideal places for the long baking, or drying out, of biscuits. Their importance in providing easily transportable sustenance is reflected in the Elizabethan records of sailors' daily allowances on board ship that included 'a pound of biscuit'. From early recipes we learn that biscuits could be made from stale bread pounded to breadcrumbs, flavoured with spices, bound with syrup and then dried in the oven, or were an ideal way to use up scraps of dough from bread-making. Their popularity eventually resulted in recipes being developed specifically for biscuits, which gave rise to an astounding range of assorted bakes. In Victorian times, biscuits were purchased by weight, scooped out of bins if the cheaper kind, or carefully removed from glass display cabinets with silver tongs if the more expensive sort; so much nicer than having them packaged in plastic and left on a shelf. The crispness and excellent keeping qualities of biscuits make them a delicious store-cupboard staple and, when they are past their prime, they form the basis of some of our most classic desserts.

# SHORTBREAD

'*Some persons ... hold themselves entitled, after two or three times receiving a piece of shortbread and a glass of elder-flower wine, to ask the lady who has given them such refreshment in marriage.*'
The Trials of Margaret Lyndsay, *1823*

Scotland is famous for its shortbread, and the word usually conjures up images of tartan boxes with pale, creamy, sugared finger biscuits or wedges nestled inside. Traditionalists might argue that the very best shortbread needs nothing more than butter, sugar and flour in its ingredients list, and there's certainly much to savour in the purity of flavour that this produces. However, looking through old baking books, I was surprised and delighted to find that many old recipes contained much bolder flavourings full of candied peel, chopped nuts and caraway comfits. Modern recipes seem positively plain in comparison. Maybe these bold flavourings inspired bold actions.

While I cannot offer any guarantee of spontaneous proposals of marriage, the three shortbread recipes I have chosen, all deliciously different in their own contrasting ways, do hint at the variety that can be achieved beyond the traditionally plain biscuit with which we are all familiar.

# ABERDEEN SHORTBREAD
*1893*

A fabulously crisp biscuit with bags of flavour from candied orange.

**MAKES 20–30 BISCUITS, DEPENDING ON SIZE AND SHAPE**

*340g butter, softened*  
*225g sifted caster sugar*  
*113g ground rice*  
*113g candied orange peel, cut into*  
  *small pieces*

*450g plain flour*

*1 x 5cm plain, round biscuit cutter*

Cream the butter in a stand mixer or with electric beaters for 5 minutes until soft. Add the sugar and cream together for 10 minutes until the mixture is light, almost white and fluffy. Mix in the ground rice and candied peel then gradually work in the flour. It will form a very soft dough.

Lay out some cling film and tip the dough on to it. Use the cling film to press the dough into a ball. Try to avoid touching it with your hands as the high butter content means it will melt very easily. Lay another sheet of cling film over the top of the dough and roll it to a thickness of 2–3cm. Chill in the fridge for at least 30 minutes.

Preheat the oven to 150°C/130°C fan/gas 2. Line two baking sheets with baking parchment.

Remove the chilled shortbread from the fridge and roll it out to 1cm thickness. Using a 5cm plain round cutter, cut out biscuits and transfer to the prepared baking sheets, leaving at least 3cm between each one to allow for spreading. Bake until golden and the edges are just beginning to darken, about 20 minutes.

# AYRESHIRE SHORTBREAD
*1901*

This biscuit is deliciously crumbly, with melt-in-the-mouth buttery richness. I like to use a loose-bottomed flan tin, which gives pretty fluted edges, but use any suitable tin that you have.

MAKES I LARGE CAKE OF SHORTBREAD, TO BE CUT INTO 10–12
SMALLER PORTIONS

*112g plain flour*
*112g rice flour*
*112g butter, plus extra for greasing*
*56g caster sugar, plus extra for*
*sprinkling*

*2 tbsp double cream*
*1 egg yolk*

*1 x rectangular, loose-bottomed*
*flan tin (35 x 12cm), or similar*

Preheat the oven to 150°C/130°C fan/gas 2. Lightly grease the flan tin.

Put the flours, butter and sugar into the bowl of a food processor and blitz until the mixture resembles breadcrumbs.

In a separate bowl, whisk the cream and yolk together and add this to the flour mix. Blitz again to combine.

Tip the mixture into the tin and press down evenly. It should be 1–2cm thick. Prick evenly with a skewer and mark the edges neatly with the tines of a fork.

Bake until lightly golden, about 35–45 minutes. The exact time will depend on the size and shape of your tin.

Cut into fingers while warm, sprinkle with caster sugar then leave to cool completely in the tin.

# MEG DODS' SCOTTISH SHORTBREAD

### 1829

*The Cook and Housewife's Manual* by Mistress Margaret Dods was actually written by Christobel Johnston, author and wife of an Edinburgh publisher. Meg Dods is the name of a fictional character in Sir Walter Scott's novel *St Ronan's Well* (1823). The formidable hostess of the Clekum Inn was said to be modelled on Miss Marian Ritchie, landlady of Scott's local inn, The Cross Keys, at Peebles. The cookery book that bore her name was a great success, and was especially notable for the section on traditional Scottish dishes.

Completely the opposite of the plain, pale golden fingers of traditional shortbread, this recipe is packed with candied peel and chopped nuts and is an absolute riot of flavours.

MAKES I X 24CM CAKE OF SHORTBREAD, TO BE CUT INTO 18–20
SMALLER PORTIONS

*370g plain flour*
*80g cornflour*
*90g caster sugar*
*300g butter, plus extra*
*  for greasing*
*60g candied orange peel, diced*
*30g candied citron peel, diced*

*60g chopped blanched almonds*
*nibbed sugar, for sprinkling*
*caraway seeds, for sprinkling*
*  (optional)*

*1 x 24cm spring-form cake tin*

Preheat the oven to 170°C/150°C fan/gas 3. Grease and line the base of the tin with baking parchment.

Put the flours, sugar and butter into the bowl of a food processor and blitz until the mixture resembles fine breadcrumbs. Tip the mixture into a separate bowl and add the candied peel to the mixture, together with the chopped nuts. Mix all together lightly.

Tip the shortbread mixture into the prepared tin and smooth over. Press lightly into place, but don't compact the mixture into a hard mass.

Crimp the edges with the tines of a fork and prick the centre neatly with a skewer. Scatter nibbed sugar and caraway seeds (my 21st-century substitution for caraway comfits), if liked, over the top of the shortbread.

Bake for 45–60 minutes until golden brown and cooked through. Cool in the tin for 10 minutes then transfer to a wire rack to cool completely.

# BATH BISCUITS
*1675–1700*

Dr William Oliver (1695–1764) is thought to have invented the Bath Oliver biscuit when his initial creation, the Bath Bun, proved too fattening for his patients 'taking the waters' in the ancient spa town. The good doctor's surprise that a yeast bun enriched with butter, eggs and sugar and decorated with dried fruit, candied peel and sugared caraway comfits should have such an effect on his patients is a little perplexing, but there you go. The upshot was a less indulgent bakery item that proved so successful, it was the making of a fortune for Dr Oliver's coachman, Atkins. When Dr Oliver died, in his will he left Atkins the princely sum of £100, some flour (the quantity ranges from 1–100 sacks of the finest wheat flour, depending on which version of the story you read) and the recipe for Dr Oliver's biscuits. With these riches Atkins opened a successful shop in the city. However, as the date of this recipe suggests, unless Dr Oliver was a particularly precocious five-year-old, it's unlikely that his creation was entirely original. A far more likely turn of events would be that Dr Oliver tweaked, and possibly perfected, an already existing recipe such as this one.

You don't have to be taking the waters in Bath to enjoy these biscuits. They make a delightful snack in themselves and are the ideal accompaniment to cheese. They're so simple to whip up—imagine how much nicer it is to enjoy your own crackers fresh from the oven than it is to open a packet of something baked an indeterminate time beforehand and preserved in plastic wrapping.

MAKES 18–20 BISCUITS

*225g strong plain flour, plus extra for dusting*
*½ tsp fast-action yeast*
*32g caster sugar*
*40g butter*

*1 tsp caraway seeds (optional)*
*warm water, to mix*

*1 x large (7–9cm) plain round biscuit cutter*

In a small bowl, mix together the flour, yeast and sugar.

Melt the butter and stir it into the mixture while hot. Add the caraway seeds, if liked. Mix with warm water to a firm paste then cover and set aside to rise in a warm place for 1 hour.

Preheat the oven to 170°C/150°C fan/gas 3. Line 2 or 3 baking sheets with baking parchment.

Roll out the paste thinly on a lightly floured work surface. Dock the paste by pricking it all over with a fork then cut it into biscuits using a large, plain round cutter. Lay the biscuits on the prepared baking sheets and bake for about 15 minutes until crisp.

Transfer to a wire rack to cool.

# *JUMBLES*
## *1685*

The word 'Jumble' is derived from the Arabic word *gemel*, meaning 'twin', and was originally used to describe sweetened dough biscuits formed into double circles or figures-of-eight. Later, the word came to describe biscuits of a whole range of shapes and sizes which were popular for centuries. There is no single recipe for Jumbles, rather there are several types of crisp biscuit made with a variety of ingredients. The simplest recipes are a mixture of almonds, sugar and egg, similar to almond paste, which were formed into fancy shapes and designs and baked, or rather dried, in a cool oven. They were flavoured with rose or orange-flower water and were either gilded or iced for decoration. Other recipes call for flour and butter, and flavourings of seeds, brandy and sack.

One Jumbles recipe with a great story attached is the one known as Bosworth Jumbles. It is alleged that they were the speciality of the cook to Richard III, and a favourite of the King. The recipe was supposedly discovered on Bosworth Field battlefield in 1485, after the King's forces had been defeated. This anecdote really caught my imagination: battle biscuits! How awesome must these biscuits have been, to warrant taking the recipe into battle? And how disappointing for the King that his cook then lost the recipe? Picture King Richard, downhearted, disconsolate, staring at defeat on the battlefield, consoling himself with 'Well, at least we can all have a nice biscuit' only to have a courtier lean forward and murmur 'Sire, about that ...'. Historical accounts tell of the King's final, furious cavalry charge, deep into enemy lines. I'm not saying this was due to the loss of the biscuit recipe, but when you fancy a little smackerel of something and it's not available, lashing out in irritation is quite understandable.

The Bosworth Jumbles recipe makes a very sweet, crisp biscuit, but the high proportion of sugar and butter means that it doesn't hold its shape during baking. Since part of the popularity of jumbles has

always been the decorative shapes it can be rolled into, I've chosen a recipe from a couple of centuries later: it's much better for holding its shape in the oven.

MAKES ABOUT 30–40 BISCUITS, DEPENDING ON SIZE

*150g plain flour, plus extra for
  dusting
112g caster sugar
35g butter
40g ground almonds*

*½ tsp aniseed
1 egg
a little double cream, to mix*

Put the flour, sugar, butter, almonds, aniseed and egg into the bowl of a food processor and blitz until the mixture resembles breadcrumbs.

With the motor running, slowly add a little cream in stages until the mixture comes together in a soft dough.

Tip out the mixture and knead until smooth. Wrap in cling film and chill for 30 minutes.

Preheat the oven to 170°C/150°C fan/gas 3. Line two baking sheets with baking parchment.

Dust your work surface lightly with flour, remove the chilled dough from the fridge and roll it into thin ropes. Form the ropes of dough into various designs: 'S' shapes, knots, curls.

Lay the biscuit shapes on the prepared baking sheets and bake for 15–18 minutes until lightly browned.

Transfer to a wire rack to cool.

# KNIGHT'S BISCUITS
*1669*

These biscuits come from the collection of recipes gathered by the English diplomat and courtier Sir Kenelm Digby (1603–1665), and published from his notes by a faithful servant some years after his death. Although called 'Excellent Small Cakes' in the original manuscript, the instructions place them firmly in the biscuit category.

Stuffed full of sweet, sharp currants, they require very little added sugar and, with just a hint of spice, they're almost a Restoration version of a Garibaldi biscuit—except crisper, with a much more pleasant flavour and less cardboard-y overtones. The original cakes were iced with a mixture of egg white and icing sugar, but I think they are lovely left plain.

Sir Kenelm's original recipe is for quantities suitable for his own privileged household, which must have been extensive as I have had to scale down the original recipe drastically in order to produce a more manageable quantity of biscuits. Since this is still a substantial amount (35–40 biscuits), if you think this might be too daunting, I suggest halving the recipe, except for the yolk.

These biscuits do keep very well in an airtight box or tin but are so tasty, I don't believe they'll stay there for long.

**MAKES 35–40 BISCUITS**

*450g plain flour*
*225g caster sugar*
*225g butter, softened,*
  *plus extra for greasing*
*1 egg yolk*
*100ml double cream*

*450g currants*
*½ nutmeg, grated*
*2 tbsp cream sherry*

*1 x 7cm fluted round biscuit cutter*

Preheat the oven to 110°C/90°C fan/gas ¼.

Sift the flour on to a baking tray and dry in the oven for
20 minutes. Remove the flour and increase the oven temperature
to 200°C/180°C fan/gas 6. Grease and line two baking sheets with
baking parchment.

In a bowl, cream together the sugar and butter. In a jug, mix the
egg yolk with the double cream and stir this into the mixture in the
bowl along with the remaining ingredients. Mix well until you have
a soft dough. Since the quantity of dough is quite large, cut it in
half and work with just one piece at a time.

Roll out the dough until it's approximately 8mm thick. As the
dough will be soft and sticky, the best way to do this is to roll it
between two sheets of cling film. Cut out the biscuits using the
fluted round cutter and prick them all over with a fork. Transfer to
the prepared baking sheets, leaving a 2cm space between each one.

Bake until light-golden brown, about 15–20 minutes. Transfer to a
wire rack to cool.

# LACE MERINGUES
*1690*

These meringues can be cut, shaped and embellished in ways far beyond the swirls and blobs that usually present the limit of meringue artistry. The effect of the oven on the raw biscuit paste is almost magical. They go in as flat discs of what looks like royal icing and come out looking like snowflake puffs. The tiny amount of ingredients required only adds to the sense of alchemy.

I've found these biscuits under a variety of names in various handwritten manuscripts, usually with the title of 'orange bisket' or 'lemon bisket', but also abbesses, gentilesses, puff jumbles, bisketillons and bisket bread. The original recipe called for gum dragon, which used to be a common ingredient and has always sounded exotic and mysterious to me. Three hundred years ago it would have been prepared by hand, by steeping hardened resin in rosewater overnight before grinding it in a pestle and mortar. Nowadays, it's readily available, already prepared. Known by its proper name of gum tragacanth, it is mostly used to stabilise sugar paste for creating delicate and lifelike sugar flowers. It can be obtained from sugarcraft suppliers and online. You can make these little puffs without the gum tragacanth, but the paste is a little more difficult to handle.

**MAKES 15–20 MERINGUES, DEPENDING ON SIZE**

*250–300g icing sugar*
*½ tsp gum tragacanth (optional)*
*zest of 1 orange or lemon*
*1 egg white*
*cornflour, for dusting*
  *(optional)*

*1 x 7–8cm fluted round biscuit*
  *cutter, plus mini pastry cutters*
  *(or a thimble) in shapes of choice*

Preheat the oven to 140°C/120°C fan/gas 1. Line a baking sheet with baking parchment.

Place 3–4 tablespoons of icing sugar in a small bowl and mix in the gum tragacanth, if using.

In a separate bowl, mix together the zest and egg white then add the gum tragacanth mixture. Mix until well combined and smooth. Continue adding icing sugar, a spoonful at a time, until the mixture comes together into a smooth and rollable paste. It might take quite a large amount of sugar, depending on the water content of the egg white and how much flavouring was added.

Lightly dust the work surface with cornflour or icing sugar and roll out the paste to a thickness of 3–4mm. Dust your pastry cutters to stop the paste sticking, and cut out the biscuits. To make circular puffs, cut out circles with the 7–8cm cutter then, using mini pastry cutters (or, as the original recipe suggests, a thimble), cut out patterns in each disc of paste. Alternatively, to make individual puffs, use mini cutters in a variety of shapes. Whatever shape you choose, press the cutters straight down to get a clean cut and do not twist. This will help the biscuits to rise evenly.

Transfer the biscuits to the lined baking sheet. Bake circular biscuits for 6–7 minutes until puffed, risen and crisp; smaller biscuits for 4–5 minutes. Allow to firm up on the baking parchment for 5 minutes then transfter to a wire rack to cool completely.

## VARIATIONS

Substitute the citrus zest with 15g ground almonds and 3–4 drops of rose or orange-flower water for a more subtle-flavoured biscuit.

For real wow-factor, use a little food colouring to tint the paste. A variety of bright shades is particularly eye-catching.

# *LEMAN'S BISCUITS*
*1830*

In 1795 Michael Leman (or Lemann; there's some disagreement) leased premises on Threadneedle Street in the City of London and set up a 'Biscuit Manufactory'.[2] It soon won a reputation for the quality of its bakes, with entire batches selling out within minutes of being drawn from the oven.[3]

Mr Leman took out no patent on his recipes. Whether this was deliberate or not is debatable, but it proved to be a cunning business move for, by not specifying the exact recipes of his bakes, Mr Leman effectively thwarted the aspirations of other city bakers to discover the secrets of his success.[4] Nevertheless, imitation recipes did appear in some 19th-century cookery books and, eventually, a rival biscuit-maker appeared in the guise of one Mr Moxhay who, after failing to buy the biscuit-making business of a neighbour in Gracechurch Street, promptly turned his shoemaker's shop into a bakery and proceeded to carve out a new career as a biscuit-maker.

Moxhay later joined forces with a former foreman of Leman's bakery and opened a rival establishment directly opposite the Leman factory. Nevertheless, both businesses appear to have prospered, Leman's surviving two moves, first to London Wall and thence to St Swithin's Lane,[5] and Mr Moxhay expanding his interests into both property and shipping.[6] Eliza Acton gives a recipe for Threadneedle Street Biscuits, though whether they imitate Leman's or Moxhay's isn't clear.

The fame of the Leman's Biscuit spread far and wide. I found a number of old Australian newspaper advertisements announcing the arrival of new shipments of the biscuits, thereby demonstrating both their popularity and, after a lengthy sea voyage, their keeping qualities. As if to reinforce their desirability, I also found them mentioned in a description of the arrival in Sydney of young female immigrants, keen to start a new life in the land down under:

*'Another lot—these look genteel; they are dressed for the occasion: one has been a favourite; it has been rumoured that, at sea, she ate Leman's biscuit; the steward, to her, has been attentive—liberal with the captain's store.'* [7]

What juicy gossip: the hushed tone practically drips with disapproval. Now extremely curious about these impressive biscuits, I immediately thought up a new slogan for them: Leman's Biscuits —so good, you'll trade your reputation for them!

It turns out that, for a plain biscuit, Leman's Biscuits really are rather satisfying. They cleverly walk the line between sweet and savoury and are suitable for both adults and children. The outside is crisp and the inside, while still crisp enough to be a biscuit, is of a much lighter, and more delicate, texture. Some sources suggest stuffing them into pockets to nibble on during energetic excursions. The addition of cheese and pieces of fruit make a simple, yet tasty, picnic meal.

MAKES 20–24 SQUARE BISCUITS

*225g plain flour, plus extra for dusting*
*1 tsp bicarbonate of soda*
*56g butter*
*28g sugar*

*150ml warm milk, to mix*

*1 x 5cm fluted square biscuit cutter*

Preheat the oven to 140°C/120°C fan/gas 1. Line a baking sheet with baking parchment.

Put the flour, bicarbonate of soda, butter and sugar into the bowl of a food processor and blitz until the mixture resembles breadcrumbs.

Tip the mixture into a bowl and slowly add the milk, working it into the mixture until it comes together in a firm paste.

Knead the dough until smooth then roll it out thinly (5mm) on a lightly floured surface and cut into 20–24 square biscuits, using the biscuit cutter (or a knife or pizza wheel). Transfer to the lined baking sheet and prick the centres of the biscuits neatly 4 or 5 times with a fork.

Bake the biscuits gently until crisp, dry and evenly browned, about 12–15 minutes. Transfer to a wire rack to cool.

# ROUT BISCUITS
*19th century*

A rout was a particular type of social occasion, popular in Georgian England. In London, routs followed a specific format, which was to be strictly observed. City routs were events attended by the 'ton', the contemporary slang for what we would today call the 'in-crowd'. Full evening dress was expected and the main purpose of the rout was to pay respects to the hostess and chat with acquaintances. A book published in 1825 and snappily entitled *Domestic duties; or, Instructions to young married ladies, and the regulation of their conduct in the various relations and duties of married life* by Mrs William Parkes, listed everything the social ingénue might need to stage her own successful rout.

To prepare the house for a rout, the hostess should remove all furniture from the public rooms and replace it with space-saving benches along the walls. Good lighting, pleasant floral decorations (but no greens, yellows or oranges, as their reflections would turn guests' complexions bilious), and light refreshments in a side room were also required. The hostess should be dressed in suitable evening garb and be ready at the door to greet guests between the hours of 9 p.m. and midnight.

In theory, this all seems fairly simple and straightforward, but what happened in practice was closer to a rugby scrum, or the first day of the January sales. A dismayed Frenchman, Monsieur Louis Simond, recounted the London rout scene in his chronicle of a tour of Great Britain in 1810–11:

*'Nobody sits; there is no conversation, no cards, no music; only elbowing, turning, and winding from room to room; then, at the end of a quarter of an hour, escaping to the hall door to wait for the carriage, spending more time upon the threshold among footmen than you had done above stairs with their masters. From this rout you drive to another, where, after waiting your turn to arrive at the door, perhaps*

*half an hour, the street being full of carriages, you alight, begin the same round, and end it in the same manner.'* [8]

All of which sounds thoroughly frazzling and unpleasant. According to Mrs Parkes, however, the purpose of the evening was not to enjoy oneself at all, but to gather enough gossip to keep conversations lively until the next social event.

*'Few expect any gratification from the rout itself; but the whole pleasure consists in the anticipation of the following days' gossip, which the faintings, tearing of dresses, and elbowings which have occurred, are likely to afford. To meet a fashionable friend next day in the park, without having been at Lady A —'s, would be sufficient to exclude the absentee from any claim to ton, while to have been squeezed into a corner with the Marchioness of B —, or the Duchess of C — is a most enviable event, and capable of affording conversation for at least ten days.'* [9]

The refreshments available were usually small, light biscuits and cakes that could be easily consumed without the need for a plate. These biscuits are ideal, and because they are essentially all made from the same biscuit mix formed into a variety of shapes and dressed with fruits, nuts and icing, they are a simple way to give the impression of a great deal of effort at the outlay of very little.

MAKES 30–40 BISCUITS, DEPENDING ON SIZE AND SHAPE

*112g ground almonds*
*112g caster sugar*
*112g sponge-cake crumbs*
*zest of 1 orange*
*1 tsp orange-flower water*
*3 large yegg olks, beaten*
*fondant icing, chopped nuts,*
   *crushed biscuit crumbs, glacé*
   *fruits, nuts, conserve, jam or fruit*
   *curd, to decorate*

*1 x small, round plain or scallop-edged biscuit cutter (plus 1 x 4 or 5cm plain or scallop-edged cutter, optional)*

Put all the ingredients except the yolks and decorations into a bowl. Gradually add the beaten yolks, stirring continuously, until the mixture comes together in a paste. How much of the yolks is needed will depend on the moisture in the rest of the ingredients.

Using about 15–20g dough per shape, make the paste into whatever shapes you like. Keep the size small and dainty. Traditional designs might include knots, fleurs-de-lys, 'S' scrolls, 'C' scrolls and shell spirals.

*To make a cone*

Roll out the paste and cut out circles with a small, round plain or scallop-edged, cutter. Dampen the edges with water and wrap the circles around your finger to make a cone shape.

*To make a two-sided basket*

Cut the paste with a 4cm scallop-edged cutter and pinch together the opposite sides to make a two-ended basket shape. Turn the basket 90 degrees and pinch again to form the handle.

*To make a three-cornered basket*

Cut the circles using a 5cm cutter. Dampen the edges with water then lift the edges of the basket at three points and press towards the middle.

Place your shapes on a chopping board and set aside to dry for 2–3 hours or overnight.

When you're ready to cook your biscuits, preheat the oven to 200°C/180°C fan/gas 6. Line two baking sheets with baking parchment.

Transfer your biscuits to the lined baking sheets and bake for 10–15 minutes until golden and the edges are just touched with brown. (Overbaking will cause the biscuits to lose their shape.) Remove from the oven and transfer to a wire rack to cool.

Once the biscuits have cooled, decorate the edges of the shapes with fondant icing. For hollow shapes such as cones and baskets, pipe icing around the basket edge and dip into chopped nuts, or crushed biscuit crumbs. Fill with glacé fruits, nuts, conserve, jam or fruit curd.

# SHAVINGS
*17th century*

The ability of biscuits to crisp up on cooling was noted by cooks
and bakers hundreds of years ago, and recipes for thin biscuits rolled
around sticks while still warm from the oven can be found in many
mid 17th-century manuscripts. Another, easier method was to lay
the warm biscuits over a rolling pin until they had cooled enough
to hold their shape. I found one such recipe with the title 'Bent
Biscuits', which seemed a very practical, no-nonsense, 'call a spade
a spade' title. Fabulous!

The shapes you can make are limited only by your imagination.
Usually, they are a variation on a circle, curved in various ways,
but the design I've chosen is called 'Shavings'. Long lines of batter
are laid out on baking parchment and, once baked, turned around
a long spoon handle. The biscuits hold their spiral shape and
resemble the curled shavings from planed wood, as might be seen
on a carpenter's workshop floor. My grandfather had just such a
workshop and, amongst other carpentry jobs, used to make wooden
furniture for my doll's house. Just seeing these biscuits brings back
memories of him working in his workshop while I played with the
paper-thin curls of wood as a child.

Do not bake too many of these biscuits at a time, as they firm up
extremely quickly. I suggest making no more than three at once and
to begin with, just two. Also, you will be limited by the number of
long-handled spoons you possess.

MAKES 15–20 BISCUITS, DEPENDING ON SIZE

*113g icing sugar*
*85g plain flour*
*60g ground almonds*
*1 tsp vanilla extract*
*egg whites, beaten, to mix*

*30g butter, melted*

*1 x piping bag fitted with an 8mm*
*plain nozzle*

Preheat the oven to 220°C/200°C fan/gas 7. Line a baking sheet with baking parchment and make 2 parallel folds along the long sides, 30cm apart. These will act as a guide when piping the batter and help keep the biscuits a uniform length.

In a bowl, mix together the icing sugar, flour, ground almonds and vanilla extract. Whisk in enough egg whites to make a soft batter then fold in the melted butter.

Pour the batter into the piping bag. Be sure to close off the tip of the bag before you fill it, to prevent the batter coming straight out again.

Pipe three 30cm lines, well spaced apart, between the 2 folds in the baking parchment. The mixture will spread a little but you can straighten any wobbly edges with a dough scraper or palette knife.

Bake for 4–7 minutes until set and the edges of the biscuits are just touched with brown.

*Rolling the biscuits*
You need to work quickly to roll all the biscuits before they set.

Have your 3 long spoons ready. Remove the baking sheet from the oven, but keep the parchment paper on it: the residual heat will help keep the biscuits soft. Hold the head of one of the spoons in one hand and use your thumb to hold one end of the biscuit against the spoon handle. With your other hand, quickly wind the biscuit around the handle. Set aside to cool. Repeat for the other biscuits.

Pipe 3 new lines of batter and return the baking sheet to the oven. The first biscuits will have cooled enough for you to remove them from the spoon handles before the next batch is cooked.

# SHREWSBURY CAKES
*Based on 17th- and 19th-century recipes*

Shrewsbury is about an hour from where I live, but I only became aware of Shrewsbury Cakes while flicking through numerous cookery books and manuscripts. No matter the decade, it seemed there was a Shrewsbury Cake recipe of some description almost everywhere I looked. After a more organised search I found no fewer than 74 recipes for these English shortbread biscuits, ranging in date from 1621 to 1865.

Despite finding so many, the recipes seemed to lack cohesion, with a wide range of textures and flavourings being scattered across the centuries. Some recipes had the traditional shortbread 1-2-3 proportions of sugar, butter and flour, while others were rich, with equal quantities of all three. These differing proportions meant that the biscuits were cooked at a range of temperatures, with oven heat described from anything between very cool to very hot. The early recipes favoured light and delicate flavourings of rosewater, nutmeg and cinnamon. Later, these became more robust, with caraway, cloves and mace, while the biscuit size grew to an impressive 12cm diameter. In the 19th century, the bold flavours faded from popularity and a smaller, lighter, more dainty biscuit, with just a hint of lemon, became fashionable.

There was such a great deal of variety over the centuries that it was difficult to establish exactly which elements constituted a Shrewsbury Cake. Nevertheless, using a range of sources, it was possible to glean little details here and there, of a more general idea of the biscuit's attributes. For example, in the summer of 1602 an Edward, Lord Herbert of Cherbury, sent some biscuits to his guardian with a note to *'Measure not my love by the substance of it, which is brittle, but by the form of it, which is circular.'*

A note in a handwritten manuscript advised that two ounces (56g) of dough made a penny cake, and four (112g) made a two-penny cake. This raised my eyebrows somewhat because even the smaller of the two quantities is still quite a substantial amount of dough for a single biscuit. However, the impressive size was supported by other sources which claimed that the biscuits should be the size of one's hand, and be made by cutting around a small wooden trencher or wooden dish. It became apparent from other recipes that the key characteristics of a Shrewsbury Cake were that it should be large, thin, circular, sweet and crisp.

I've chosen four recipes; three from the 17th century, and one from the late Victorian era. The three older recipes hint at the diversity of popular flavourings that graced the century, and are a refreshing change from our vanilla- and chocolate-obsessed times. The proportions of sugar, butter and flour vary slightly in each recipe, which also gives the biscuits greater variety, but if you have a preference for one particular biscuit texture, you could just use that recipe and swap in the different spice combinations to your liking.

# HANNAH WOOLLEY'S SHREWSBURY CAKES
*1672*

MAKES 15–20 BISCUITS

| | |
|---|---|
| *225g plain flour, plus extra for dusting* | *1 tbsp rosewater* |
| | *1 egg* |
| *85g sugar* | |
| *112g butter* | *1 x 8cm plain round biscuit cutter* |
| *1 tbsp ground cinnamon* | *(or use lid from tin/jar)* |

Put the flour, sugar, butter, cinnamon and rosewater into the bowl of a food processor and blitz until the mixture resembles breadcrumbs. Whisk the egg and add it gradually to the mixture, while the motor is running. You might not need all the egg, so add a little at a time and wait until it has been thoroughly mixed in before adding more. Stop when the mixture comes together in a ball.

Tip out the dough on to a lightly floured work surface and knead it until smooth. Wrap it in cling film and chill in the fridge for at least 30 minutes.

Preheat the oven to 170°C/150°C fan/gas 3. Line a baking sheet with baking parchment.

Remove the chilled dough from the fridge and roll it out thinly to 3–4mm. Cut out the biscuits, using a large 8cm plain round cutter. If you don't have one, improvise using a suitable lid from a jar or tin. I use the lid of my coffee tin.

Place the biscuits on the lined baking sheet and bake for 7–8 minutes until golden. Transfer to a wire rack to cool.

# JANE NEWTON'S SHREWSBURY CAKES
*1675*

MAKES 10–15 BISCUITS

*170g plain flour, plus extra for*
  *dusting*
*56g sugar*
*112g butter*
*2 tsp ground cinnamon*

*2 tsp rosewater*
*1 egg*
*1 tsp caraway seeds*

*1 x 10cm plain round cutter*

Put the flour, sugar, butter, cinnamon and rosewater into the bowl of a food processor and blitz until the mixture resembles breadcrumbs.

Whisk the egg and gradually add it to the mixture while the motor is running. You might not need all the egg, so add a little at a time and wait until it has been thoroughly mixed in before adding more. Stop when the mixture comes together in a ball.

Tip out the dough on to a lightly floured work surface and scatter the caraway seeds over it. Knead the dough until smooth, wrap it in cling film and chill in the fridge for at least 30 minutes.

Preheat the oven to 180°C/160°C fan/gas 4. Line a baking sheet with baking parchment.

Remove the chilled dough from the fridge and roll it out thinly, to 3–4mm. Prick it all over, using a fork or biscuit docker, and cut out biscuits using a large, plain round 10cm cutter. Place them, well spaced out, on the lined baking sheet and bake for 7–8 minutes until golden. Transfer to a wire rack to cool.

# ELIZABETH GODFREY'S SHREWSBURY CAKES
*1686*

**MAKES 15–20 BISCUITS**

*225g plain flour, plus extra for dusting*
*112g sugar*
*170g butter*
*1 egg yolk*

*1 tsp ground coriander*
*1 tsp ground mace*
*2–3 tbsp cream sherry, to mix*

*1 x 8cm plain round cutter*

Put the flour, sugar, butter, yolk and spices into the bowl of a food processor and blitz until the mixture resembles breadcrumbs.

Gradually add the sherry to the mixture, while the motor is running, a spoonful at a time. Depending on the moisture content of your butter and flour, and the size of the egg yolk, this will be between 2 and 3 tablespoons. Stop when the mixture comes together in a ball.

Tip out the dough on to a lightly floured work surface and knead until smooth. Wrap in cling film and chill for at least 30 minutes.

Preheat the oven to 180°C/160°C fan/gas 4. Line a baking sheet with baking parchment.

Remove the chilled dough from the fridge and roll it out thinly, to about 3–4mm. Prick the dough all over using either a fork or a biscuit docker. Cut into biscuits using an 8cm plain round cutter.

Place the biscuits, well spaced out, on the lined baking sheet and bake for 7–8 minutes until golden. Transfer to a wire rack to cool.

# HARRIS & BORELLA'S SHREWSBURY CAKES

*1890s*

MAKES 25–30 BISCUITS

*225g plain flour, plus extra for
    dusting
112g caster sugar
140g butter
zest of 1 small lemon*

*1 egg*

*1 x 6cm plain, round biscuit cutter,
    or similar*

Put the flour, sugar, butter and lemon zest into the bowl of a food processor and blitz until the mixture resembles breadcrumbs.

Whisk the egg and gradually add to the mixture, while the motor is running. You might not need all the egg, so add a little at a time and wait until it has been thoroughly mixed in before adding more. Stop when the mixture comes together in a ball.

Tip out the dough on to a lightly floured surface and knead until smooth. Wrap in cling film and chill for at least 30 minutes.

Preheat the oven to 200°C/180°C fan/gas 6. Line a baking sheet with baking parchment.

Remove the dough from the fridge and cut it in half. Put one half back in the fridge. The dough will be easier to handle if you just work with half of it at a time. Roll the dough out thinly, to about 3–4mm thick. Cut out the biscuits, using a 6cm plain, round cutter.

Place the biscuits, well spaced out, on the lined baking sheet and bake for 7–8 minutes until golden and tinged with brown at the edges. Transfer to a wire rack to cool.

# NAPLES BISCUITS
*Mid to late 17th century to present day*

These biscuits must qualify as one of the oldest biscuits still sold today, and they are very straightforward to make. Over the years they have taken many names, including 'Funeral Biscuits', 'Boudoir Biscuits' and 'Ladyfingers', but they are probably most familiar to us today as sponge fingers.

The Naples Biscuit is a fatless sponge biscuit that has been dried in the oven after an initial baking. It can be stored almost indefinitely for use in a number of recipes. Gated biscuits were often used as a thickener in puddings and sauces and the biscuits themselves were the basis for sack creams (creamy trifles flavoured with fortified wine) and more elaborate trifles. They were also served alongside popular creams, fools and syllabubs to provide a contrasting crunch to the smooth, rich desserts. They are ideal for dipping.

In the late 18th and 19th centuries it became the fashion, especially in Yorkshire and Lincolnshire, to serve them to mourners at funerals in much the same way children today receive party bags to take home.

*'But if at the funeral of the richer sort, instead of hot ale they had burnt wine and Savoy biscuits, and a paper with two Naples biscuits sealed up to carry home for their families. The paper in which these biscuits were sealed was printed on one side with a coffin, cross-bones, skulls, hacks, spades, hour-glass, &c.; but this custom is now, I think, left off, and they wrap them only in a sheet of clean, writing paper sealed with black wax.'* The Gentleman's Magazine, 1802

No doubt the images printed on the paper, combined with the brittle, dry biscuits within, were intended to remind the mourners of their own mortality. Later accounts describe an official announcement of death on the paper. These packages could then be sent to relatives who were unable to travel to the funeral.

Possibly in an attempt to create a lighter, frothier image, in the early part of the 20th century they were renamed 'Boudoir Biscuits'. The imagery this conjured up was much more popular than that created by their previous incarnation and they have remained popular enough to this day to be used in trifles and Charlottes or indeed, as they were centuries ago, for dipping into creamy desserts.

Seventeenth-century recipes were flavoured with rosewater, orange-flower water, ambergris, musk, or caraway, and sometimes were not flavoured at all. I've chosen orange-flower water as it's so light and delicate, but feel free to substitute any flavourings you wish. If using vanilla extract, use just ½ teaspoon. This recipe is essentially a proportional one, so it's easy to scale up if a greater quantity is required.

**MAKES 20–30 BISCUITS**

*4 eggs, separated*  
*the weight of 2 eggs in caster sugar*  
*1 tsp orange-flower water*  
*the weight of 2 eggs in plain flour*

*caster sugar, for dusting*

*1 x piping bag fitted with a*  
*plain 1.25cm nozzle*

Preheat the oven to 200°C/180°C fan/gas 6. Line a baking sheet with baking parchment and make 2 folds in the paper to act as guides when piping the batter and to help keep the biscuits a uniform size. They should be about 10cm apart.

In a bowl, whisk the whites to soft peaks. Gradually add half the sugar, a teaspoon at a time, and whisk to stiff peaks. Set aside.

In a separate bowl, whisk the yolks with the orange-flower water and the remaining sugar until light and creamy, 5–10 minutes.

Fold the egg whites into the yolks and gradually fold in the flour until just combined then stop mixing.

Fill the piping bag with the mixture and pipe the biscuits in even rows on to the baking sheet, leaving a 2cm space between each one for them to spread into. Don't worry if the edges of the biscuits aren't perfectly straight and even, they can easily be trimmed with a knife if necessary.

Dust the biscuits with caster sugar then lift the edge of the paper and shake off any excess sugar.

Bake for 10–15 minutes until crisp and golden. Remove the biscuits from the oven but leave them on the paper until cold before attempting to remove them. If they seem a little moist, return them to the cooling oven to finish drying.

# PEARL BISCUITS
*1890s*

Pearl Biscuits are essentially a variation of Naples Biscuits, made with egg whites only and with slightly different proportions of sugar and flour. They are wonderfully pale and shimmering, as their name so aptly suggests. They can be used in the same way as Naples Biscuits, possibly when a more striking appearance is desirable, against a dark damson fool or with a pale lemon syllabub.

**MAKES 20–30 BISCUITS, DEPENDING ON SIZE**

| | |
|---|---|
| *150ml egg whites* | *icing sugar, for dusting* |
| *1 tsp orange-flower water* | |
| *165g caster sugar* | *1 x piping bag fitted with a* |
| *85g plain flour* | *plain 1.25cm nozzle* |

Preheat the oven to 180°C/160°C fan/gas 4. Line a baking sheet with baking parchment and make 2 folds in the paper, about 10cm apart, to act as guides when piping the batter.

In a bowl, whisk the egg whites with the orange-flower water to soft peaks. Gradually add the sugar, a teaspoon at a time, and whisk to stiff peaks. Gradually fold in the flour until combined. Do not over-mix.

Fill the piping bag with the mixture and pipe the biscuits in even rows on to the baking sheet, leaving a 3cm space between each one. Don't worry if the biscuits aren't perfectly straight, they can easily be trimmed later.

Dust with icing sugar then lift the edge of the paper and shake off the excess. Leave to sit for 15 minutes until the icing sugar has partially dissolved, then bake on the bottom shelf of the oven for 10–15 minutes until crisp, but still pale. Leave the biscuits on the tray in a warm place overnight to dry out completely.

# RATAFIAS
*1770*

These macaroon-style biscuits were extremely popular in the 17th and 18th centuries. Much like Madeira cake, which came to be known by the drink that traditionally accompanied it, they were usually enjoyed with a glass of the almond-flavoured liqueur known as Ratafia.

Carefully baked and dried, if properly stored these biscuits stay crisp and tasty for a long time. They are perfect for serving with delicate creams, fools and syllabubs, to give a fantastically crunchy contrast in texture. You can also use them in trifles, in place of sponges: their very dryness makes them ideal for soaking up whatever alcohol you like to slosh in and they will hold their shape much better. Alternatively, just enjoy them with a cup of something for elevenses.

Traditionally, ratafias contained both sweet and bitter almonds, the bitter almonds giving the biscuits a distinctive flavour. However, a hydrogen cyanide concentration of between 4 and 9mg per nut makes bitter almonds somewhat hazardous in high quantities so, if you like a strong almond flavour, add a few drops of almond flavouring, to taste.

**MAKES 40–50 SMALL BISCUITS**

*75ml egg whites*
*115g ground almonds*
*225g caster sugar*

Preheat the oven to 150°C/130°C fan/gas 2. Line 2 baking sheets with baking parchment.

In a bowl, whisk the egg whites to stiff peaks. Fold in the ground almonds then stir in the sugar, a little at a time, until incorporated.

Using a piping bag or teaspoon, drop the mixture on to the lined baking sheets. The mixture will spread during cooking, so make the drops no larger than 2–3cm in diameter and space them 3cm apart.

Bake for 30–40 minutes until golden brown and crisp.

Slide the baking parchment on to wire racks to cool. Leave the biscuits on the paper until they are completely cold, when they will be easier to remove.

Stored in an airtight box or tin, they will keep very well and stay crisp for a long time.

# 3

# GINGERBREAD

*'And I had but one penny in the world, thou should'st have it to buy gingerbread.'* Love's Labor's Lost, *William Shakespeare*

Gingerbread was one of the first sweetmeats, originally made by mixing breadcrumbs, spices and honey and then pressing the mixture into moulds to dry. It was sometimes decorated with cloves and box leaves and occasionally even gilded. Elizabeth I used to present favoured dignitaries visiting court with their likenesses in gingerbread.

At some point, gingerbread split into two separate forms: cake and biscuit. Both forms are popular throughout the UK, with great numbers of local varieties and specialities. Whatever your personal taste, there's sure to be a recipe that's just right for you. This chapter gives a glimpse of some of the delicious forms gingerbread can take.

# BROONIE
*1890*

F. Marian McNeill was a Scottish traditionalist and folklorist, born in Holm, on Orkney, in 1885. In her celebrated book on Scottish food customs and traditions, *The Scots Kitchen*, first published in 1929, she remembers that Broonie was the first recipe she ever collected. She recalls, at the age of five or six, wanting to know how to make her playmate's lunchtime snack. As an adult, armed with the list of ingredients she'd memorised as a child, she was able to work out the correct proportions.

This loaf cake has a wonderful texture from the oatmeal and is like a lighter, milder version of parkin. As with all treacle-based cakes, it also has great keeping qualities if kept wrapped up in an airtight box or tin. I made a large loaf for some friends and they were still enjoying it three weeks later!

**MAKES I LARGE LOAF CAKE**

| | |
|---|---|
| *170g medium oatmeal* | *1 egg* |
| *170g plain flour* | *150ml milk* |
| *1 tsp ground ginger* | *150ml natural yoghurt* |
| *¾ tsp baking powder* | |
| *60g butter, plus extra for greasing* | *1 x 2kg/28cm loaf tin, or similar* |
| *30ml treacle* | *capacity* |
| *112g soft brown sugar* | |

Preheat the oven to 180°C/160°C fan/gas 4. Grease and line the loaf tin with baking parchment.

Sift the oatmeal, flour, ginger and baking powder into a bowl.

Put the butter, treacle and sugar into a pan and warm gently until the butter is melted and the sugar dissolved. Remove from the heat.

Whisk the egg and add to the dry ingredients, together with the warm treacle mixture.

Stir the milk and yoghurt together and gradually add to the mixture until a 'dropping' consistency is formed (it should drop freely off a spoon). Use more milk if necessary.

Pour the mixture into the prepared tin and smooth the surface. Bake for 1–1½ hours until well risen and firm in the middle.

Set aside to cool in the tin.

# COCONUT GINGERBREAD
## 1845

Originally a poet, Eliza Acton is considered by many to be the first to write a cookery book as we would recognise it today. Her *Modern Cookery for Private Families* (1845) was the first to separate a list of ingredients from the methodology, and was aimed specifically at small households. Additionally, the author's observations on potential problems, and recommendations for subtle variations that were included, emphasised Eliza's personal experience with the recipes (unlike many of her contemporaries and a great number of cookery authors that were to follow). The book was an immediate success and remained in print for almost 60 years. She was to write only one other—*The English Bread Book* (1857)—in which she voices her strong views against the adulteration and processing of food (an opinion that would be echoed by Doris Grant almost a century later: see entry for The Grant Loaf, page 299).

This is Eliza's recipe for Coconut Gingerbread Cakes, scaled down to a manageable quantity. The bite-sized cakes are dark with the glossy richness of traditional gingerbread, the added coconut giving a lighter, moister texture as well as a more complex flavour. Fresh coconut is a little time-consuming to prepare, but very much worth the effort.

**MAKES 24 BITE-SIZED CAKES**

| | |
|---|---|
| *80g fresh grated coconut* | *110g treacle* |
| *75g plain flour* | *40g soft dark brown sugar* |
| *75g ground rice* | *40g butter, plus extra for greasing* |
| *2 tsp ground ginger* | |
| *zest of 1 lemon* | *1 x 24-hole mini-muffin tin* |

*To prepare the fresh coconut*
Preheat the oven to 200°C/180°C fan/gas 6.

With a sharp-pointed implement, poke a hole through one of the 3 'eyes' located at one end of the coconut. There is always one that is weaker than the other two, so if the one you try first seems too hard, try one of the others. Shake out the coconut water.

Put the coconut in the oven for 20 minutes. This will crack the coconut shell and also help loosen the flesh from the shell.

Wrap the coconut in a clean hand towel and strike it against a hard surface to break the shell into pieces.

Ease the white flesh from the hard shell and remove the dark skin with a sharp knife or vegetable peeler. Grate the white flesh either by hand or using a food processor.

*To make the coconut gingerbread*
Mix the flour, ground rice, ginger and lemon rind in a bowl and set aside.

Put the treacle, sugar and butter into a saucepan and heat gently until the butter is melted and the sugar dissolved. Remove from the heat.

Add the dry ingredients to the warm treacle mixture and stir to combine. Stir in the coconut and then set the mixture aside to cool.

Preheat the oven to 120°C/100°C fan/gas ½. Grease the cups of the muffin tins well.

Divide the cooled mixture into 20g pieces, roll each piece into a ball and drop them into the greased mini-muffin cups.

Bake for 30 minutes then transfer to a wire rack to cool.

# HONEYCOMB GINGERBREAD
## *1830*

This is a beautifully light and crisp biscuit, ethereally thin to the point of translucency, and yet so simple to make. The original recipe called for the cooked biscuit sheet to be cut into squares and then rolled around the handle of a wooden spoon, like brandy snaps, but just breaking it into shards is easier and I much prefer the informal, organic look that this gives. During baking, the large grains of demerara sugar melt and leave behind lace-like honeycomb pockets.

This recipe is adapted from the cookery book of Mrs Catherine Emily Dalgairns. *The Practice of Cookery* was first published in Edinburgh in 1829 and was a bestseller for over 30 years, being displaced only by the publication of Isabella Beeton's *Book of Household Management* (1861). Mrs Dalgairns was not Scottish. She was born and raised on Prince Edward Island, in what is now Canada. She married into a well-to-do Scottish family and eventually settled in Dundee, embracing the traditional food of her adopted country with gusto. Her book was compared favourably to the acknowledged cookery powerhouses of the day, Mrs Eliza Rundell and Dr William Kitchener:

> '..and though we shall not put away Rundell and Kitchener for Mrs *Dalgairns, she is far more copious than they are, far more various and to us more novel.'* The Spectator

This wafer-thin gingerbread will absorb moisture easily and, in doing so, will lose its snap and crispness. To keep it at its best, store in an airtight container or resealable food bag as soon as it is cold.

MAKES 20–30 DELICATE WAFERS OR 3 HUGE, INDULGENT SLABS

*40g butter*

*80g treacle*

*zest and juice of ½ lemon*

*80g plain flour*

*80g demerera sugar*

*¾ tsp allspice*

*1½ tsp ground ginger*

Preheat the oven to 140°C/120°C fan/gas 1. Line a baking sheet with baking parchment.

Put the butter and treacle into a small pan and warm gently over a low heat until melted. Stir to combine then add the lemon zest and juice. Set aside to cool until just warm.

Mix the remaining ingredients thoroughly in a bowl. Add the warm treacle mixture to the dry mix and stir until thoroughly blended. (If you add the treacle while it is too warm, it will dissolve the sugar grains and the resulting gingerbread will be less delicate.)

Spread the paste thinly on to the lined baking sheet. The broader the piece of paste, the more tricky it will be to bake thoroughly. Better to roll it into three or four long, narrow pieces than one large, broad one. If the spreading is proving difficult, cover the paste with a second sheet of parchment and use a rolling pin to roll it thinly.

Bake for 15–18 minutes then remove from the oven and transfer to a wire rack to cool. If the cooled biscuits are a little soft, return them to a 110°C/90°C fan/gas ¼ oven, turn off the heat and allow them to cool in the oven. Break into shards to serve or store.

## VARIATIONS

You can experiment with other liquid sugars such as golden syrup, maple syrup or agave nectar instead of the treacle, to give a milder taste. Omit the spices for the mildest version of all. One way to avoid the biscuits becoming soft is to coat them with melted chocolate. Use tempered chocolate (see page 339) for a crisp and shiny coating. All credit to Sheila, my next-door neighbour, for this cunning solution to a sticky problem!

# OLD WELSH GINGERBREAD

*Traditional*

This is a mild and gentle gingerbread loaf that is loved by all, especially children. Rather surprisingly, it contains no ginger, but is delicious nonetheless, with jewels of candied peel studding each slice. This is typical of the gingerbread that used to be made for Welsh fairs and other celebrations such as the Mabsant. The Mabsant was a traditional Welsh holiday in celebration of the vilaage's patron saint, and was an occasion of great gaiety. An early 19th-century Mabsant is described below:

*'Worthy too of all remembrance were a couple of old women who had baskets of gingerbread and cakes there for sale. These wily crones passed along from one to the other of them as they sate on the benches, complimenting the vain girls on the prettiness of their dress, or of their persons, and the young men on their good dancing; and thus coaxed the simple-hearted creatures into a purchase of their sweetmeats. Great was the delight of the rustic lovers at treating their sweethearts to a pennyworth of gingerbread!'* [10]

To measure the treacle accurately, open the tin and stand it in a small pan of water. Heat the water slowly until the treacle has warmed and moves easily in the tin, then pour out as required.

**MAKES I LARGE LOAF CAKE**

*340g plain flour*
*2 tsp baking powder*
*112g butter, plus extra*
*   for greasing*
*170g demerara sugar*
*60g mixed candied peel, chopped*
*   into 1cm pieces*

*150ml milk*
*170g treacle, warmed*

*1 x 2kg/28cm loaf tin, or similar*
*   capacity*

Preheat the oven to 170°C/150°C fan/gas 3. Grease and line the loaf tin with baking parchment.

Put the flour, baking powder and butter into the bowl of a food processor and blitz until the mixture resembles breadcrumbs. Tip the mixture into another bowl and stir in the sugar and candied peel.

In a jug, add the milk to the warmed treacle and stir until combined.

Add the warm liquid to the dry ingredients and stir to combine.

Pour the mixture into the prepared tin and bake for 1½ hours, or until the loaf is cooked.

Set aside to cool in the tin.

# HONEY GINGERBREAD
*1824*

This gingerbread can also be found under the name 'Queen's Gingerbread', although exactly which queen it refers to is unclear. Going by the date alone, it might refer to the tragic but popular Queen Caroline of Brunswick, relegated below Mrs Fitzherbert in her husband King George IV's affections, and repelled at bayonet point from attending his coronation. However, it's far more likely to be a much older recipe, given a change of name at an opportune time. Perhaps the name has something to do with the recipe being 'fit for a queen', with its delicate flavourings of honey, spices and rich jewels of candied peel.

As with the Old Welsh Gingerbread (see page 116), this recipe contains no ginger. Possibly the warming spiciness of ginger was considered too excitable for ladies of delicate and refined constitutions. Nevertheless, this biscuit can certainly provide plenty of very enjoyable taste sensations and for all its lack of ginger, is surprisingly feisty. Personally, I found the quantity of cardamom suggested a spice too far, but I didn't want to leave it out just because of my own personal tastes, so I would suggest that you use it with caution. Additionally, the overall flavour can be varied quite surprisingly merely by using a range of differently flavoured honeys and sugars.

You can use slivered or flaked almonds if you prefer, or even unblanched almonds, although I think the paleness of the blanched almonds is a nice contrast to the golden brown of the biscuit. These are best baked as a sheet, but cut before they go in the oven. The biscuit would harden too quickly to cut after baking, and cutting before baking ensures neatness and minimal spread.

MAKES 1 SHEET OF DOUGH ABOUT 40CM SQUARE, TO BE CUT INTO
AS MANY BISCUITS AS YOU LIKE

160g plain flour
30g candied orange peel, cut into
    5mm pieces
30g candied lemon peel, cut into
    5mm pieces
30g blanched almonds, roughly
    chopped

2 tsp ground cinnamon
1 tsp freshly grated nutmeg
¼ tsp ground cloves
¼ tsp ground mace
¼ tsp ground cardamom (optional)
100g caster sugar
120g honey

Preheat the oven to 170°C/150°C fan/gas 3.

Sift the flour into a bowl. Add the candied peel, nuts and spices and stir well.

Put the sugar and honey into a pan and warm gently until the sugar is dissolved.

Pour the warmed mixture into the dry ingredients and stir to make a thick paste.

Roll out the warm paste until it's about 5mm thick. This is best done between 2 pieces of baking parchment. Discard the top piece.

Score the gingerbread into rectangular biscuits of roughly 3 x 6cm—i.e. cut through the paste but leave it as a single sheet to bake.

Slide the baking parchment, complete with the cut biscuits, on to a baking sheet and bake for 12–15 minutes until golden and slightly risen.

Divide the cooked paste into biscuits while warm and transfer to a wire rack to cool.

# WHITE GINGERBREAD
*Traditional*

Don't be fooled by this pale confection which, like the previous recipe, is made without treacle. Just because it lacks the dark, glistening menace of a traditional gingerbread doesn't mean it pulls any punches in the flavour department. This is not a biscuit for the soft and dainty for, unlike the previous recipe, it is positively bursting with ginger. No, that is not a typo, this recipe really does call for 30g ground ginger. Before you start picturing some kind of trial-by-ordeal endurance taste test, let me reassure you that, while the flavour is strong, it's more comforting and warming than fire-breathing madness. Just the thing to enjoy with a hot drink next to a roaring fire.

MAKES 12–15 BISCUITS

*112g butter, softened*  
*112g sugar*  
*1 egg, separated*  
*pinch of salt*

*225g plain flour*  
*¼ tsp baking powder*  
*30g ground ginger*

Preheat the oven to 170°C/150°C fan/gas 3. Line a baking sheet with baking parchment.

Cream the butter and sugar together until light and fluffy. Add the egg yolk and salt and mix thoroughly to combine.

Sift the flour, baking powder and ginger together in a separate bowl.

In another bowl, whisk the egg white to firm peaks.

Gradually add alternate spoonfuls of flour and whisked egg white to the creamed butter and sugar, retaining as much lightness as possible.

Drop rounded spoonfuls of the mixture on to the lined baking
sheet. To make this easier I use a small ice-cream scoop that holds
about 1½ tablespoons of mixture.

Bake for 30–40 minutes in the bottom of the oven, until baked
through but still rather pale in colour.

Transfer to a wire rack to cool.

*l–r: Honey Gingerbread, White Gingerbread, Parliament Cakes*

# PARLIAMENT CAKES
*18th century*

The landlady Mrs Flockhart is a minor character in the novel
*Waverly* by Sir Walter Scott. Although the novel is set during the
1745 Jacobite rising, it would appear that Scott based the character
on a real person. A Mrs Flockhart ran a tavern and grocery on the
Potterrow in Edinburgh that was much visited by Scott's father.
The Widow Flockhart, or 'Lucky Flykie' as she was more generally
known, was much respected in the neighbourhood and, in the late
18th century, her establishment was frequented by many politicians
and notable gentlemen, including Sheriff Cockburn, Lord Melville,
the banker Donald Smith, and Dr William Cullen.

On arrival, Mrs Flockhart's respected guests would proceed to
the parlour and partake of the refreshments she had laid out.
Occasionally this would be a substantial meal in the form of a
casserole, served on the bunker seat of the window of an adjacent
closet barely large enough for the necessary chair. Just why the
eminent gentlemen of Edinburgh would elect to sit on a cupboard
and eat stew from a windowsill is puzzling to say the least, but it's
a great comic image. It was more usual, however, for guests to opt
for a 'wee dram' of brandy, rum or whisky, and some home-made
gingerbread, in the form of either white or brown 'quality cakes',
circular 'snaps' or small, rectangular biscuits. The popularity of
the biscuits amongst the distinguished guests led them to become
known as Parliament Cakes, or Parlies.

These biscuits are fantastically crisp and crunchy, with just the
right amount of ginger to give a great flavour without any
uncomfortable afterburn.

MAKES 30–40 SMALL, SQUARE BISCUITS

*225g plain flour*  *1 tsp ground ginger*
*1 nutmeg, grated*  *115g treacle*
*1 tsp bicarbonate of soda*  *56g soft brown sugar*
*½ tsp cream of tartar*  *30g butter*
*1 tsp ground cinnamon*

Preheat the oven to 150°C/130°C fan/gas 2.

Sift the flour and other dry ingredients, except the sugar, into
a bowl. Put the sugar, treacle and butter into a pan and warm gently,
stirring, until the butter is melted and the sugar dissolved. Pour
this warm treacle mixture into the dry ingredients and mix to
a firm paste.

Roll the paste out to about 2–3mm on a sheet of baking parchment
and cut into small squares with a 3–4cm diameter, but leave the
sheet of dough intact. Slide the baking parchment on to a baking
sheet and bake for 25–30 minutes until the biscuits are slightly risen
and cooked through.

Separate the squares while still warm then transfer to a wire rack
to cool.

# 4

# PASTRY

The tradition of using pastry to hold a baked filling is long and varied. Historically, as with pies, the pastry for tarts was used merely as a vessel to hold a filling, and was rarely eaten. However, whereas pies were lidded to help retain moisture, tarts were genearlly left uncovered in order that the filling be left on display, allowing cooks to present the traditionally sweet fillings to their best advantage. Even if a pastry lid were required for baking, it would often be removed and cut into smaller shapes before being arranged attractively around the dish before serving. Originally filled with rich custards as a means of using up egg yolks (the whites were used for clarifying wines and for starching collars), the range of tart fillings broadened to include a wide variety of different and delicious fillings.

# MINCE PIES
*Traditional*

Mince pies are a traditional British offering during the Christmas season, but at almost no other time in the year. Perhaps the mix of fruit, fat, sugar, spices and alcohol that brings to mind cold winter nights and roaring fires, proves too incongruous if you happened to bite into one on a warm summer's evening.

The ancestors of these sweet pastries contained actual meat, the thought of which sends shudders of horror through most of us with our 21st-century taste buds accustomed to sweet mince pies. But consider Moroccan tagines with dates and apricots, or Normandy pork with cream and prunes, and it's not such a wacky idea. I used to think that just beef was used, but old cookery books reveal a whole range of recipes for different meats. Esther Copley (1838) included five different recipes for mincemeat in her cookbook, the main ingredients being beef, tripe, neat's tongue, eggs and oranges. Mrs Rundell (1815) has four: three of them without meat, and Hannah Glasse's 'best' mince pies also include layers of meat. Furthermore, Glasse has a mincemeat recipe for Lent, which has become my favourite for its lack of suet and sugar, and its light, fresh flavour. With such guilt-free mincemeat it is possible to make the pastry a little indulgent. I love the contrast of crisp crunchy pastry with soft filling, and for this, you can't beat puff.

Traditional puff pastry involves repeated rolling and folding of a 50/50 mix of flour and butter. Although delicious, it is very rich and time-consuming to make. Luckily, these days you can buy ready-made puff pastry, either in blocks or ready-rolled, in regular or all-butter versions with considerably less butter content than home-made puff pastry, with just as good a flake. It's practically the healthy option!

The recipe is all about the assembly. It specifies ready-rolled pastry, but this is simply for convenience, block pastry is also fine. It might seem straightforward to make mince pies from ready-made puff pastry, especially if it is already rolled, but a few subtle tips and tricks, some of them gleaned from professional bakers' handbooks from the 19th century, will make a world of difference to both the appearance and taste of your pies.

Before we start, a word about baking tins: use shallow tart tins, usually no more than 3cm deep, for this recipe—cupcake tins will be too deep and won't allow the pastry to really rise and shine.

**MAKES 24 MINCE PIES**

*2 sheets ready-rolled, all-butter
puff pastry
1 x quantity of Guilt-free
Mincemeat (see page 322)
milk, for brushing
caster sugar, for sprinkling
butter, for greasing*

*flour, for dusting*

*2 x 12-hole mince pie tins, or
shallow tart tins (no more than
3cm deep)
1 x fluted pastry cutter (slightly
wider than top of pie hole)*

Preheat the oven to 200°C/180°C fan/gas 6. Grease the mince pie tins.

Unfurl the pastry on a lightly floured work surface. Using a fluted pastry cutter slightly wider than the top of the pie holes, cut as many circles as possible from each sheet and set them aside. These will (mostly) be the lids for the mince pies.

Gather the scraps and re-roll them to the same thickness as the original sheet and, again, cut out as many circles as possible. The re-rolled pastry circles, which won't rise as well or as evenly as those from the first roll, will make the bottoms of the mince pies. It makes use of as much of the pastry as possible, and allows for a sky-high pastry top.

Lightly place each of the pie bottoms into the holes in the tin. Using your thumb, press down on to the middle of one of the pastry discs then gradually move your thumb around the base of the tin, thinning the pastry on the base and easing it up the sides of the tin. This will give a thin, crisp base and sides that puff upwards.

Repeat until all the holes are lined with pastry. (You may need to use some of the pastry discs reserved for lids.) Using a pastry brush, moisten the edges of the pastry bottoms with a little water. (It is easier to do it now than when the mincemeat has been added.) Put a heaped teaspoon of mincemeat into the middle of each pie. Do not spread the mincemeat out.

Now you are ready to lid your pies. Take a pastry lid and moisten its edges with water. Lay it on one of your pies and press the sides and lid together just inside the edges, about 5mm from the edge. (If you squash the edges together, the puff pastry won't puff up during cooking.) If, like me, you find that this proves too fiddly for your fingers, using the end of a teaspoon handle works marvellously. Once the edges are sealed, press down gently on the dome of mincemeat to spread it out inside the pie. The top of the pie will flatten and the sides will be pressed outwards and upwards. This opens up the top of the pie like a flower and will help the puff pastry to soar during cooking.

Repeat until all the pies are sealed then brush the tops with milk and sprinkle with caster sugar. Cut one or two vents in each lid to let the steam out.

Bake for about 15 minutes, turning the trays round after 10 minutes to ensure an even colour.

Transfer to wire racks to cool.

These pies are best served warm. To reheat, arrange on a baking sheet and put into a cold oven. Turn the oven to 140°C/120°C fan/ gas 1 and warm the pies for 10 minutes.

# BLACK AND WHITE TARTS
## 1651

These unique tarts are striking both to look at and to taste. The dark filling is a rich mixture of fruit, the white a soft, delicately flavoured cream. I also love this recipe for its ease of preparation, making it ideal for a stress-free special occasion. Each component—the pastry cases, and each of the fillings—is prepared separately and then combined just before serving. Make the fillings the day before to allow the flavours to fully develop but bake the pastry on the day for maximum flaky crispness.

These tarts were traditionally served heaped high on platters, a different filling in each pile. The original manuscript from which this recipe comes goes on to suggest two additional fillings, of red (rosehip jelly) and yellow (egg-yolk custard), but I think the black and the white look stunning together and makes for a wonderful contrast. To add an extra dimension to these tarts, gently heat the black filling just before serving—the contrast of the warmed, sweet-sharp fruit with the chilled, creamy white filling, together with the crunch of the crisp pastry, is divine.

MAKES 8 TARTS

_For the black filling_
1 Bramley apple, peeled, cored and
  cut into chunks
75g prunes, stoned and chopped
75g currants
1 tsp ground ginger

_For the white filling_
150ml egg whites
300ml double cream
sugar, to taste
rosewater, to taste

_For the pastry_
400g block ready-made puff
  pastry, chilled
flour, for dusting
beaten egg white, for glazing

1 x round pastry cutter (optional)
kitchen foil

*To make the black filling*
Put the apple, prunes and currants into a small pan over a medium heat. Add 300ml of cold water and cover. Simmer until the apple is cooked and fluffy and the currants and prunes have softened.

Take the mixture off the heat and either transfer to a food processor or blend with a hand blender, then return the purée to the saucepan, add the ginger and stir. Heat gently and continue stirring until any excess liquid has evaporated and the mixture holds its shape.

Cover and chill in the fridge until required.

*To make the white filling*
This is basically a custard made with egg whites instead of yolks.

Whisk the egg whites with 3 tablespoons of the cream.

In a pan over a medium heat, heat the rest of the cream to almost boiling, then remove from the heat and pour slowly into the egg white mixture, whisking all the time. When all of the hot cream has been added, return the mixture to the pan over a medium heat and continue to whisk until the mixture has thickened.

Remove from the heat and add sugar and rosewater to taste. (The strength and flavour of rosewater can vary wildly, so add 1 teaspoon to begin with, then add extra as required.)

Continue to stir until the mixture has cooled. Keeping the mixture moving will help prevent it separating—use a stand mixer or hand whisk to speed up this task.

Cover and chill in the fridge, preferably overnight.

*To make the pastry cases*
Cut the block of pastry in half and put one piece back in the fridge; it's easier to work with two small pieces of pastry than one large one, and reduces the chances of it tearing. Lightly dust a work

surface with flour and roll out the pastry to a thickness of about 5mm then slide it on to a chopping board and put it in the freezer for 10 minutes. (Cutting out the tarts will be much easier if the pastry is very cold and firm.) Repeat with the second piece of pastry.

Preheat the oven to 220°C/200°C fan/gas 7. Line a baking sheet with baking parchment.

Remove the first sheet from the freezer and cut out the tart bases. I use a loose-bottomed tartlet tin as a cutter, because the crinkled edges make the finished tart rather attractive, but any shape will do. Lay the bases on the prepared baking sheet.

Remove the second sheet of pastry from the freezer and repeat. These discs will make the tart rims. Using a sharp knife, or smaller pastry cutter, cut out the centre of each pastry shape, leaving a 2cm rim around the edge. Discard the centre portion of pastry.

To join the rims to the bases, wet the edges of the pastry bases with cold water then lift the pastry rims on to the bases, lining up the edges neatly. Press the pastry circles and rims together gently but firmly—avoid pressing on the edges otherwise they might not rise properly. Prick the centre of the bases with a fork to allow the steam to escape and so help prevent the middle of the tart cases from rising. Carefully brush the pastry circles with beaten egg white. Don't brush the cut edges as the egg white will glue the layers together and prevent the pastry from rising.

Bake for 5 minutes then turn the baking sheet 180 degrees and bake for another 5 minutes, or until the cases are well risen and golden brown. (If the centres of the pastry cases have risen slightly, gently press them back down with the back of a spoon while still hot.) Transfer to a wire rack to cool.

*To assemble the tarts*
Fold a sheet of foil several times until you have a strip that holds its shape. The precise length will depend on the size of your tarts.

You will need one strip for each tart case. Spray the foil strips with cooking oil and bend them into 'S' shapes. Tuck one strip inside the rim of each tart.

Spoon some of the white filling into each tart case on one side and the black filling into the other half. Using a wooden cocktail stick, ease the fillings away from the sides of each foil strip and remove it. Smooth the fillings together with the cocktail stick.

Serve with pouring cream, if liked.

to make layd tarts

to make ye blacke tarke
malligo
take a pound of prunes, and a pound of reasons, 6:
promwaters pared and sliced, put them into a skillet
and fill it with water, boyle it on a soft fire couer
it and stire it often for fear of burning, when it is
boyled to a mash rub your pulpe through a strayner
and when it is strayned set it on coales, put in suger
and rose water a litell, and make it hott with ginger
stire it well together and when your tart is raised up
with an edge harden it in ye ouen and when it is
hardened enough take them out and fill them and let
it not goe any more into ye ouen, but eate it soe
    to make the white tarte layde
take halfe a pinte of creame, 4: or 8: whites of egg
take out ye tredells, and beate them uery well with
a litell cold creame, and when your creame boyles take
it of ye fire, and put in ye eggs stire them together
and set it on a quicke fire and boyle it thicke all
wayes stiring it then put it forth and stire it till it is
cold and fill your tart as before seasone it with suger
and rose water
    to make yallow tarte
you may put ye yolks of ye eggs into ye creame
and not ye whites and season it with suger and rose
water a litell ginger if you please and boyle it as before
    in ye other

# CHOCOLATE MERINGUE PIE
## 1777

The use of chocolate in British recipe books goes back a surprisingly long way, as far as the 17th century. English cookery writer Hannah Glasse (1708–70) mentions it several times in *The Art of Cookery Made Plain and Easy* (1747), but never in an actual recipe. Just as with her muffin recipe, where she careers off at a tangent to give instructions for building your own baking griddle, with chocolate she takes the 'back to basics' approach to the extreme by giving two separate instructions for making it, beginning with roasting and grinding your own cocoa beans. Over the years, Hannah Glasse has been the butt of much mirth for the (incorrectly quoted) 'first catch your hare' phrase. Much funnier, and much more accurate, would be 'first roast your beans'.

The only other reference to chocolate in her book is her recipe for Sham Chocolate, where she suggests making a custard with cinnamon, cream, sugar and egg yolks and serving it in a chocolate cup. Maybe the cups were supposed to fool everyone—if it's served in a chocolate cup, it must be chocolate! I can only imagine this working with someone who had no idea what chocolate was. What larks, Hannah!

I found two printed recipes for chocolate tart in 18th-century recipe books, both of which are just as delicious today as they were then, and probably more so, given the quality of the ingredients we now have available. The first, from 1737, seems to be missing a few instructions, but is essentially a chocolate custard baked in a pastry shell, and finished by brûléeing sugar on the top just before serving. Delicious as this sounds, the recipe I have chosen is Charlotte Mason's meringue pie with a chocolate and lemon filling. Nowadays we usually pair chocolate with orange, so I was excited to try this variation and I wasn't disappointed! Both the candied and fresh lemon adds a real zing to the rich, dark custard. The billowy meringue and crisp pastry make this seemingly simple dessert a real feast of textures and flavours.

I've tweaked the original recipe in order to present all elements of the dish at their very best. Each component of the tart is prepared separately so it can then be assembled just before serving. Alternatively, you could pour the custard straight into the cooled pastry case, leaving just the meringue to make.

SERVES 6–8

400g block ready-made puff
  pastry, chilled
flour, for dusting
butter, for greasing

*For the filling*
30g cornflour
3 egg yolks
2 tbsp milk
50g cocoa powder
50g caster sugar
300ml double cream
1 cinnamon stick
zest of 1 lemon

pinch of salt
30g candied lemon peel

*For the meringue*
3 egg whites
pinch of salt
a few drops lemon juice
220g granulated sugar
1 sachet (7g) powdered egg white

1 x 20cm loose-bottomed tart/
  cake tin
cook's thermometer (optional)
kitchen blowtorch (optional)

*To make the pastry case*
Grease the tart or cake tin. On a lightly floured surface, roll out the puff pastry to 5–8mm thick. (Too thin and it won't be sturdy enough to hold both the filling and the meringue topping.) Line the prepared tin with the pastry. It should cover both the base and sides and will shrink slightly, so don't trim the excess, and prick holes in the pastry on the bottom of the tin with a fork to help prevent it from rising. Cut some baking parchment to size and place it on top of the pastry. Fill with baking beans, beads or uncooked rice and place in the fridge for 30 minutes for the pastry to chill and relax.

Preheat the oven to 220°C/200°C fan/gas 7.

When you're ready to bake the pastry, remove the tin from the fridge and bake for 10 minutes, then remove the baking parchment and baking beans/beads/rice and return to the oven for a further 10–15 minutes, until the pastry case is fully cooked. Transfer to a wire rack and set aside to cool.

*To make the filling*
First mix the cornflour, yolks and milk together in a bowl until smooth. Put the cocoa powder, caster sugar, cream, cinnamon stick, lemon zest and salt into a small pan over a low heat and warm gently, stirring all the time, until the sugar is dissolved. Increase the heat and, just before it reaches boiling point, remove the pan from the heat and slowly pour the mixture over the egg yolk mixture, whisking continuously. When the mixture is thoroughly combined, pour it back into the pan and continue heating and stirring until it thickens. Do not let the mixture boil.

Once the mixture has thickened, remove the cinnamon stick and stir in the candied lemon peel. Either pour the filling straight into the cooled pastry case, or into a bowl to cool. Whichever you choose, cover with cling film, making sure it is fully in contact with the surface of the custard to prevent a skin forming.

*To make the meringue*
First put the egg whites, salt and lemon juice in a mixer bowl and whisk slowly until frothy, then fast until you have stiff peaks. Mix 20g of the granulated sugar with the powdered egg white and gradually add this to the whisked egg whites. Allow each spoonful to dissolve before adding the next. Beat to stiff, glossy peaks. Set aside.

Make a sugar syrup by heating the remaining 200g granulated sugar with 100ml cold water in a pan over a low heat, stirring until the sugar dissolves. Increase the heat and let the syrup simmer until it reaches 115°C, or when the syrup forms a soft sticky mass when dropped in cold water (soft-ball stage). Remove the pan from the heat and allow the bubbles to subside. With the beaters running, pour the sugar syrup in a thin stream down the side of the bowl into the beaten whites. Avoid pouring the hot syrup on to the beaters as this will cause splashes. Continue whisking until the bowl is cool to the touch and the meringue is stiff, 10–15 minutes.

*To assemble the pie*
Trim the excess pastry from the edges of the cooked pastry case, then remove the pastry case from the tin and place it on a serving plate. If you've not yet filled the tart, give the custard a stir and pour it into the case, smoothing the surface with a palette knife. Spoon the meringue on top of the filling, making sure it reaches the pastry at the edge of the tart. Swirl the meringue with a fork.

With a blowtorch, lightly caramelise the top of the meringue. If you don't have a blowtorch, heat the grill on your oven to the highest setting and slide the tart underneath for a few seconds (keep an eye on it!). Remove, turn the plate and repeat until browned to your satisfaction.

# COCONUT ALMOND TARTLETS

*1890s*

The recipe for these pretty little tarts has been adapted from a professional Victorian baker's handbook for the trade. The mixture of coconut and almond results in a chewy filling and the cornflour pastry is crisp and not overly sweet. If you can find nibbed sugar, it makes a very pretty addition to the top.

**MAKES 12–15 TARTLETS**

*For the pastry*
225g plain flour
60g cornflour
140g butter, plus extra for greasing
85g caster sugar
zest of 1 lemon
1 egg
iced water

*For the filling*
70g egg whites
1 tsp vanilla extract
140g sugar
50g ground almonds
50g desiccated coconut

*nibbed sugar, for sprinkling
(optional)
icing sugar, for dusting*

*1 x 24-hole mini-muffin tin
1 x round pastry cutter (slightly
    larger than the diameter of the
    muffin cups)
1 x piping bag fitted with a 1cm
    plain nozzle*

Put all the pastry ingredients, except the egg, into the bowl of a food processor and blitz until the mixture resembles fine breadcrumbs. With the motor still running, tip in the beaten egg and let the motor run until the mixture comes together into a ball. If the mixture looks dry, add a little iced water, a tablespoon at a time, until it comes together. Switch off the machine and tip out the pastry on to a lightly floured work surface.

Gently knead the dough until it becomes smooth then wrap in cling film and chill in the fridge for 30 minutes.

Grease the cups of the mini-muffin tin. You will probably only need yo use 12–15 of the cups.

Remove the chilled pastry from the fridge, cut it into 2 pieces and roll one half out to about 3mm thick.

Cut out circles of pastry and line the mini-muffin cups. Repeat with the second piece of pastry. Chill in the fridge until required.

When you're ready to cook the tartlets, preheat the oven to 170°C/150°C fan/gas 3.

To make the filling, in a bowl whisk the egg whites and vanilla together to soft peaks. Slowly add the caster sugar, a tablespoon at a time. Continue to whisk the mixture to stiff peaks.

Add the ground almonds and coconut and stir until thoroughly combined. The mixture should be a little loose so that it 'settles' when dropped from a spoon. Add a few drops of cold water if it seems rather stiff.

Spoon the filling into the piping bag and pipe it into the pastry cases, until they are three-quarters full. Sprinkle the tops with nibbed sugar, if using.

Bake for 10–12 minutes until the filling is risen and lightly browned. Dust with icing sugar while still hot and transfer to a wire rack to cool.

These tartlets are best eaten within 1–2 days.

# FRUIT FANCIES

*19th century*

These attractive little tartlets were an absolute treasure to find in an old Victorian baker's handbook. I was intrigued by the use of fresh fruit and also the cake crumbs used to add texture to the filling. Obviously, for a baker, it is sound business sense not to waste any of your expensive ingredients and any creations that can make use of the leftovers of other baked items are going to be deliciously efficient. I love finding a recipe that uses up scraps from some other dish, especially when they turn into something so delightful.

What you end up with by following this recipe is a fabulously refreshing morsel that is so much more than the sum of its parts. Similar to a Bakewell tart, the filling resembles a firm sponge, but with the novelty of having the fresh taste of fruit. The pastry case is light and crisp and makes a very neat container.

I've made these little tartlets in a mini-muffin tin, to give dainty, bite-sized portions, but you can make them in almost any size tartlet tin. For a less formal finish, leave them un-iced; that way it is easy to see the different flavours by the colour of the filling.

MAKES 24–30 MINI TARTLETS

*For the pastry*
*225g plain flour, plus extra for*
  *dusting*
*60g cornflour*
*140g butter*
*85g caster sugar*
*zest of 1 lemon*
*1 egg*

*For the filling*
*150g caster sugar, plus 30g*
*150g apple purée, or other fruit*
  *purée of your choice*
*1 egg, separated*
*60g ground rice*
*30g sponge-cake crumbs*
*zest and juice of 1 lemon*

*(ingredients continued overleaf)*

*For the topping*                 *2 x 24-hole mini-muffin tins, or*
*150g icing sugar*                *small, individual tartlet tins*
*a little egg white*              *1 x 5cm round pastry cutter*
*a little green food colouring*   *1 x piping bag fitted with a 1cm*
*candied apple pieces, diced*     *plain nozzle*

Put all the pastry ingredients, except the egg, into the bowl of a food processor and blitz until the mixture resembles breadcrumbs.

Whisk the egg then gradually add it to the mixture while the motor is running until the mixture comes together in a ball. If the mixture looks dry, add a little iced water, a tablespoon at a time, until it comes together into a soft paste. Tip out the pastry on to a lightly floured surface and knead a little until smooth. Wrap in cling film and chill in the fridge while you make the filling.

Mix the 150g sugar, the apple pulp and egg yolk in a small pan over a medium heat. Stir until the sugar is dissolved and the mixture has thickened. Remove from the heat and stir until cool.

Whisk the egg white to soft peaks then whisk in the remaining 30g sugar to make a firm meringue. Fold this into the apple mixture.

Mix the ground rice and cake crumbs and stir into the apple mixture together with the lemon zest and juice. Set aside.

Preheat the oven to 200°C/180°C fan/gas 6. Grease the mini-muffin tin.

Remove the chilled pastry from the fridge and roll it out thinly to 3mm thickness. Cut out circles of pastry and line the mini-muffin cups. Prick the pastry bottoms with a fork to help prevent them from rising.

Fill the piping bag with the fruit filling and fill the pastry cases to three-quarters full.

Bake for 12–15 minutes until the pastry is cooked and the filling is risen and slightly browned. Remove from the tin and transfer to a wire rack to cool.

*To ice*
For the topping, mix the icing sugar with a little egg white to a smooth, soft pouring consistency and add a tiny amount of food colouring.

Level the top of the tartlets by slicing off any excess filling. The pastry rim should form a natural barrier for the icing.

Spoon the icing over the top of the tartlet filling and spread it to the edges.

Place 2 candied apple cubes on each iced tartlet and set aside to dry.


## VARIATIONS

Any fruit purée can be used to flavour the filling. The purée needs to be quite firm, so avoid any excess moisture. When making the purée, cook for a little longer with the sugar if needed. The sharper the fruit, the better and more refreshing the flavour in the finished tartlet. Damson or blackberry makes a beautiful purple filling and gooseberries keep it delicately pale. Try to add decoration on top of the tartlets that hints at the flavour within.

# FANCHONETTES
*1830*

The great Marie-Antonin Carême cooked for many of the crowned heads of Europe, including the Emperor Napoleon, the young George IV (the Prince Regent), Tsar Alexander I and James Rothschild. Fanchonettes appeared on Carême's menu for 6 July 1829 at Château Rothschild, and by the following year, they could be found in Richard Dolby's *Cook's Dictionary*.

This recipe initially caught my attention because the name gave absolutely no clue as to what the recipe was. Upon reading, I discovered it to be a delicate, early version of a lemon meringue pie. The origin of the name 'Fanchonettes' is a little hazy. My best stab at the reasoning behind the name is through the French 'fanchon', meaning kerchief, referring to the soft folds of meringue, but I'm not completely convinced, so I'd be interested in any other theories.

So what is a Fanchonette like? Crisp puff pastry, a soft lemon and almond custard, and a lightly toasted meringue topping—I thought it was amazing: recognisable as a lemon meringue pie but just different enough to be tantalisingly unusual. The filling isn't as strongly flavoured as the lemon meringue pies we know today, but I think this is part of its attraction: lemon meringue pie is punchy and sharp in flavour, whereas this has an altogether more delicate and subtly-flavoured filling.

MAKES 6–8 FANCHONETTES, DEPENDING ON SIZE OF TINS

*500g block ready-made puff*
  *pastry, chilled*
*butter or cooking spray or oil,*
  *for greasing*
*flour, for dusting*

*For the meringue*
*2 egg whites*
*a few drops lemon juice*
*pinch of salt*
*112g caster sugar*

*(ingredients continued overleaf)*

*For the filling*
30g butter
60g plain flour
90g sugar
60g ground almonds
zest of 1 lemon
2 egg yolks
1 egg
pinch of salt
300ml milk

*6–8 individual deep, loose-bottomed tart tins*
*1 x piping bag fitted with a plain 1.5cm nozzle*

Preheat the oven to 220°C/200°C fan/gas 7.

Grease your tart tins. On a lightly floured surface, roll out the pastry to about 5mm thick and use it to line the tart tins. Line the pastry with baking parchment then cover with baking beans, beads or uncooked rice, and blind bake for 8 minutes. Take the tins from the oven, remove the parchment and the beans/beads/rice and return to the oven to crisp the bottom of the pastry for 3–4 minutes. Remove from the oven and set aside.

Reduce the oven temperature to 170°C/150°C fan/gas 3.

Put all the filling ingredients into a small pan over a low heat and whisk until thickened. Pour this mixture into the pastry cases and return to the oven for 15–20 minutes until almost set.

While the tart filling is cooking, make the meringue. Put the egg whites, lemon juice and salt into a bowl and start whisking on a slow speed. Once the eggs have become frothy, increase the speed a little and add a spoonful of the sugar. Allow each spoonful to dissolve before adding the next. Keep gradually increasing the speed of whisking as you add the sugar until the meringue is light, fluffy and will stand in stiff peaks. Spoon the meringue into the piping bag.

Remove the tarts from the oven and pipe the meringue on to the hot filling. The original recipe called for 7 little points of meringue around the edge of each tart, and then a large one in the middle. Alternatively, you can just have a single mound of meringue.

Return the tarts to the oven until the meringue is crisp and golden, about 15 minutes.

# JAM TARTS
*Traditional*

*The queen of hearts,*
*She made some tarts,*
*All on a summer's day,*

*The knave of hearts*
*He stole those tarts,*
*And with them ran away.*

*The king of hearts*
*Call'd for those tarts,*
*And beat the knave full sore;*

*The knave of hearts*
*Brought back those tarts,*
*And said he'll ne'er steal more.*

I always assumed that the tarts in this 18th-century poem[11] were jam tarts, and I think that for most of us nowadays, jam tarts are viewed strictly as nursery food. This is a shame, because in the past they were a deceptively simple means whereby ladies of the household were able to demonstrate their skill and expertise in preserving the bounty of summer for enjoyment during the long, lean winter months.

Although recipes specifically labelled 'jam' are few and far between in the cookery books and manuscripts of the 17th and 18th centuries,[12] what they do contain are a great number of recipes for preserving fruits whole—what today we would call 'conserves'.

Pastry tarts were an ideal way to display these delicate confections to their maximum advantage, and the use of scraps of pastry to divide the tarts into sections allowed several different types of preserve to be served in one tart without becoming jumbled together. The greater the number of different preserves served, the more impressive the store cupboard—and, by extension, the more skilled the lady of the house.

*'Eight was considered a reasonably good show, but a diamond pattern of twelve different jams was really showing off.'* [13]

The scraps used to decorate these often complex and detailed pastries were also a means by which skill could be both demonstrated and judged. These scraps would be teased into wafer-thin ribbons which were then twisted, plaited, woven and coiled into ingenious designs that enhanced the finished dishes. However, too much decoration could be counter-productive—excessive use of pastry decorations hinted at poor judgement when determining how much pastry to make, and designs with the simplest ornamentation using the smallest amount of dough implied great skill in judging the precise quantity of pastry to make.

Jam Tarts: the housewife's humble-brag.

## A GUIDE TO IMPRESSING WITH JAM TARTS

*Equipment*
Jam tarts should be made in shallow tins or on pie plates. Since the filling will be preserves of the best quality, a little will go a long way, and there can't be many of us who would gladly eat large quantities of jam.

Traditional jam tart trays, holding a dozen at a time, are fine for individual servings, but their small size leaves little room for decoration. Larger, family-size tarts baked on a pie plate give much greater scope for decoration and the wide lip allows for a well-defined edge to which cross-bars of pastry can be secured. The downside of tarts made in large plates is that the individual servings destroy the pattern, and what ends up on the plate is a mere sliver of the beauty of the original.

A happy medium can be found in Yorkshire pudding tins, with 4 shallow indentations that are large enough to decorate while small enough to be deemed an individual serving.

Silicone trays should be avoided. It is the heat of the metal baking trays that helps crisp up the pastry. Their rigidity also makes the moving of tarts, both before and after baking, much easier.

*Pastry*
Sweetened shortcrust pastry is a great choice for jam tarts, but it can be awkward to work with when it comes to room temperature, so allow a generous chilling time and return it to the fridge if necessary.

The more pastry is handled, the tougher it becomes, so try not to re-roll your trimmings endlessly. Gather them all together, chill, roll them out once and chill again. Make all your decorations from this one large sheet.

*Fillings*
Pastry needs a hot oven to bake properly. Jam has already been cooked in order to get it to set. Putting jam into a raw pastry case means that it will effectively be cooked twice, and invariably boil over to produce a sticky mess. Even if it doesn't boil over, it will have lost most of its delicate colour and flavour. Far better to fully cook the pastry unfilled—also known as blind baking—and then fill the tarts just before serving. Alternatively, for tarts and fillings that are generally cooked together (treacle tart, apple tart), partially pre-baking the pastry can improve the finished dish immensely and help avoid the dreaded 'soggy bottom'.

*Decoration*
When it comes to decoration, pretty much anything goes; you're limited only by your imagination. Cut pastry strips with a sharp knife or pizza wheel for perfectly straight edges. Use a pastry wheel for serrated edges. Moisten the ends of the strips and press them firmly on to the rim of the pastry bottom to secure them.

Here are a few easy suggestions for introducing variation:
- Lay your strips flat across the tart to make a simple check pattern. Use cloves to 'pin' the strips where they cross.
- Twist the strips into spirals as you lay them down.
- Weave your strips under and over one another for a basketweave pattern.
- Plait 3 thin strips and use as above.
- Make a pastry rim to neaten the appearance of your tart once the strips are in place by covering the ends.
- Leaves—cut diamond shapes and use a knife blade to mark the leaf veins.
- Flowers—roll strips of pastry (a patterned edge can be very effective) into spirals.
- Shapes—use mini pastry cutters and use the shapes either individually or to make a decorative border. Any simple shape can look very effective when repeatedly overlapped. Fiddly, though.


## TRADITIONAL DESIGNS

Here are some suggestions for tart designs to get you started, as recorded by Miss Dorothy Hartley in her magnificent book *Food in England*. Line your pie plate with the pastry of your choice, cut a covering strip of pastry for the rim of the tart, if required, then proceed with your chosen design.

DESIGNS FOR SINGLE FLAVOUR FILLINGS:

*The Gable*
This design resembles the battlements of a castle and is probably the easiest and simplest to do. Moisten the edge of the tart with water. Make an even number of cuts, 3cm apart, all around the rim of the tart. Fold down alternate flaps of pastry to make a crenellated edge. Fold over the remaining flaps just halfway, making a double thickness of pastry. Brush the pastry with a syrup of sugar dissolved in a little milk, and bake blind.

### The Tail

Roll any pastry trimmings into a circle and, with a sharp knife, cut a spiral. Moisten the top of the tart with water. Lay the outer end of the spiral on the edge of the tart and let the rest of it coil into the centre of the tart over the filling. Neaten the rim of the tart with a strip of pastry or overlapping shapes. Bake.

### The Lattice

This effect is achieved by criss-crossing strips of pastry over a tart filling. These strips can be plain or decorative, laid flat or twisted, or even woven. Use cloves to anchor the pastry strips together where they overlap. Neaten the edges of the tart by laying a pastry rim over the ends of the strips. Brush the pastry with milk syrup and bake.

DESIGNS FOR TWO-FLAVOUR FILLINGS:

### The Well

Use pastry strips or plaits to create a circle in the centre of the tart. Decorate the border of the tart, brush with sugar syrup and bake blind. Fill the inner circle with a dark jam such as blueberry or blackcurrant. Fill the outer circle with a lighter, contrasting preserve such as greengage plum or lime curd, to give the impression of an overhead view of a well in a grass lawn.

### The Red Cross

Cut a covering strip of pastry for neatening the edge of the tart; set aside. From the remaining pastry scraps, use 4 thin strips of pastry shaped into right angles to divide the tart into quarters, leaving space between the pastry strips to create the shape of a cross in the centre. Moisten the ends of the strips and press them into the pastry rim. Lay the covering strip of pastry over the rim of the tart, neatening the edge and covering the ends of the dividing strips. Brush the pastry with milk syrup, and bake blind. Fill the four quadrants with one flavour and the centre cross with a contrasting flavour. Sweetened cream cheese with raspberry jam gives a striking effect.

DESIGNS FOR MULTIPLE-FLAVOUR FILLINGS:

*Cross Tart*
Divide the tart into quarters by running two strips of pastry at
right-angles to each other across the middle of the tart. The strips
can be plain, plaited or twisted. Moisten the ends of the strips and
press them into the pastry rim. Cut a longer, flat strip and lay it over
the rim of the tart, neatening the edge and covering the ends of the
dividing strips. Glaze and bake blind. Fill each quarter with
a different preserve.

*Slits Tart*
Cut a covering strip of pastry for neatening the edge of the tart; set
aside. Roll an oval the width of your pie plate, using the remaining
scraps. Cut lengthways down the middle then cut a slit lengthways
down the middle of each half. Pull the pastry apart to create the
shape of a capital D. Moisten the pastry with water and then lay
both D-shaped pieces of pastry back to back, with a small space
in-between. Your tart should be divided into 5 crescents. Glaze and
bake blind. Fill each section with a preserve of a different colour.

*Epiphany Tart*
The Epiphany Tart is the very pinnacle of understated boasting in
the jam-tart world. The design itself is simple—6 strips of pastry
are arranged into a 6-pointed star (commonly called the Star of
David) and the rim neatened with a covering strip of pastry. Glaze
and bake blind. The tart is thus divided into 13 sections, supposedly
representing Jesus and the 12 disciples, which are then filled. To
create this tart with all 13 sections filled with a different kind of
preserve was impressive indeed.

# MAIDS OF HONOUR

*Tudor*

*'Granny turned a page.*
*"What about this one? Maids of Honour?"*
*"Weeelll, they starts out as Maids of Honour," said Nanny, fidgeting*
*with her feet, "but they ends up as Tarts."*
Maskerade *by Terry Pratchett*

I love a recipe with a good story behind it, and if ever there was a pastry with a good tale to tell, it is the Maid of Honour.

Several tales, even. Much like a game of Chinese whispers, the elements of the story seem to change over time. Some versions claim the tarts were named by King Henry VIII after he discovered some ladies of the court enjoying a dish of pastries.[14] Other variations have him discovering the recipe in a locked chest and passing it on to Katherine of Aragon's lady-in-waiting, Anne Boleyn, who then made them for the King.[15] The palace is sometimes Hampton Court, and sometimes Richmond. A slightly grisly version involves having the kitchen maid who first created the pastries imprisoned in the palace grounds so that she could produce the tarts solely for the royal household.[16] The sovereign has also been variously identified at times as Elizabeth I, George II and George III,[17] although it would seem that, by all accounts, the Georges were rather busy 'bunning' down in Chelsea (see page 269). All in all, it's a bit of a pick-and-mix-and-match-your-monarch anecdote. Whatever the true story, naming these pastries Maids of Honour might only date from the 18th century,[18] but their reputation for being naughty, delicious treats was widespread many decades before, and should be again.

**MAKES 12 TARTLETS**

*For the filling*
95g caster sugar
1 egg
1 egg yolk
75g butter, plus extra for greasing
zest and juice of 1 lemon
a little freshly grated nutmeg
30g ground almonds
60g well-drained curd cheese
25ml double cream

*For the pastry*
450g block ready-made puff
  pastry, chilled
icing sugar, for dusting
flour, for dusting

1 x 12-hole shallow tartlet tin
1 x 5cm plain, round pastry cutter

In a bowl, whisk the caster sugar, egg and yolk until light and fluffy.

Melt the butter and drizzle it slowly into the eggs and sugar while continuing to whisk. Add the lemon zest and juice, nutmeg and ground almonds.

Press the curd cheese through a fine-meshed sieve and add to the rest of the ingredients. Stir thoroughly to combine. Lastly, stir in the cream. Cover and put in the fridge to chill.

Preheat the oven to 220°C/200°C fan/gas 7. Grease the tartlet tin.

Roll out the puff pastry thinly on a lightly floured surface and cut out circles using a 5cm plain cutter.

Press the pastry circles into the prepared tin. Using your thumbs, gently press the pastry into the base of each tartlet, so as to make the centre thinner and almost translucent, and allowing the rim edges of the pastry to ease upwards. This will ensure crisp bottoms to the tartlets and give the edges room to puff around the filling.

Spoon in about 1 tablespoon of the filling. Do not overfill as the filling will puff up greatly during cooking and sink again as it cools.

Bake for 8–10 minutes until lightly browned then transfer to a wire rack to cool. Lightly dust with icing sugar before serving.

# MINI CHEESECAKES
*1660*

A generalisation of the difference between American and British cheesecakes is that those from across the pond tend to be cooked, while in Britain we currently favour uncooked cheesecakes, set with either chocolate or some form of gelatine. However, the baked cheesecake is actually a very old British dish which originally crossed the Atlantic Ocean in the customs and cookbooks of the Pilgrim Fathers.

While food tastes in Britain in the 17th and 18th centuries evolved alongside international trade developments and contact with other cultures, the colonists of the New World were almost living in their own little time capsule, with very little innovation in the food they prepared and ate. The first cookbook published in the US was actually an English one, *The Compleat Housewife*, written by E. Smith and originally published in England in 1727, and it would be another 50 years before a cookery book written by an American author was published in North America (Amelia Simmons's *American Cookery*).

Cooked cheesecake recipes appear in a number of early British cookbooks. The redoubtable Robert May, author of arguably the first major English cookery book (which he published in 1660 at the grand old age of seventy-two), included no fewer than ten cheesecake recipes. Instructions for similar pastries can be traced even further back, to the court of Richard II, where they were recorded in the recipe rolls of the time.[19] Richard II, of course, is believed to have invented the handkerchief. I like to think it was not because the boy king couldn't bear to see members of the court wipe their runny noses on their sleeves, rather it was because he needed something to dab from his mouth the pastry flakes from the ancestors of these little cheesecakes.

MAKES 12–15 MINI CHEESECAKES

*For the filling*
170g well-drained curd cheese
112g butter, softened, plus extra
  for greasing
2 eggs
1 tbsp brandy
15g ground almonds
40g caster sugar
¼ tsp ground cinnamon
zest and juice of 1 lemon

2 tbsp orange-flower water
currants, for sprinkling

*For the pastry*
450g block ready-made puff
  pastry, chilled
flour, for dusting

1 x 12-hole shallow tartlet tin
1 x 5cm fluted pastry cutter

Preheat the oven to 220°C/200°C fan/gas 7. Grease the tartlet tin.

Rub the curd cheese and the butter through a fine sieve into a bowl.

Whisk the eggs with the brandy until frothy, then stir in the ground almonds, sugar, cinnamon, lemon zest and juice and orange-flower water. Pour this mixture into the bowl with the butter and cheese and combine thoroughly. NB: If the mixture is looking 'curdled', either whizz it in a blender or use a hand blender to froth it to smoothness.

Roll out the puff pastry thinly on a lightly floured surface and cut out circles, using a 5cm fluted cutter.

Press the pastry circles into the prepared tin. Using your thumbs, gently press the pastry into the base of each tartlet, so as to make the centre thinner and almost translucent, allowing the rim edges of the pastry to ease upwards. This will ensure a crisp bottom to the tartlets and give the edges room to puff around the filling.

Spoon in about 1 tablespoon of the filling. Be careful not to overfill the tarts—the filling will puff up greatly during cooking and then sink again as it cools.

Sprinkle some currants on to each cheesecake—6–8 is about the right quantity. The filling will puff up around them. If you put the currants into the tartlets first, they will remain in a layer on the bottom of each cheesecake.

Bake for 8–10 minutes until puffed and lightly browned then transfer to a wire rack to cool.

# RICH ORANGE TART
*1695*

This recipe was actually entitled 'The Best Orange Pudding', and written in the margin in a different hand was the comment 'good'. Since I was keen to include an orange-flavoured pudding but was having trouble choosing between the more than 50 handwritten recipes I'd found, I decided the anonymous endorsement of two separate cooks was good enough. I always trust personal recommendations over a printed recipe, and with manuscript recipe books, if someone liked a recipe enough to go to the trouble of writing it out, and another has tried it and deemed it good also, it's tantamount to a guarantee that you're on to a winner.

There is a whole range of these types of rich custard tart, one of the earliest being Lady Elinor Fettiplace's Tart of Eggs (1604) and the most famous being Bakewell Pudding. There is much discussion as to when the Bakewell pudding was first created, and by whom. One account is that sometime in the 1850s, Ann Wheeldon, the flustered cook of Mrs Greaves at the Rutland Arms Hotel in Bakewell, put strawberry jam on the bottom of a pastry shell instead of spreading it over the cooked custard filling. The result was so well received that the dish became a regular menu item.

This is both a charming anecdote and also utterly believable. Tarte Tatin has similar origins as a mistake that turned out to be better than the intended dish. There are, however, recipes for Bakewell Pudding that date earlier than the mid-19th century. The earliest known printed recipe appears in *The Magazine of Domestic Economy* of 1836, while an even earlier one turned up recently in a handwritten recipe book dated 1811. It was entitled 'Bakewell Pudding—Duke of Devonshire' and when you consider that the seat of the Duke of Devonshire is at Chatsworth House, less than 5 miles from Bakewell, it becomes an even more interesting version. The flavour layer consisted of 'any kind of sweetmeat or preserve' topped with a rich sugar, butter and egg-yolk mixture.

But I digress. The original recipe for this rich orange cake calls for puff pastry, but the filling is so rich, a plain shortcrust is a much better choice. The filling sinks slightly on cooling, a light crust forming over it.

SERVES 6–8

| *For the shortcrust pastry* | *For the filling* |
|---|---|
| *60g lard* | *112g butter* |
| *60g butter, plus extra for* | *3 egg yolks* |
| *greasing* | *112g caster sugar* |
| *240g plain flour, plus extra for* | *30g candied orange peel, chopped* |
| *dusting* | |
| *ice-cold water, to mix* | *1 x 20cm loose-bottomed cake* |
| | *or tart tin* |

Put the lard, butter and flour into the bowl of a food processor and blitz until it resembles breadcrumbs.

With the motor running on low, gradually add cold water, a spoonful at a time, pausing after each one to let the water be fully absorbed. When the mixture comes together in a ball, stop the machine and tip it out on to a lightly floured surface.

Knead a few times until smooth then wrap in cling film and chill in the fridge for 30 minutes.

Grease the cake or tart tin.

Roll out the chilled pastry thinly on a lightly floured surface to about a 5mm thickness. Slide the loose bottom from the tin under the pastry and then fold the edges of the pastry inwards towards the centre of the base. Return the base to the tin then unfold the pastry, easing it into the edges of the tin and against the sides.

Return the pastry to the fridge and chill again for 20 minutes, so that the pastry can relax and be less prone to shrinkage.

Preheat the oven to 180°C/160°C fan/gas 4.

Lay some baking parchment over the pastry in the tin and fill with baking beads, uncooked rice or dried beans.

Bake the pastry case for 10 minutes then remove from the oven and remove both the baking parchment and the beads/rice/beans. Return the pastry case to the oven and bake for another 5 minutes. Remove and set aside.

Turn the oven temperature down to 140°C/120°C fan/gas 1.

To make the filling, warm the butter until it's just melted.

Mix the yolks with the sugar and the chopped candied orange peel. Add the warm melted butter and stir to combine.

Pour the filling into the pastry case and smooth the top.

If the edges of the pastry are in danger of becoming too dark, cover them with a folded strip of foil to keep them from burning.

Bake for 35–40 minutes until the filling has set and a thin crust has formed on the surface. Set aside to cool.

Trim the excess pastry from the edges and serve the tart with pouring cream, if liked.

# RASPBERRY TART WITH CREAM
*1777*

This delicate tart comes from a rather neglected 18th-century cookery book by Mrs Charlotte Mason that deserves to be better known than it is today. Mrs Mason was the first to suggest menus, or 'Bills of Fare', as she called them, for households of limited income. She begins with more than 30 menu suggestions of, by our standards, very generous three-course meals, although it was the fashion at this time for all dishes to be placed on the table at the same time. One such menu included a haunch of beef, two roasted rabbits, greens, carrots and cauliflower, all finished off with a large steamed Cumberland pudding, rich with apples and dried fruits. She continues with numerous suggestions for meals consisting of up to 19 different dishes, and then includes more ideas for cod suppers.

The rest of her book is packed with recipes for every conceivable type of dish, sweet and savoury: confectionery, vegetables, pies, pastries, wines, spirits, puddings, creams and giam (jam). She even includes a calendar of seasonal produce—a rare sight in even our modern cookery books.

I came upon Mrs Mason's recipe for Raspberry Tart by backtracking through various other recipe books. It sounded a very fresh and simple dish, and I was keen to find the original author because it has been cheerfully plagiarised for more than 200 years. Now I can appreciate that it is possible that recipes for similar dishes can evolve independently, but that doesn't seem to be the case here. Some well-respected names in the culinary world, including John Farley, Mrs Rundell and even Hannah Glasse, have blithely taken Mrs Mason's recipe into their own collections. Plagiarism aside, if these names considered the recipe worthwhile purloining then it's a great recommendation.

The original recipe called for raspberries to be baked with sugar under a pastry lid. The lid was then removed and the cream custard poured into the (now) tart. The dish was returned to the oven to cook the custard. In the intervening (almost) 250 years since this recipe was written, we have come to enjoy many advancements in food production, which has led to much larger and juicier raspberries. The original method created too much juice for the tart to hold together with my initial trial of this recipe, so I have made a few minor adjustments that make for a deliciously simple dessert, while staying true to Mrs Mason's original dish.

SERVES 6–8

400g block ready-made puff
  pastry, chilled
300g fresh raspberries
1–2 tbsp caster sugar, for
  sprinkling
300ml double cream

3–4 tbsp icing sugar
3 egg yolks
flour, for dusting

1 x 20cm loose-bottomed tart/
  cake tin

Grease and line the tart or cake tin with baking parchment. On a lightly floured surface, roll out the pastry to a little larger than the tin and line the tin with it. Leave the excess pastry attached. Prick holes in the bottom of the pastry, using a fork, to help keep it from rising too much. Cover lightly with cling film and chill in the fridge for 30 minutes. (This helps the pastry relax and prevents it from shrinking too much during cooking.)

Preheat the oven to 220°C/200°C fan/gas 7. Remove the tin from the fridge and discard the cling film.

Cut a piece of baking parchment to size and lay it over the pastry base and sides. Cover it with baking beans, uncooked rice or baking beads. Blind bake the pastry for 8 minutes then remove it from the oven, discard the parchment and beans/rice/beads and return the tart to the oven for a further 5 minutes.

Check to see if the centre of the tart has puffed up. If it has, run a knife around the edge of the top layer of puffed pastry and remove it (this will allow the layers underneath to dry out and thus avoid the dreaded 'soggy bottom'). Return it to the oven for 2–3 minutes to further dry the bottom of the tart then take the tin out of the oven and set it aside to cool. If the edges of the pastry seem to be browning too much, cover them with a folded strip of foil.

Lower the oven temperature to 150°C/130°C fan/gas 2.

Once the tin has cooled, place it on a baking sheet and arrange the raspberries inside the tart. Stand them upright, 3cm apart. Sprinkle lightly with caster sugar.

Sweeten the double cream with the icing sugar. Add the egg yolks, and whisk to combine. Gently pour the cream mixture into the tart, between the raspberries. Try to keep the raspberries upright and in place. Just their tips should be visible above the cream.

Return the tart to the oven for 20–30 minutes until the custard is almost set. There should still be some slight wobble in the middle of the tart. Set aside to cool.

Trim the excess pastry from the tart edges with a sharp knife and serve the tart slightly warm or at room temperature.

# MARY EATON'S SPRING FRUIT PUDDING

*1822*

I found this recipe in a manuscript belonging to the Johnson family from Lincolnshire that had been continuously maintained and added to for almost 140 years. It was called 'Spring Fruit Pudding from Miss Burford' and it caught my eye because of its novelty; the notion of eating fruit in spring is odd given that there is usually little home-grown fruit available until the earliest soft fruit in May.

Then there's the fact that, although definitely a dessert, this isn't a pudding in the contemporary sense—a sponge boiled for hours in a floured cloth—it is a puff pastry tart. Also, the fruit concerned is rhubarb, which is technically a vegetable, although poached gently with sugar, it has a wonderfully tart and refreshing flavour.

In the pre-refrigeration era, after long winter months surviving on increasingly musty apples and pears, and candied and preserved fruit, fresh new stalks of rhubarb must have been a welcome sight. The very earliest rhubarb crops are the delicate, pale coral-pink stems of forced rhubarb available from the tail end of winter until Easter, the technology for which was developed in the early 1800s. However, for this recipe I used maincrop rhubarb, the mature stems producing a fresh, avocado-green filling.

I've changed little from the original recipe, merely specifying quantities where none were given and reducing the amount of butter in the filling. I like its sharpness, but you can adjust the quantity of sugar to your own taste. The filling is beautifully light, gently spiced and creamy-smooth, halfway between a curd and a custard, but without all the guilt-ridden cream.

Despite the implied provenance, I discovered that this recipe actually comes from Mary Eaton's *The Cook and Housekeeper's*

*Complete and Universal Dictionary* (1822). Mary's recipe is actually called Rhubarb Pudding, but at the end she does comment that it would make a good spring pudding, and I think that it deserves this refreshing title as per the manuscript, for without it I would have overlooked this delight of a dessert.

A pretty effect can be produced by doubling the recipe and then separating the chopped stalks into 'mostly green' and 'mostly pink'. Making the filling in two batches results in two contrastingly-coloured—but equally delicious—mixtures. These can then be served either separately, or side by side in the same tart case for a very striking look. Any extra filling can be kept chilled and is delicious served over cereal or just enjoyed by itself.

The following instructions are for making individual serving tarts, but you can also make 1 large (20–24cm) tart.

SERVES 6–8, EITHER AS I LARGE TART OR SEVERAL INDIVIDUAL
TARTS

*400g block ready-made puff*    *2 cloves*
  *pastry, chilled*    *100g sugar*
*1 egg white, beaten, for glazing*    *55g butter*
*flour, for dusting*    *½ nutmeg*
    *1 egg*
*For the filling*    *3 egg yolks*
*400g rhubarb*
*pared rind of 1 lemon*    *6–8 loose-bottomed individual*
*1 x 5cm cinnamon stick*    *tart tins*

*To make the pastry cases*
Preheat the oven to 220°C/200°C fan/gas 7. Line a baking sheet with baking parchment.

Cut the block of pastry in half and put one piece back in the fridge; it's easier to work with 2 small pieces of pastry than one large one, and reduces the chances of it tearing.

Lightly dust a work surface with flour and roll out the pastry to about 5mm thick then slide it on to a chopping board and put it in the freezer for 10 minutes. (Cutting out the tarts will be much easier if the pastry is very cold and firm.) Repeat with the other piece of pastry.

Remove the first sheet from the freezer and cut out the tart bases. I use a loose-bottomed tartlet tin as a cutter, because the crinkled edges make the finished tarts rather attractive, but any shape will do. Lay on the prepared baking sheet.

Remove the second sheet of pastry from the freezer and repeat. These discs will make the tart rims. Using a sharp knife, cut out the centre of each pastry shape, leaving a 2cm rim around the edge. Discard the centre portion of pastry.

To join the rims to the bases, wet the edges of the pastry bases with cold water then lift the pastry rims on to the bases, lining up the edges neatly. Press the pastry circles and rims together gently but firmly, but avoid pressing on the edges otherwise they might not rise properly. Prick the centre of the bases with a fork to allow the steam to escape and so help prevent the middle of the tart cases from rising. Carefully brush the pastry circles with beaten egg white. Don't brush the cut edges as the egg white would glue the layers together and prevent the pastry from rising.

Bake for 5 minutes then turn the baking sheet 180 degrees and bake for another 5 minutes, or until the cases are well risen and golden brown. (If the centres of the pastry cases have risen slightly, gently press them back down with the back of a spoon while still hot.)

Transfer to a wire rack to cool.

*To make the filling*

Wash and chop the rhubarb roughly into cubes and put into a pan with a well-fitting lid. To make 2 different-coloured fillings, double the recipe and divide the rhubarb into red and green pieces then cook them in separate pans.

Using a peeler, remove the rind of the lemon and add to the pan, together with the cinnamon stick, cloves and sugar.

Stir, cover and place on a very low heat until the rhubarb has softened and breaks down easily when pressed with the back of a spoon, about 20–30 minutes. Stir occasionally. There is no need to add any liquid as there is more than enough in the rhubarb.

When the rhubarb is ready, remove the pan from the heat and pick out and discard the spices and the lemon peel.

Add the butter to the pan and stir until melted. Grate the nutmeg into the pan. Stir well and taste. Add more sugar if the mixture is too sharp.

Beat the egg and the yolks together then add to the fruit mixture in the pan, whisking vigorously to avoid the mixture curdling.

Return the pan to the low heat and whisk until the eggs have cooked and the mixture has thickened. To ensure the very smoothest and lightest of mixes, use an immersion or jug blender.

Set the filling aside to cool then chill in the fridge until required.

Spoon some of the rhubarb filling into each tart case and smooth the surface. Serve with pouring cream, if liked.


*To assemble two-colour tarts*

Fold over a sheet of foil several times until you have a strip that holds its shape, and spray it with cooking oil. you will need one strip for each tart case. Bend each strip into an 'S' shape and tuck one inside the rim of each tart.

Spoon the green filling into each tart case on one side and the pink filling into the other half.

Using a wooden cocktail stick, ease the fillings away from the sides of each foil strip and lift it out. Use the cocktail stick to smooth the fillings together.

## HANDY HINTS

- The filling can be made the day before required.
- The pastry bases can be rolled out and cut out, covered well with cling film and left in the fridge until required. Glaze and bake them just before your guests arrive (allowing time for cooling), and they will be light and crisp and at their very best.
- Optional: Dust the pastry cases with icing sugar before filling.
- Optional: If you've made the two-colour version, you can serve both flavours together in each pastry case for a striking effect.

# SPICED DAMSON TART
### 1654

Damsons are a delicious variety of small, wild plum, peculiar to the UK and a familiar sight in the woods and hedgerows of my home counties of Worcestershire, Herefordshire and Shropshire. The fruit is the size of a large grape, and the skins have a characteristic bluish bloom. Their flavour is extremely astringent and they are usually too sharp to eat raw, and so their bounty tends to be preserved in conserves, jams and jellies. For the more adventurous, damson gin and damson wine are also very delicious, with a well-made damson wine considered by some to rival a vintage port.

I chose this recipe because it was a little out of the ordinary against the many recipes for preserves or alcohol. After a few trial bakes, I arrived at a dessert that I was happy with that showcases the fruit to its best advantage, looks stunning and makes a very special occasion dessert: crisp pastry with a soft, sweet damson custard topped with a set layer of damson purée. If you can't find damsons, use any sharp-tasting plum. Greengages would be equally impressive. I've selected the cornflour sweet pastry for this tart because I like its crispness, but you can use your own favourite pastry recipe if you prefer.

SERVES 6–8

_For the pastry_
225g plain flour, plus extra for
    dusting
60g cornflour
140g butter, plus extra
    for greasing
85g caster sugar
zest of 1 lemon
1 egg
1 egg white, beaten, as required

_For the filling_
500g damsons
125g sugar, plus extra to taste
200ml red wine
2 tsp ground cinnamon
1 tsp ground ginger

*For the custard*
4 egg yolks
2 tbsp cornflour
80ml clotted cream

*For the topping*
2 sheets gelatine

1 x 20cm loose-bottomed tart tin

*To make the pastry*
Grease the tart tin.

Put all of the ingredients for the pastry, except the egg and egg white, into the bowl of a food processor and blitz until the mixture resembles breadcrumbs. Lightly whisk the egg and gradually add it to the mixture while the motor is running until the mixture comes together in a ball. Add a little extra egg white (which will enrich the pastry; you could use water instead) if necessary.

Tip the pastry on to a lightly floured work surface and knead a little until smooth then roll it out to about 5mm thickness and line the prepared tart tin. Don't trim the edges. Chill in the fridge for 30 minutes.

Preheat the oven to 200°C/180°C fan/gas 6.

Remove the chilled pastry from the fridge. Cut parchment paper to the size of the tin and line the inside of the tart. Cover the paper with baking beans, beads or uncooked rice to keep the pastry from rising while it's baking. Bake for 10 minutes then remove from the oven and discard the parchment and the beans/beads/rice. Return the tart to the oven for a further 10 minutes to finish baking. Set aside to cool.

*To make the fruit purée filling*
Put the damsons, the 125g sugar and the wine into a small pan over a low heat. Cover and cook for 20–25 minutes until the fruit has softened. Once the damsons are soft, take the pan off the heat and sieve the fruit into a bowl, working the fruit with a spatula until just the skins and stones remain in the sieve. Scrape the pulp from the

underside of the sieve with the back of a knife. This should produce about 600ml of pulp and juice. Taste, and add the cinnamon and ginger, plus more sugar if required. Make sure the sugar is fully dissolved before adding extra. If necessary, warm the mixture over a low heat. Don't over-sweeten it as you want the damson topping to be a little sharper than the custard. Set aside 200ml of the fruit mixture.

*To make the custard*
Whisk together the egg yolks and cornflour. Continue to whisk while you pour the remaining 400ml of the fruit purée over the mixture. Keep mixing until fully combined. Return to the pan and stir over a low heat until the mixture thickens then set aside to cool slightly. When just warm, stir in the clotted cream. Trim the excess pastry from the cooked tart case, then pour the mixture into the pastry case and cover the surface with cling film to prevent a skin forming. Leave to set completely then place in the fridge to chill.

*To make the topping*
Cut the sheet of gelatine into pieces and place in a small bowl. Add 60ml of cold water and leave it to swell and become soft. This is known as blooming. Put the reserved 200ml fruit purée into a small pan and add the bloomed gelatine. Stir over a low heat until the gelatine is fully dissolved.

Remove from the heat and cool slightly.

*To assemble the tart*
Remove the pastry case from the fridge and discard the cling film. Carefully pour the fruit purée mixture over the top of the custard until it is completely covered. Return to the fridge to chill until set. This will take several hours.

Allow the tart to come to room temperature before serving. Serve with cream or ice cream.

# TAFFETY TARTS
*1690*

This recipe has such a fun-sounding name, as soon as I read it, I just had to try it.

I found a variety of recipes for these tarts in old manuscripts, each with varying degrees of detail but, in general terms, they all described a fruit tart made with peeled and sliced pippins. Pippins are a variety of what we would now call a dessert or eating apple, which was used especially for cooking. Unlike our more familiar Bramley apple, eating apples hold their shape during cooking. Nearly all the recipes I found called for the apple slices to be arranged neatly and a couple added the helpful detail of 'like slating of houses'. Of all the variations I discovered, the recipe below is the one that I found most deliciously unusual.

To produce delicate pastries such as these from a continuously cooling brick oven required great skill, especially as there was no way of setting or even reading the temperature. However, I was delighted to discover the following helpful hint included in two of the recipes:

*'...bake them in a temperate oven which you must try by throwing of flower into the oven. If the flower do sparkle, it is too hot, but if it is only brown, then set in your tarts...'*

So if the oven was hot enough to ignite the flour particles then it was still too hot. What fun it would be if our ovens today had 'sparkling flour' as a heat setting instead of 200°C which, although helpfully specific, is much less colourful.

MAKES 8 INDIVIDUAL TARTS

*For the filling*
4 eating apples
113g granulated sugar
60ml sweet sherry
zest and juice of 2 oranges

*For the pastry cases*
400g block ready-made puff
  pastry, chilled
flour, for dusting
1 egg white, beaten, for glazing

8 loose-bottomed tart tins

*Prepare the filling*
Peel the apples, cut each one into 8 wedges and remove the core. This is best done with an apple corer/slicer—not only is it much quicker, but it helps keep the apple wedges a uniform size. Cut across each wedge to make 5mm wedge-shaped slices—any thicker and they become rather too chunky to arrange neatly in the tarts; any thinner, and they risk burning before the pastry is cooked.

Put the apple slices into a pan with the sugar and sherry. Cover and heat gently until the sugar dissolves. Don't worry if there isn't much liquid to begin with, the sugar will help draw out the apple juice. Stir the apple slices in the syrup and bring to a gentle simmer. When the apple slices start to look translucent, about 2–3 minutes, remove the pan from the heat and add the orange zest. Stir gently to mix.

Return the pan to the heat and bring to a simmer for a second time. then remove the pan from the heat and stir in the orange juice. Set aside to cool.

*Make the pastry cases*
Preheat the oven to 220°C/200°C fan/gas 7. Line a baking sheet with baking parchment.

Cut the block of pastry in half and put one piece back in the fridge. It's easier to work with 2 small pieces of pastry than one large one, and reduces the chances of it tearing.

On a lightly floured surface, roll out the pastry to about 5mm thickness. You can roll it thinner if you like, but the sides of the cases won't rise as much.

Slide the sheet of pastry on to a chopping board and put it in the freezer for 10 minutes. (Cutting out the tarts will be much easier if the pastry is very cold and firm.) Repeat with the second piece of pastry.

Remove the first sheet of pastry from the freezer and cut out the tart bases. I use a loose-bottomed tartlet tin as a pastry cutter because the crinkled edges make the finished tarts rather attractive, but any shape will do.

Remove the second sheet of pastry from the freezer. This sheet will be used to form the tart rims. These can be either plain or decorative. For each pastry rim simply cut out another circle of pastry as before then, with a sharp knife, cut out the centre of the circle, leaving a 2cm rim around the edge. Discard the centre portion of pastry. To join the rims to the bases, wet the edges of the pastry bases with cold water. Lift the pastry rims on to the bases, lining up the edges neatly. Don't press the circles and rims together or they might not rise properly.

For a more decorative pastry edge, cut the pastry into shapes using a small (2cm diameter) pastry cutter. Arrange these shapes around the edge of the rim of each pastry base, overlapping them to form a continuous circle.

Prick the centre of the bases with a fork. This will allow the steam to escape and so helps prevent the middle of the tart cases from rising.

Transfer the uncooked tart shells to the lined baking sheet before adding the filling.

*Add the filling*
Starting at the edge of the tarts, arrange the cooled apple wedges neatly in a circle, with the wider edge touching the edge of the pastry circle. Lay another circle of apple slices inside, overlapping the outer one like roof tiles. Continue until each tart is filled.

Brush a little of the poaching liquid over each tart for added moisture during cooking.

Brush the pastry rings with beaten egg white, being careful not to moisten the cut edges, as the egg white would act like a glue and prevent the pastry from rising.

Bake for 8 minutes. Remove the baking sheet, rotate it 180 degrees and cook the tarts for another 7–8 minutes until the pastry is risen and golden. Be careful that the apple slices don't burn. Cover with parchment if necessary.

While the tarts are cooking, simmer the apple poaching liquid, uncovered, until enough moisture has evaporated for it to form a syrup.

When the tarts are cooked, remove from the oven and transfer to a wire rack.

Brush the apple slices generously with the syrup and allow to cool.

Serve warm or at room temperature with some double cream.

# 5

## PUDDINGS

Puddings are a great tradition in British cookery, but not one in which we indulge very often, and to our own detriment, I feel. We might not have the time or the opportunity to simmer a steamed pudding for hours these days, but there are still a great many delicious ways to round off a meal.

# BROWN BREAD
# ICE CREAM
*1807*

Ice cream was invented in Italy in the late 17th century, and I was delighted to discover four very early recipes for ice cream in the cookery manuscripts of the Wellcome Library. All of the recipes date from the mid to late 17th century, demonstrating that British cooks were familiar with the most innovative and fashionable dishes of the day.

Elizabeth Jacob's recipe (c. 1654–1685) is very simple: just sweetened cream with fruit. That of Lady Ann Fanshawe (1651 onwards), charmingly, and possibly more accurately, called 'Icy Cream', suggests flavourings of mace, ambergris and orange-flower water. The third recipe has been dated to the late 17th century. Enriched with eggs and flavoured with Spanish Water (possibly liquorice),[20] it is entitled 'The Ice Cream Made At Court'. It isn't hard to imagine the bewigged privileged members of the Royal household enjoying this simple but luxurious treat. The final recipe comes from an anonymous manuscript which suggests adding mace or orange-flower water, and then serving with some of the unfrozen, sweetened cream poured around the decanted ice cream as a garnish. All of these recipes have a similar method, using a mixture of ice and salt [21] to freeze the creams solid, a technique which changed little over the following decades until the invention of refrigeration in the 19th century.

This particular recipe is adapted from an 1807 Brown Bread Ice Cream recipe by Frederick Nutt. Lightened with Italian meringue, it is more like a frozen soufflé than a traditional ice cream, but it has the advantage of being easily made without an ice-cream maker. I have tweaked the recipe to use an Italian cooked meringue in an effort to allay any concerns over the eating of raw egg whites. The crunchy texture of the toasted breadcrumbs contrasts fantastically with the smoothness of the cream. (The Grant Loaf is ideal for the coarse breadcrumbs: see page 299).

The quantities may look small, but the ice cream is rather rich and so individual ramekin portions are ideal. They freeze in 3–4 hours, and I have successfully stored them in the freezer for up to 2 days, making them an ideal make-ahead special-occasion dessert.

SERVES 4–6

*For the toasted breadcrumbs*
*150g wholemeal breadcrumbs, the*
*coarser the better*
*190g demerara sugar*

*For the meringue*
*2 egg whites*
*pinch of salt*
*a few drops lemon juice*
*90g caster sugar*

*For the cream*
*1 tsp vanilla extract*
*150ml double cream*

*4–6 small ramekins*
*kitchen foil*
*cook's thermometer, optional*

Preheat the oven to 200°C/180°C fan/gas 6. Line a baking sheet with baking parchment.

*Prepare the toasted breadcrumbs*
Mix the breadcrumbs and demerara sugar together and spread them on the lined baking sheet. Bake for 10 minutes. Remove from the oven, stir, then bake for a further 5 minutes. Stir again, breaking up any large pieces and then set aside to cool.

*Prepare the ramekins*
Tear off a 15cm strip of kitchen foil and fold in half along its length. You will need 4–6 strips of folded foil.

Wrap a strip of foil firmly around each ramekin, making a collar that stands 3–4cm above the rim. Use sticky tape to keep it tight.

*Make the meringue*

Put the egg whites, salt and lemon juice into a mixer bowl. Whisk slowly until frothy, then fast until they form stiff peaks. Gradually add 2 tablespoons of the caster sugar. Whip to stiff, glossy peaks. Keep the mixer running on low while you prepare the sugar syrup.

Slowly heat the remaining 60g sugar and the water in a pan over a low heat until all the sugar is dissolved then heat on high to 115°C or until the syrup forms a soft sticky mass when dropped in cold water (soft-ball stage). Remove the pan from the heat and allow the bubbles to subside.

With the beaters running, pour the sugar syrup down the side of the bowl into the whisked whites in a thin stream, then continue whisking until the bowl is cool to the touch and the meringue is stiff. This will take between 10 and 15 minutes.

*Prepare the cream*

Add the vanilla extract to the double cream and whip to soft peaks. Stir in the cooled caramelised breadcrumbs then fold in the meringue gently but thoroughly.

Divide the mixture evenly between the prepared ramekins, cover lightly with cling film and place in the freezer until required.

*To serve*

Remove from the freezer and set aside to soften slightly, about 15–20 minutes. Remove the foil collars and set the ramekins on to serving plates. Serve with the remaining caramelised breadcrumbs on the side.

# FRUIT FOOL
*17th century*

Short of enjoying fruit freshly picked, a fool is one of the simplest, yet most delicious, of English desserts. A coarse purée of fruit is stirred through sweetened, whipped cream and then spooned into a serving dish. It's that simple. With some crisp ratafia biscuits, or elegant sponge fingers to dip or scoop, a fruit fool is a fabulous way to enjoy the freshest summer fruit, and it requires practically no skill whatsoever to produce.

The word 'fool' is thought to come from the French verb 'fouler', which means 'to tread', as in treading grapes. For the modern interpretation of this dessert it seems a perfectly reasonable supposition, but it's not really convincing when you consider the earliest fool recipes. Back in the 16th century a fool was a rich custard made with a mixture of cream, eggs, sugar and spices, and occasionally served over crustless, sliced white bread. It was an early example of what would go on to become that other classic, trifle.

Fruit fool works best with tart and sharp-tasting fruits like damsons and rhubarb, which need only a little cooking to be at their best. Damsons are small, wild plums, about the size and shape of a large grape, with dark purple skins that have a characteristic bluish bloom. Too sharp to eat raw, their skins are especially bitter, and so they are best cooked and sieved to remove both skins and stones. Gooseberry fool is an absolute classic, especially good with the addition of a little elderflower cordial. This gives an aroma of the finest muscat grapes, from which many delightful dessert wines are made. You can also use crushed fresh red berries and other soft fruits for a simpler version, but try not to over-sweeten the mixture.

There are a number of ways to make a fruit fool: you can sweeten the fruit and keep the cream plain, or lightly sweeten the cream and leave the fruit mostly unsweetened. Alternatively, lightly sweeten both fruit and cream: it's very much down to personal preference.

This recipe can be made with any type of fruit, just adjust the quantity of sugar accordingly. If you're using fruit that will need cooking, prepare it the day before, as the purée will need to be chilled before it is mixed into the whipped cream.

SERVES 4–6

| | |
|---|---|
| *450g damsons* | *2–3 tbsp icing sugar, to taste* |
| *sugar, to taste* | *300ml double cream* |

Put the damsons into a pan over a low heat and add 125ml cold water. Cover and simmer gently until the fruit has broken down then sieve the softened fruit to remove the skins and stones. Add sugar to taste.

In a bowl, add 2–3 tablespoons of icing sugar to the cream to sweeten it slightly. Whip the sweetened cream until it forms stiff peaks. Be careful not to over-whip. The liquid fruit purée will loosen the cream to a delicate softness.

Fold the chilled fruit purée into the whipped cream to give a rippled effect.

Serve with crisp Ratafias (see page 105) or Naples Biscuits (sponge fingers, see page 101) for dipping.

## VARIATIONS

*Fruit Purée*
Any fruit purée can be made into fruit fool, but the best flavours come from sharper fruits. The purée should be thick to avoid a sloppy finished dish.

*Apple, Quince, Pear*
Sharpen with lemon juice and zest.

*Gooseberries and Rhubarb*
Both very juicy. Reduce the cooking water to 2–3 tablespoons.
Crush gently when tender.

*Cranberries, Blueberries*
Simmer until soft, sharpen with lemon juice and mash.

*Soft Fruits*
Trim and chop the fruit and sprinkle with a little caster sugar.
Cover and set aside for 30–60 minutes to draw out the juices. Crush
to a coarse purée then stir through the whipped cream.

*Cranachan*
This traditional Scottish dessert is a version of a fruit fool. Toast
50g medium or coarse oatmeal in a dry pan until golden. Sprinkle
some raspberries with sugar and set aside. Flavour the whipped
cream with 2 tablespoons each of honey and whisky. Spoon some of
the softened, sweetened raspberries into the bottom of some serving
glasses, and fold the rest through the cream, together with the
cooled, toasted oatmeal. Spoon into the glasses and serve with crisp
shortbread. For more texture, use rolled oats instead of the oatmeal.

*Additional Flavourings*
Elderflower cordial is fantastic when paired with gooseberries.
Rosewater goes well with raspberries or rhubarb. Orange-flower
water brings a delicate aroma to apricots, rhubarb or peaches.

*Winter Fools*
The cold winter months have a glimmer of cheer in that it is the
season for citrus fruits. Zesty winter fools can be made by folding
through a rich curd made from any number of citrus fruits. Lemon,
orange, pink grapefruit and lime are all readily available, and for a
short time, Seville oranges can also make a fabulous curd. To save
Seville oranges to make curd later in the year, grate the zest and
squeeze the juice and mix together. Freeze the mixture in ice cube
trays—the zest and juice of 1 Seville orange will make one large
ice cube.

*Healthier/Low Fat Option*
Replace the double cream with a firm, creamy natural yoghurt.
Even the creamiest of yoghurts contains just a fraction of the fat
content of double cream. If the yoghurt seems too runny, drain
it through a fine mesh sieve for 12 hours until it firms up. You
will need to increase the amount of sugar in order to combat the
sharpness of the yoghurt, or use a purée of really sweet fruit such as
stoned dates, figs and dried bananas. Simmer the fruit in apple juice
with a little lemon zest and/or lemon juice until soft, then chill and
fold through the yoghurt.

# LACE PANCAKES THE BEST WAY
*1625*

I like recipes with the word 'best' in the title: it implies that the author has tried a number of variations and has decided that this recipe should stand above all others. I found this one in a manuscript book dated 1654–c.1685. Several things about it piqued my interest: the recipe title boldly claimed these to be 'The Best'; the batter was generously spiced; and it was mixed with water rather than milk (specifically stating that pancakes made with milk or cream are not as good). Now I've only ever known pancake batter to be mixed with milk, so I decided to take up the thrown gauntlet and scribbled the recipe down on my 'To Do' list.

A few days later I stumbled across a website containing scanned pages from 17th-century Dutch recipe books. Someone had painstakingly transcribed the Middle Dutch text and, when I showed it to my husband (who happens to be Dutch), curious as to whether he could still read and understand the Dutch from hundreds of years ago, I pointed at a random recipe from a book dated 1667 and asked him if he could translate it for me. And here's where it gets a bit spooky—he read out, word for word, the same instructions I had seen but days before, including the note about mixing the batter with water rather than milk or cream.

This coincidence had me puzzled for quite a while until I discovered the missing link between the printed recipe and the household manuscript: in fact the recipe had originally been printed in Gervase Markham's *The English Hus-wife* in 1615. While this doesn't explain how it got to appear in a Dutch printed book in the middle of a selection of pancake recipes, it's fun to see how the habit of copying and passing on a recipe from someone else's cookbook was alive and well in the 17th century.

So—what are the pancakes like? I couldn't make you sit through all this rambling and not get to the crux of the matter. One word: delicious. Not as heavy or as stodgy as milk-mixed pancakes. And the spices are wonderful.

MAKES ABOUT 10 REGULAR PANCAKES, OR 18 LACE PANCAKES

*2 eggs*
*½ tsp ground cloves*
*½ tsp ground mace*
*½ tsp ground cinnamon*
*½ tsp grated nutmeg*
*pinch of salt*

*plain flour, to thicken*
*melted butter, for cooking*
*icing sugar, for dusting*
*lemon juice or syrup or other*
*   topping, to serve*

In a large bowl, whisk the eggs thoroughly. Add 250ml cold water, the spices and salt and whisk again. Add flour, a spoonful at a time, until the mixture has thickened to your liking. The batter will have a pouring consistency somewhere between single and double cream.

Cook the pancakes as you would normally in flat circles or have fun creating lace pancakes.

*For lace pancakes*
Pour the pancake mixture into a squeezy bottle. You can buy them, but an empty squeezy ketchup bottle, well washed, is ideal and has the advantage of a lid you can close if you don't want to cook all your batter at once.

Melt some butter in a frying pan and drizzle the batter into it in swirls and loops, making a lacy pattern. Flip the pancake over when the underside is browned and briefly cook on the other side.

Serve dusted with icing sugar, and finish with a squeeze of lemon juice, syrup or a topping of your choosing.

# QUIRE OF PANCAKES
*1714*

A quire of paper is one-twentieth of a ream and, depending on the type of paper, usually equates to either 24 or 25 sheets. This recipe, then, is for a stack of rich, cream pancakes, wafer-thin as paper, served as a cake. Instead of serving the pancakes individually, the pancake pile is cut into wedges, like a cake, and served with a dusting of icing sugar and a rich sauce.

This is an adaptation of Mary Kettilby's 1714 recipe, but recipes for this style of pancake stretch back into the 17th century. Although the unusual method of stacking the pancakes is implied in the older recipes, Mary Kettilby's is the first to give detailed instructions and to give the dish its descriptive name. A further instruction, from a much older recipe, was to cook the batter 'in a pan no bigger than a trenchard plate', which is similar in size to a modern side plate. The smaller the diameter of the pancakes, the greater the number you could make from the batter and thus the greater and more impressive the height of the stack. Cooking the pancakes on one side only makes the individual layers easy to see in the sliced portions, with the browned undersides of each pancake being separated by a creamy white upper layer.

This recipe is an ideal make-ahead dessert for a special occasion. The pancakes can be prepared in advance and stacked when needed then gently warmed in the oven while the sauce is being heated.

**MAKES ABOUT 30 SMALL, THIN PANCAKES**

*35g butter*
*200ml double cream*
*3 egg yolks*
*2 egg whites*
*25g plain flour*
*25ml cream sherry*

*1½ tsp orange-flower water*
*25g caster sugar, plus extra for*
  *sprinkling*

*(ingredients continued overleaf)*

*For the sauce*

60ml cream sherry                    *icing sugar, for dusting*

60ml lemon juice

35g sugar

In a pan over a low heat, warm the butter in the cream until melted then set aside to cool.

In a bowl, whisk together the egg yolks and whites.

In a separate bowl, mix the flour to a paste with the sherry and stir into the whisked eggs. Add the orange-flower water and caster sugar then mix in the cooled cream. Set aside for 2 hours to allow the flavours to mingle.

*To cook*

Heat a small frying pan (about 12–15cm in diameter). Prepare the pan by cooking a throwaway pancake. The mixture is so rich, the cooking process also prepares the pan for the next pancake, so no additional butter is required. Alternatively, use a tiny amount of butter to grease the pan before cooking the first pancake.

For each pancake, spoon in about 1 tablespoon of batter. It will froth up and bubble, and you'll need to tilt the pan to make sure the mixture spreads evenly. (I put the batter into a squeezy bottle.)

Fry until golden brown on the bottom and edges. Do not turn it over, but slide the pancake on to a plate and sprinkle with caster sugar. Continue with the rest of the batter, stacking the cooked pancakes one on top of another, each sprinkled with a little sugar.

*For the sauce*

Put all of the sauce ingredients into a small pan with 60ml cold water and simmer gently until reduced to a syrup.

Serve dusted with icing sugar and drizzled with the sauce.

# LEMON CREAM WITHOUT CREAM

*17th century*

This recipe will appeal to anyone who has to avoid dairy yet still craves a creamy, indulgent pudding. It was a pleasant surprise to find a dairy-free recipe in such an old manuscript, although it was probably not created specifically with those of limited diet in mind. A more likely explanation is that it was for use in times when cream was scarce, such as in the depths of winter, when the main concern was for the animals just to survive until spring.

This cream has a light and delicate consistency and is a fabulous make-ahead dessert for a special occasion. Make the day before required and keep covered in the fridge.

**SERVES 4**

*zest and juice of 2 lemons*
*2 eggs*
*60ml egg whites*
*1 tsp rosewater*

*4 tbsp caster sugar (or more),*
  *to taste*
*lemon peel, to decorate*

Pour the juice from the lemons over the zest and leave to steep for 1 hour.

Whisk the eggs, whites and rosewater together until very light and frothy. Add the lemon zest and juice and 4 tablespoons of cold water. Whisk until well combined. Add the sugar and whisk until it is dissolved. Taste and add more sugar if required.

Pour into a heatproof bowl and set over a pan of simmering water, making sure the bottom of the bowl does not touch the water. Whisk until thickened like custard, about 8 minutes.

Remove from the heat and lay cling film on the surface to prevent a skin forming. Set aside to cool then transfer to the fridge to chill until required.

Before serving, pour into glasses and decorate each dessert with a curl of lemon peel. Serve with Naples Biscuits, Pearl Biscuits or Ratafias (see pages 101, 104 and 105).

# SEVILLE ORANGE DELIGHT

*20th century*

This fabulous hot pudding is another example of the sense of alchemy that cooking can sometimes create. A simple set of ingredients is combined like a sponge cake and lightened with egg white. However, what emerges from the oven is decidedly different from the dish that goes into it, but is delicious nonetheless. The mousse-like mixture separates into a delicate soufflé sponge on top of a rich custard-like sauce. I was both surprised and delighted to find the original recipe in an old Women's Institute collection, because it seemed so unusual. Recipes from the WI tend to be wholesome and nutritious and, to be honest, for the most part a little on the plain side. This was a refreshing surprise.

Back in the 1970s, I remember seeing adverts for a rather more solid, chocolate packet-mix version of this dessert. The TV family gasped in wonder because 'the sauce is on the bottom!'. Watching was as close as I ever got to tasting it, though, because in our house, puddings were made from scratch, not bought in a packet. The one rare exception to this rule was Angel Delight. An occasional (bordering on rare) table appearance, it was everything our regular puddings weren't and, consequently, was a huge favourite. Packed with artificial sweeteners, colouring and flavourings, it was the antithesis of regular fare in our house and, consequently, perpetually yearned-for.

The quantities here are for four individual servings, baked in ramekins. I think that even the most ordinary of desserts can be made to appear much more special when served as an individual-sized portion. This serving suggestion elevates this simple pudding to dinner party elegance, when a slice or a spoonful would seem rather homely by comparison.

**SERVES 4**

30g butter, softened, plus extra  
 for greasing  
85g sugar  
zest and juice of 1 Seville orange  
1 egg, separated

1 heaped tbsp self-raising flour  
pinch of salt  
150ml milk

4 small ramekins

Preheat the oven to 180°C/160°C fan/gas 4. Grease your ramekins.

Cream the butter and sugar together until light and fluffy. Add the orange zest and juice, then beat in the egg yolk. Add the flour and salt then slowly add the milk. In a separate bowl, whisk the egg white to stiff peaks and fold into the mixture.

Spoon the mixture into the ramekins and place them in a roasting tin. To make a water bath, pour cold water around them so that it comes halfway up the sides of the ramekins. Bake for 25–30 minutes until the puddings are risen and lightly browned. The cooking time will depend on the size of your ramekins. Serve immediately, as the puddings will deflate as they cool.

## VARIATIONS

*Lemon/Lime*  
A straight swap with the Seville orange.

*Orange*  
Use the zest and juice of ½ orange and ½ lemon. The pudding needs sharpness to offset the sugar, and just using sweet oranges makes it too sweet.

*Large Pudding*  
If you'd prefer to make just a single pudding, double the recipe and cook in the water bath in a buttered casserole for 45–60 minutes.

# MALVERN SUMMER PUDDING
*1868*

Summer Pudding is a simple bread and berry dish that is a regular on lunch tables across the UK during soft fruit season. Words such as 'classic' and 'quintessential' are often bandied around when summer pudding crops up in conversation but, compared with other well-known British desserts, it is a comparative youngster. While recipes for syllabub and trifle date back hundreds of years, summer pudding has only been appearing in print for just over a century. Although there is much debate and a number of differing theories as to its origins, the earliest published recipe we have for Summer Pudding can be found in a book entitled *Sweets ('Part One)*, No. 6 in the 'Queen' cookery books, collected and described by S. Beaty-Pownall (1904). There is always the possibility of an earlier recipe being discovered, of course, but until one does, this claims the title.

As with a number of other recipes in this book, there is a little more to this story than meets the eye. While I agree that the 1904 recipe for Summer Pudding is the earliest in print, to my mind it's difficult to dismiss older recipes that call for lightly stewed berries to be poured into a bread-lined basin which is then weighted and left to stand for several hours, purely because the name is different to the one we use today.

For years I'd read articles that mentioned something called 'Hydropathic Pudding', described as being a version of summer pudding served in Victorian spas (its lightness and freshness a relief from the heavy suet and steamed puddings of the day). I searched fruitlessly—no pun intended—for some evidence in print of this version and was beginning to wonder if this particular story was a myth.

Eventually I came across the recipe in an undated (although I suspect 1880s) Victorian publication entitled *More Tasty Dishes*. It is clearly Summer Pudding in all but name. Following the lines of the healthy dessert even further back, the recipe appears in another guise—Malvern Pudding—as early as 1868 in *Warne's Model Cookery and Housekeeping Book*. A spa town of renown since the 17th century, Malvern is surrounded by the lush, fruit-filled landscapes of Herefordshire and Worcestershire that overflow with the fresh berries required for this pudding.

It is the simplicity of ingredients which makes this dish such a success, and so they should always be of the very best quality available. The mixture of berries can be whatever you have to hand, although raspberries and redcurrants are traditional. I like to include some dark and juicy blackcurrants for contrast. The bread should be slightly stale so that it holds its shape when it soaks up the fruit juices. Slice it thinly, about 1cm, to keep the pudding delicate. Although it is tempting, DO NOT use factory sliced bread. It doesn't absorb juices well and makes the surface of the pudding slimy, which is definitely not the texture we're aiming for: think sponge just on the point of maximum absorption. If you're not confident about slicing the bread evenly and thinly yourself, many bakeries have machines that will slice a loaf for you.

Some recipes recommend dipping the bread into the juices before lining the bowl to make for an even colour, but this is a mistake. As the pudding stands overnight, the dry bread draws juice from the warm fruit like a sponge and, in doing so, also draws itself closer to the berries. This 'tightening up' gives the finished pudding some firmness, which helps it stand up once turned out. To overload the bread with juice beforehand would mean that this firming would not take place and would make for a very sloppy pudding. Any uneven colouring in the bread can be rectified before serving by using a pastry brush to paint over the patches with extra juice once the pudding is turned out.

SERVES 6–8

| | |
|---|---|
| *400g redcurrants* | *slightly stale white bread, cut into* |
| *200g blackcurrants* | *about 12 x 1cm-thick slices, crusts* |
| *400g raspberries* | *removed* |
| *125g caster sugar, plus extra* | |
| *to taste* | *1 x deep, round pudding basin* |

*Prepare the fruit*

Strip the currants from the stalks using a fork. Hold the stalk in one hand and comb downwards with the fork to remove the berries. Hull the raspberries and pick out any small leaf pieces.

Put the fruit into an ovenproof bowl and sprinkle with the sugar. Toss gently to combine.

Put the bowl into the oven and turn the heat on to 110°C/90°C fan/gas ¼. Leave the berries to warm for 30 minutes.

*Prepare the bowl*

Choose a deep, round pudding basin and, with a pastry brush, just dampen the insides of the bowl. This will help the cling film stick, and it can be smoothed over easily.

Tear off 2 strips of cling film. Lay the first across the bowl one way, and smooth it close to the sides of the bowl. Lay the second strip at right angles, and make sure all of the sides of the bowl are covered.

Cut a circle of bread to fit into the bottom of the basin and place it there. Set aside 1 slice of bread to make the cover and cut the remaining slices lengthways into strips about 3cm wide.

Line the sides of the bowl with the bread strips, overlapping each one slightly so that there are no gaps for the berries to leak through. Err on the side of caution and use extra bread to be on the safe side.

When the berries have been warming for 30 minutes, remove from the oven and stir gently. Try to keep the berries as whole as possible. There should be quite a lot of juice. Taste to see if more sugar is required and add accordingly. Stir again to combine the extra sugar and to help it dissolve.

Spoon the warm fruit into the bread-lined bowl, using a slotted spoon. When full, add a little of the remaining juice just until it is visible between the berries. Cover and chill the remaining juice for later.

Put the lid of bread (cut to fit) on top of the pudding and fold over the ends of the cling film. Place a saucer on top and add some weights—a couple of tins will do. Leave in the fridge overnight to firm up.

*To serve*
Remove the pudding from the fridge and remove the weights and saucer. Fold back the cling film.

Place the serving dish over the basin and turn upside down to turn out the pudding. Gently lift off the basin and remove the cling film.

With a pastry brush, gently paint over any uneven colouring of the bread with the leftover juice.

Serve with pouring cream, if liked.

# SYLLABUB
## 1690

A syllabub is a sweet and creamy dessert that has been popular for centuries and, somewhat surprisingly, hasn't really changed over the years. Early versions resembled ice-cream floats in that a rich, sweetened and delicately flavoured cream sat above a refreshing alcoholic drink below. It was served in a special glass adorned with a spout, enabling guests to sip the drink from below while delicately spooning off the indulgent topping. Syllabubs originally had to be made and served almost immediately, before the frothy topping evaporated. It was later discovered that reducing the quantity of wine and spirits a little allowed the cream to hold its shape once whipped, and keep fresh for several days. Syllabubs of this style were known as 'everlasting syllabubs'.

A syllabub is a perfect make-ahead dessert, because the flavours only improve with time. Served with some crisp Naples or Pearl Biscuits (see pages 101 and 104), it is an elegant finish to a meal.

SERVES 6–8

225ml sweet dessert white wine
60ml Madeira wine
pared peel and juice of 2 lemons
sprig of fresh rosemary

112g caster sugar
½ nutmeg
600ml double cream

Day 1
Pour the dessert wine and Madeira into a container with a lid and add the lemon peel and juice.

Gently bruise the rosemary by rolling it with a rolling pin, and add it to the mixture, then stir in the sugar until dissolved. Cover the container and leave to marinate at room temperature overnight.

*Day 2*

Strain the liquid into a large bowl and add a good grating of nutmeg.

Pour in the cream and beat with a wire whisk until it just holds its shape, being careful not to overbeat or it will curdle.

Keep in a cool place until required. Spoon into glasses to serve and decorate with some pared zest and a sprig of rosemary. This syllabub tastes delicious served with Naples or Pearl Biscuits (see pages 101 and 104).

## VARIATIONS

The basic recipe can be varied simply by changing the alcohol. Any white wine can be used: the most popular used to be the Riesling wines from Germany. White wine is most common, although I have also found recipes that use reds, even as strong as claret. One country version I discovered used equal parts ale and cider.

Other fortified wines that could be substituted include brandy, sweet sherry, Marsala or ginger wine.

Seville oranges or limes can be substituted for the lemons, and ground mace makes an unusual replacement for the nutmeg.

# TRIFLE
*1694*

I often think Trifle is a bit hard-done-by in the naming stakes.
Alongside its close companion, Fool, it has definitely drawn the
short straw, as a trifle means something of little consequence.
Certainly some trifles of my childhood qualify for this label. I've
seen more than my fair share of hundreds and thousands bleed their
colours into a bright yellow custard skin over a tin of fruit cocktail
and a lake of sherry with sponge fingers floating in it. This is sad,
because this is a mere shadow of what a trifle should be.

Properly made, a trifle is so much more than the sum of its parts.
The etymology of the word trifle ultimately comes from the old
French 'truffe', meaning deception, and I think that this is a much
more accurate description of what lies at the heart of a trifle.
Seemingly ordinary ingredients are combined to make a complex,
delicate, astonishing dessert that deserves a fabulous return to
our tables.

Trifle is an excellent way to use up biscuits and cake that are past
their first flush of youth. Do not try this recipe with freshly baked
sponge cake, because it doesn't end well. When I was young, I
decided I was going to make the best trifle ever, creating each
element from scratch. I was having no truck with dry sponge fingers
so, with the arrogance of youth, I decided to bake some deliciously
light and delicate sponge to go into the base of the trifle bowl. Alas,
when I started to drizzle the alcohol over them, my delicate sponges
turned into sherry sponge soup cocktail. This recipe was developed
to use dry biscuits and cake for a very good reason: they absorb the
sprinkled alcohol well and will also hold their shape.

Each layer of this trifle has its own flavour and texture. The syllabub
on the top is firm and creamy and flavoured with lemon and
rosemary, while the silky-smooth custard is delicately perfumed
with mead, contrasting with the sharpness of the raspberry jam and

crunch of the almonds. Finally, crumbly and moist biscuits lie in the bottom of the bowl.

The recipe for a trifle, even one as elegant as this, is more of a guideline than a strict list of instructions that must be adhered to without fail. If you use all of the syllabub and custard, they will make a trifle to serve 6–8 people generously, but you could just as easily use a proportion of them as they both keep well. You can also scale the quantities up or down to suit your own requirements.

Both the syllabub and the custard can be made ahead of time, so the trifle can be assembled when required. You don't have to use mead in the custard: any fortified wine such as Madeira, Marsala or ginger will do, but delicious, made-from-scratch, rich egg custard is also a joy in itself, with no additional flavours needed. Try to find a straight-sided glass bowl to serve your trifle, as the different layers of ingredients make much of its visual appeal.

SERVES 6–8

*1 x quantity of Syllabub (see page 210)*

*For the custard*
*4 egg yolks*
*2 tbsp cornflour*
*50g sugar*
*400ml double cream*
*3 tbsp mead*

*To finish*
*sponge fingers and ratafias*
*2 tbsp sweet or cream sherry, or to taste*
*1 tbsp brandy, or to taste*
*seedless raspberry jam*
*flaked almonds, for sprinkling*
*assorted nuts, dried fruit and candied peel, to decorate*

TWO DAYS BEFORE:
Mix the syllabub flavourings and allow to steep overnight.

DAY BEFORE:
Make the syllabub and the custard.

*To make the custard*
Put the yolks and cornflour into a bowl and mix together.

Put the sugar and cream into a pan and heat gently until the sugar has dissolved. Increase the heat until bubbles appear around the edge of the pan. You do not want the cream to boil.

Remove the pan from the heat and pour a little of the cream on to the egg mixture while whisking. When the cream has been thoroughly mixed into the eggs, add a little more and whisk again. Continue until all the hot cream has been whisked into the eggs. Pour the mixture back into the pan and return it to the gentle heat.

Keep whisking while the mixture heats until it thickens. Again, do not let it boil otherwise your eggs will curdle and your cream will split. (If this happens, you can fix it by quickly pouring it into a blender, or a food processor, or even using an immersion blender, and mix it vigorously until it comes together.) Add the mead and stir thoroughly.

Pour the custard into a heatproof container and lay cling film on the surface to prevent a skin from forming. Cover and chill when cooled until required.

*To assemble the trifle*
Break the sponge fingers in half and lay them in the bottom of your trifle bowl. Sprinkle the ratafias over the fingers.

Mix together the sherry and brandy and sprinkle over the biscuits. Add more if liked, but try to stop short of the biscuits breaking down into mush.

Drop teaspoons of raspberry jam over the biscuits—warm the jam if it's a little stiff—and scatter with flaked almonds.

Pour the custard over the top. Spoon the syllabub on top of the custard and strew with the nuts and fruit. Chill before serving.

# 6

# SMALL CAKES

Easier and quicker to whip up than large cakes, small cakes and buns are fun for all. Perhaps it's their size that contributes to this air of frivolity—or maybe it's a more historical significance. There's a certain ceremony attached to the slicing of a large cake, acknowledging the time, effort and expensive ingredients involved in its creation, but a small, individual cake or bun is much more light-hearted. In the Regency era, routs were elegant parties and gatherings typically attended by the characters in the novels of Jane Austen. Cookbooks of this time are littered with recipes for rout cakes and cupcakes, adding to their association with a party atmosphere and so it's not difficult to see how the term 'bun fight' was coined to describe a fun get-together.

# KING & QUEEN CAKES

These are probably the oldest types of small cake baked in Britain. A King Cake is rather like a cross between a scone and a Garibaldi biscuit: relatively large with a firm consistency, ostentatiously rich with currants and sack (a fortified wine similar to modern sweet/ cream sherry), and delicately spiced with mace. In contrast, Queen Cakes are a much more delicate affair, more closely resembling small sponge cakes familiar to us today, also with flavourings of mace and currants. I like to think they were developed at the same time, to be served side by side: the large sturdy King Cakes alongside the smaller, delicate Queen Cakes, but I suspect that it is unlikely.

The earliest King Cake recipe I found dates from the middle of the 17th century. It was most likely created to celebrate the restoration of the monarchy and Charles II's return from exile in 1660. Its popularity was short-lived, possibly because the rich ingredients became too expensive, or because the lighter Queen Cakes held more appeal. Queen Cakes appear a little later and for some reason, became so popular they remained a favourite for over 300 years. During the 18th century it became fashionable to bake them in a variety of intricately shaped tins, which no doubt added to their charm. Sadly, over time, the flavourings faded until, by the late 19th century, many recipes employed just a hint of lemon or almond to complement the currants.

The recipes I have chosen, with their warm flavour of mace, hark back to the cakes' first flush of popularity. At the height of their fame Queen Cakes were baked in heart-shaped tins, but any small, decorative shape will do. I've found that baking King Cakes in Yorkshire pudding tins works best, keeping the cakes well-shaped in their shallow dimples. The recipe will make 12 cakes, but I don't have three Yorkshire pudding tins myself—who does? However, baking in batches with this mixture is fine because it doesn't mind hanging around. I have found no appreciable difference in texture between the first batch and the last.

# KING CAKES
*1685*

**MAKES 12 SMALL CAKES**

| | |
|---|---|
| *450g currants* | *1 egg* |
| *300g plain flour* | *1 egg yolk* |
| *2 tsp ground mace* | *100ml cream sherry* |
| *150g caster sugar* | *140ml clotted cream* |
| *150g butter, plus extra* | |
| *for greasing* | *3 x 4-hole Yorkshire pudding tins* |

Grease the Yorkshire pudding tins.

Put the currants into a heatproof bowl and put the bowl in a cold oven. Turn the oven to 110°C/90°C fan/gas ¼ and leave the currants to warm through for 15 minutes.

Meanwhile put the flour, mace, sugar and butter into the bowl of a food processor and blitz until the mixture resembles breadcrumbs. Tip into a large bowl and set aside.

Lightly whisk the egg, yolk, sherry and cream together until smooth. Set aside.

Take the warmed currants from the oven and tip them into the dry mixture. Toss to mix.

Increase the oven temperature to 170°C/150°C fan/gas 3.

Make a well in the middle of the dry mixture and pour in the liquids. Gently fold together until thoroughly mixed. Divide the dough into 100g pieces. Lightly grease your hands with butter and roll the dough into balls. Put a ball of dough into one of the Yorkshire pudding tin holes and press to flatten. The dough will

spread out to fill the hole during baking. This prevents the edges from getting too thin and running the risk of burning. Repeat with the remaining balls of dough.

Bake for 20–25 minutes until the cakes are golden and browning slightly at the edges. Transfer to a wire rack to cool. I've found the best way to do this is to lay the rack over the cakes and upturn the tins. The cakes come out cleanly and then quite happily cool upside down.

The original recipe claimed that these cakes would last three months, but they taste so good, I honestly don't think they'll last a week.

# QUEEN CAKES
*1694*

These cakes intentionally have no baking powder in them: their diameter is small enough for the eggs to provide sufficient rise without any need for additional raising agents. If you try these little cakes and, on reflection, would prefer to use either self-raising flour or to add a teaspoon of baking powder then, by all means, do so.

MAKES 12–18 SMALL CAKES

*170g butter*
*170g caster sugar*
*3 eggs*
*2 tsp ground mace*
*170g plain flour*
*100g currants*
*milk, as required*

*1 or 2 x 12-hole cupcake or bun tins*
*paper cases (fairy cake cases are ideal)*

Preheat the oven to 180°C/160°C fan/gas 4. If your butter is chilled, cut it into cubes and drop into hand-hot water for 10 minutes to soften.

Drain the butter and whisk until light and fluffy. Add the sugar and continue to whisk on high speed for 5 minutes.

Add the eggs, one at a time. Make sure each one is thoroughly mixed in before adding the next.

Sift the mace with the flour and whisk it into the mixture, a spoonful at a time.

Fold in the currants. Add a little milk if the mixture seems stiff. The batter should be of a dropping consistency (it should fall off a spoon easily).

Line your cupcake or bun tin with paper cases. For preference, use small fairy cake cases, but if you only have large muffin paper cases, then by all means use those, just remember to lengthen the cooking time a little.

Spoon the batter into the cases, filling them no more than two-thirds full.

Bake for 15 minutes until risen and golden. Turn the tin around after 10 minutes to ensure even browning. Transfer to a wire rack to cool.

# HAZELNUT RASPBERRY SLICES

*1797*

These tempting little cakes come from *The Diary of a Farmer's Wife, 1796–1797*, written by Anne Hughes at the close of the 18th century. The simple sponge is brightened up with a dusting of chopped and toasted hazelnuts and, when cooled, is filled with a mixture of raspberries and cream cheese and cut into individual cakes. Anne credits her cousin Floe with the introduction of these little delicacies, which were baked for the summer wedding of Anne's maid, Sarah.

Anne originally used a mixture of raspberry jam and butter to fill the cakes, but I have changed this for a lighter and fresher filling.

**MAKES 12–15 SANDWICHED FINGER CAKES**

*150g butter, softened*
*150g caster sugar*
*3 eggs*
*150g self-raising flour*
*milk, as required*
*100g chopped roasted hazelnuts*
*200g cream cheese*
*200ml double cream*
*2–3 tbsp icing sugar, to taste*

*250g fresh raspberries*

*icing sugar, for sprinkling*

*1 x large, shallow tray-bake tin*
*or Swiss roll tin*
*1 x piping bag fitted with a plain*
*1.5cm nozzle*

Preheat the oven to 170°C/150°C fan/gas 3. Grease and line a large, shallow tray-bake tin. A swiss roll tin is ideal, if you have one.

Cream the butter and caster sugar together until light and fluffy. Whisk in the eggs, one by one, making sure each one is thoroughly combined before adding the next.

Gradually sift in the flour until thoroughly combined. The mixture should have a dropping consistency (it should drop off a spoon easily). If it seems too heavy, mix in a little milk to loosen.

Spread the mixture evenly into the prepared tin. Sprinkle the surface with the chopped, roasted hazelnuts and bake for 30–40 minutes until risen and golden brown.

Transfer to a wire rack to cool.

*To make the filling*
Put the cream cheese and cream into a bowl and whisk together until fully combined. Add icing sugar to taste—2–3 tablespoons should be sufficient.

Add the raspberries and mix gently to combine. The raspberries will break down a little and the cream will turn a delicate pink.

*To assemble*
Cut the cooled cake in half down the middle and place one half on top of the other. Cut the stacked cakes into individual slices.

Fill the piping bag with the filling mixture.

For each cake, lift off the top layer, pipe the filling on to the bottom layer, then replace the top layer and set aside. Working this way, each cake is made up of 2 layers the exact same size without the need to mix and match.

Sprinkle the tops with a little icing sugar to serve.

# VERY GOOD SMALL RICH CAKES

*Eliza Acton, 1845*

With the popularity of cupcakes today, with their mountains of buttercream and sparkly decorations, to my mind, the cake itself seems a bit neglected. Without the cake, of course, there'd be no cupcake, but it still seems to play second fiddle to the bling of decoration in terms of visual appeal. I sometimes think that there could be any old cake under all the ornamentation.

How lovely, then, to have a recipe where the cake itself is the focus of attention, and deservedly so. Eliza Acton's 'Very Good Small Rich Cakes' is just such a recipe. It's small, making just a dozen cakes, and the title tells you everything you need to know. Delicately flavoured with lemon, cinnamon or mace, Ms Acton suggests no further embellishment. At the risk of gilding the lily, my suggestion for a special flourish would be some vanilla Depression-era Buttercream (see page 331).

**MAKES 12 SMALL CAKES**

*4 eggs*
*225g sugar*
*113g clarified butter (see page 327), melted and cooled*
*113g plain flour*
*zest of 1 lemon or ¾ tsp ground mace or 1 tsp ground cinnamon*

*1 x quantity of Depression-era Buttercream (see page 331)*

*1 x 12-hole cupcake or bun tin*
*paper cases*
*1 x piping bag fitted with a plain 1.5cm or star nozzle*

Preheat the oven to 170°C/150°C fan/gas 3. Line the cupcake or bun tin with paper cases.

In a bowl, whisk together the eggs and sugar until light and frothy.

Still whisking, slowly add the cooled, clarified butter.

Sift in the flour, add the flavouring and mix thoroughly for 10 minutes then spoon the batter into the cases, filling them no more than two-thirds full.

Bake for 12–15 minutes until risen and golden. Transfer to a wire rack to cool.

Fill the piping bag with the buttercream and pipe a generous swirl of buttercream on to the top of each cake.

# BANBURY CAKES
*1848*

Banbury Cakes are just one of a whole range of regional pastries
formed with dried fruit and pastry, and probably the richest in
terms of ingredients. Coventry Godcakes are triangular puffs of
pastry with a rich dried fruit filling, popular at New Year and Easter
as gifts from godparents to their godchildren. Eccles Cakes are
both similar and simpler fare, circular in shape and usually made
with flaky pastry instead of the richer puff. The filling is also less
rich, comprising just currants, peel, sugar and spice. Chorley Cake
is the most humble of pastries, made from just currants inside
unsweetened shortcrust pastry. An even poorer relation is the Sad
Cake sometimes found in East Lancashire. Currants are rolled in
scraps of pastry, probably originally the trimmings from the weekly
bake. 'Sad' in the local dialect refers to heaviness or toughness,
which is understandable, given the scraps of re-rolled pastry from
which it is made.

Banbury Cakes, from the Oxfordshire town, have been notable
since their first mention back in the late 1500s.[22] Over the years,
they have undergone many changes in both size and composition.
The earliest recipes are for large, fruited yeast cakes wrapped in
plain dough. This method was not unusual: the original Simnel
cakes were also made this way and the tradition continues to this
day in the Scottish New Year cake known as Black Bun.

The original Banbury Cake bakehouse was located in town at
12 Parsons Street. Back in the 17th century it was run by the White
family, or, to be more precise, by Mrs Betty White, watched from
the side lines by her idle husband, Jarvis. Betty's Banbury Cakes had
dispensed with the troublesome yeast dough and instead presented
a mixture similar to mince pies encased in a rich pastry. The shape
was described as like a diamond, of the size of a piece of glass from
a leaded window. The filling was rich with fruit, similar to that of
mince pies but, in this case, popular all the year round.

MAKES 16 SMALL CAKES

*For the filling*
30g candied orange and lemon    *zest and juice of ½ lemon*
    peel, finely chopped
60g dark muscovado sugar    *For the pastry*
125g currants    *500g block ready-made all-butter*
1 tsp ground allspice    *puff pastry, chilled*
1 tsp ground cinnamon    *flour, for dusting*
50g plain flour    *a little milk and caster sugar, for*
30g butter, melted and cooled    *glazing*

Preheat the oven to 200°C/180°C fan/gas 6. Line a baking sheet with baking parchment.

In a bowl, mix together the candied peel, sugar, currants and spices. Sift in the flour and add the cooled melted butter and lemon zest and juice. Stir to combine.

Lightly dust a work surface with flour and cut the block of puff pastry into quarters. Put three of the quarters back in the fridge.

Working with the remaining piece of pastry, roll it out into a very thin 25cm square. Cut this square into 4 smaller ones with sides of approximately 12cm. Brush the edges of all 4 pastry squares with water and put a heaped tablespoon of filling in the middle of each one. Fold in the top and bottom sides of each one to cover the filling. Dampen the remaining 2 side pieces then fold them in at an angle to form a diamond shape and press the edges to seal. Turn the pastry over and place on the lined baking sheet. Repeat this process with the remaining quarters of pastry and filling.

Brush any excess flour from the finished pastries and glaze them with milk. Sprinkle with caster sugar and bake for 15 minutes. Turn the baking tray around after 10 minutes to ensure even baking. Transfer to a wire rack to cool.

# CORNFLOUR CAKES
*1909*

These enchanting little cakes come from the fabulous recipe collection *The Cookery Book of Lady Clark of Tillypronie*. For more than 50 years, spanning almost the entire reign of Queen Victoria, Lady Clark collected recipes and jotted down notes on food, purely for her own interest. On her death in 1897, her collection comprised 16 manuscript books and numerous loose notes.

Sir John Clark described his late wife as:

*'...having been, not the mere "housewife" on culinary things intent, but an exceptionally widely-read woman, gifted with fine literary taste and judgement, a singularly retentive and accurate memory and great conversational powers.'*

When Lady Clark died, Sir John asked Catherine Freere to help select and publish recipes from his wife's collection. It would take her seven years to sort through the almost 3,000 pages of notes. One of her most impressive achievements was to eliminate, to the best of her ability, any recipe that had been previously published. The recipes that remain, therefore, are largely unknown in print and provide a fabulous resource for the food enthusiast. Another great feature of this collection is the sheer number of variations on favourite recipes. For instance, most people have a favourite form of apple cake (mine is on page 22), but if you're like me, there are also times when you just fancy something a little bit different. Lady Clark's collection boasts more than 20 versions of apple cake to explore. And this is just one recipe example.

Cornflour has a wonderful effect on the texture of biscuits: it provides that crumbly melt-in-the-mouth quality of biscuits such as Melting Moments and Viennese Whirls. What is fantastic about this recipe, quite apart from it being gluten-free, is that the cornflour has the same effect on the texture of the cakes. The sensation is quite unlike any other cake I've tasted; the sponge just seems to dissolve on your tongue. However delicious this is, these little cakes do need some sharp, contrasting flavour if they are to avoid becoming cloying. A citrus curd is ideal, so I made these cakes 'soft centred' with some fresh lemon curd hidden inside. Topped with a zesty fondant and a sliver of candied lemon peel, these little cakes are a unique afternoon treat.

MAKES 24 SMALL CAKES

*For the cake*
*80g butter, softened*
*56g caster sugar*
*1 egg*
*zest of 1 lemon*
*112g cornflour*
*pinch of salt*
*½ tsp baking powder*

*juice of 3–4 lemons (125ml)*
*zest of 1 lemon*

*For the icing*
*1 egg white*
*1 tsp lemon juice*
*150–200g icing sugar*
*a little chopped candied lemon peel*

*For the lemon curd*
*75g clarified butter (see page 327)*
  *or regular butter*
*3 eggs, lightly beaten*
*75g caster sugar*

*1 x 12-hole cupcake or bun tin*
*paper cases*
*1 x piping bag fitted with a plain*
  *1.5cm nozzle (optional)*

Preheat the oven to 200°C/180°C fan/gas 6. Line the cupcake or bun tin with paper cases.

To make the cakes, cream the butter then add the caster sugar and beat until light and fluffy. Add the egg and lemon zest and beat until well combined. Sift the cornflour, salt and baking powder together and add to the creamed butter mix, a spoonful at a time, until thoroughly combined.

Pipe the mixture into the cases, using the piping bag, filling each one no more than two-thirds full. The piping bag makes it easier to manipulate the extremely soft mixture and gives a smoother finish to the baked cakes, but if you don't have one, spoon 2 teaspoonfuls or a small ice-cream scoopful of mixture into each case instead.

Bake for 8–10 minutes until risen and golden. Transfer the cakes to a wire rack to cool.

Meanwhile, to make the lemon curd, put the butter or clarified butter into a pan. Add the remaining ingredients and stir over a low heat until thickened. Set aside to cool.

To make the icing, whisk together the egg white, lemon juice and 100g of the icing sugar. Gradually add the remaining icing sugar until you have the right consistency. The icing should be soft enough to flow, but not so soft as to run off the edges of the cakes. To test for the consistency, drizzle a little back into the bowl: if it flows easily, and the ribbon of icing stays visible on the surface for a second or so, this is perfect.

To assemble the cakes, first trim any that have risen unevenly so that they all have neat, slightly rounded tops. With a sharp, pointed knife, cut a cone of cake out of the middle of each cake and fill the holes with lemon curd. Slice off the top of the removed cones and replace the little circles of sponge back on top of the lemon curd fillings. Spread a little icing over the tops and set pieces of candied lemon peel on top of each cake.

# SHELL BREAD
*1617*

When I read old recipe books and manuscripts, the ingenuity of home bakers always amazes me. In Devon, the sycamore leaves that originally provided a simple and cheap way to protect the bottoms of Revel Buns from the ash and dust of the brick-oven floor, are now an integral part of this regional bake. In Anglesey, the Welsh shortbread Berffro Cakes (Aberffraw Cakes) were baked in the scallop shells that washed up on the shore.

The little cakes in this recipe were originally baked in buttered mussel shells, and the browned-and-cooked cake mixture would indeed closely resemble the colour of cooked mussels. To recreate the shell imagery without resorting to baking in shells, you can bake these small cakes in madeleine tins. If you don't have two madeleine tins to make the full batch, I suggest making just a half batch (using 1 egg and 1 extra yolk), because the remaining half of the cake batter will not retain its frothy lightness waiting for the first one to cook. Additionally, I've found my little cakes are sometimes, how shall I put this, 'reluctant' to come out of madeleine tins, which then require a thorough cleaning afterwards. This would add further delay to getting the second batch of cakes into the oven.

I chose this recipe because I find the lemon and aniseed flavouring refreshingly light and delicate, and with the rosewater icing it makes an unusual teatime treat.

MAKES 24 SMALL CAKES

*3 egg yolks*
*1 egg*
*112g caster sugar*
*60ml double cream*
*1 tsp ground aniseed*
*zest of 1 lemon*
*4 tbsp plain flour*

*For the icing*
*1 tsp rosewater*
*1 egg white*
*icing sugar, to mix*

*2 x 12-hole madeleine tins*

Preheat the oven to 180°C/160°C fan/gas 4. Grease the madeleine tins well.

In a bowl, whisk together the yolks, egg and sugar until light and frothy then whisk in the cream, aniseed and lemon zest. Still whisking, sprinkle in the flour, mixing until combined.

Pour the batter into the well-greased madeleine tins, filling them no more than three-quarters full.

Bake for 11–12 minutes, turning the tins around 180 degrees after 8 minutes, until the cakes are risen and golden brown.

Let the cakes rest in the tin for 2 minutes then ease around the edges with a wooden cocktail stick and transfer them to a wire rack to cool.

To make the icing, mix the rosewater and egg white together. Gradually sprinkle in icing sugar, stirring until the mixture comes together in a smooth coating consistency.

Using a pastry brush, paint the icing on to one side of the cakes and set on a wire rack to dry.

# CURRANT CAKES
*1650s*

These cakes perfectly illustrate the wariness that one should employ
when approaching old recipes: use of the word 'cake' doesn't always
refer to something we would recognise today as being a cake.
Despite technically being miniature pies, or possibly pastries, I
have included them in this chapter because they are decadently
rich, small, dainty and sweet, something I've longed to be my
whole life. This particular recipe comes from the manuscript book
of Lady Ann Fanshawe, wife of the poet and diplomat Sir Robert
Fanshawe. As staunch royalists, when civil war broke out shortly
after they married, they allied themselves with the future Charles
II and travelled with him in exile, both at home and abroad. Lady
Anne's memoirs recount how she remained at her husband's side
as they travelled through the south-west of England. After losing
most of their possessions at the hands of an unscrupulous captain
while at sea off the coast of Penzance, they were forced to use what
little they had left to forestall a mutiny. Lady Anne was put ashore
in the Scilly Isles, and it is at this point we learn that she was seven
months pregnant. The thought of making such a long and arduous
journey by land and sea today is exhausting. It is astounding that
the heavily pregnant Lady Anne managed it 350 years ago.

With Charles restored to the throne, the Fanshawe's fortunes
increased and together they travelled to Portugal and Spain in the
1660s, where Lady Anne added to her already impressive recipe
book with recipes for *escaveche* of fish, *adobado* pork, Spanish *olla*
and what must be one of the earliest recipes for the Portuguese
sponge cake *pao de lo*.

Currant Cakes could well be the ancestors of the more modern, but
less refined Banbury and Eccles cakes. In resurrecting this elegant
morsel, its spiced filling of candied peel and dried fruit all wrapped
in saffron pastry, we can literally taste the richness of the turbulent
times of the English Civil War.

MAKES 10 BITE-SIZED CAKES OR 20 PASTY-SIZED CAKES

*For the pastry*
*225ml double cream*
*pinch of saffron strands*
*225g plain flour*
*30g caster sugar*
*1 egg yolk*
*flour, for dusting*
*a little milk and caster sugar,*
*   for glazing*

*For the filling*
*113g currants, rinsed and dried*
*30g candied lemon peel, finely*
*   chopped*
*30g candied citron peel, finely*
*   chopped*
*¼ tsp ground nutmeg*
*¼ tsp allspice*
*Apple Jelly, to mix (see page 328)*

*1 x round pastry cutter, any size*

To make the pastry, gently heat the cream in a pan over a low heat until almost boiling. Remove from the heat, add the saffron and let it steep until the cream is cool.

When the cream has cooled, blitz the flour, sugar and yolk together in a food processor until well combined. Gradually add the saffron cream until the mixture comes together into a paste. Tip the mixture out and knead until smooth then wrap in cling film and chill in the fridge for 30 minutes.

Preheat the oven to 200°C/180°C fan/gas 6. Line a baking sheet with baking parchment.

To make the filling, in a bowl, mix together the currants, candied lemon and citron peels and the spices. Stir in enough apple jelly to bind the mixture together.

Roll out the pastry thinly on a lightly floured surface, to about 3–4mm, and cut out circles using a plain round pastry cutter. (The size is entirely up to you; you can make them bite-sized or pasty-sized.) Brush the edges of the circles with water.

Spoon some filling on the middle of a pastry circle and place another circle of pastry over the top. Press the edges together firmly then crimp them either by hand or with the tines of a fork. Prick holes in the top to let the steam out and place the finished cakes on to the prepared baking sheet. Repeat with the rest of the pastry circles then brush them with milk and lightly sprinkle with caster sugar.

Bake until the pastry is cooked and lightly browned. This will obviously depend on the size you have made them, but as a suggestion, small cakes will take 12–15 minutes, and larger ones 20–25 minutes.

Transfer to a wire rack to cool.

# LITTLE FRUIT CAKES
*20th century*

I love these little cakes for a number of reasons. Firstly, they're small and, to me, anything small is automatically fun. Then they are made with fresh fruit, which we don't see enough of in cakes. They are almost infinitely variable, because you can use whatever fruit you have to hand. Lastly, they eat like little cakes, but are put together like little pies. The outside is a cross between a biscuit, a pastry and a shortcake and can be moulded into whatever size and shape you like. I prefer to keep these small and dainty, and so I bake them in mini-muffin tins. A silicone mini-muffin tray will keep the cakes from getting overly crisp and make them easy to turn out.

**MAKES 24 SMALL CAKES**

*225g plain flour*
*2 tsp baking powder*
*pinch of salt*
*112g butter, plus extra for greasing*
*112g caster sugar*
*1 egg*
*a little milk, to mix*
*250ml fruit purée*

*For the glaze*
*a little milk, for brushing*
*caster sugar, for sprinkling*

*1 x 24-hole mini-muffin tin*

Preheat the oven to 200°C/180°C fan/gas 6. Grease the cups of the mini-muffin tin.

Put the flour, baking powder, salt, butter and sugar into the bowl of a food processor and blitz until the mixture resembles breadcrumbs.

Whisk the egg and slowly add to the mixture with the motor running, until the mix comes together into a soft dough. Add a little milk if the mixture seems a little dry.

Break off pieces of dough the size of a walnut and press them into the prepared mini-muffin cups. Add 1 teaspoon of fruit purée filling into each pastry cup then cover with flattened pieces of dough, pressing the edges of the dough together lightly. Brush with milk and sprinkle with caster sugar.

Bake for 12–15 minutes until slightly puffed and golden. Transfer to a wire rack to cool.

## VARIATIONS

Any flavour of fruit purée can be used, but it should be drained of excess juice before use.

# MADEIRA BUNS
## 1808

Maria Eliza Rundell was born in 1745 in Ludlow, Shropshire, a town where I spent a lot of my childhood, and not far from where I currently live. Her recipe for these buns caught my eye because not only do the ingredients and their quantities look very similar to our cake recipes today but also, rather surprisingly, unlike the more well-known Madeira Cake, it contains a healthy slug of alcohol.

Mrs Rundell's recipes and household hints were initially intended only for her daughters, but a close family friend convinced her of the value of a book aimed at the home, rather than large country houses or lowly taverns, and so *A New System of Domestic Cookery* came into print and was to remain so for over 80 years.

I found the original recipe a little on the heavy side, so I have tweaked it to take full advantage of modern raising agents. Although the alcohol in the Madeira evaporates during baking, the aroma remains and, together with the fragrant spices, makes the delicate flavour of these little cakes quite extraordinary. It's not difficult to imagine these buns gracing the sideboards of the routs and assemblies of Georgian society. They might look plain, but they need no additional decoration.

These buns make an ideal snack for morning coffee, afternoon tea, packed lunches or picnics.

**MAKES 24 BUNS**

| | |
|---|---|
| *2 eggs* | *1 tsp ground ginger* |
| *225g butter, softened* | *1 tsp caraway seeds* |
| *400g plain flour* | *150–200ml Madeira wine* |
| *2 tsp baking powder* | |
| *175g caster sugar* | *2 x 12-hole cupcake or bun tins* |
| *½ nutmeg, grated* | *paper cases* |

Preheat the oven to 170°C/150°C fan/gas 3. Line the cupcake or bun tins with paper cases.

Whisk the eggs thoroughly. In a separate bowl, cream the butter for 5 minutes until pale and fluffy. Add the beaten eggs and mix to combine. Add all the dry ingredients and mix thoroughly. Beat for a further 10 minutes until pale and light.

Stir in enough Madeira until a dropping consistency is reached— i.e. until the mixture drops freely from a spoon. Spoon the mixture into the cases, filling them no more than two-thirds full.

Bake for 15–20 minutes until golden brown, well risen and springy to the touch. Transfer to a wire rack to cool.

# PORTUGAL CAKES
*1796*

In 1661, shortly after King Charles II returned from exile, he married the Portuguese princess Catherine of Braganza. Catherine is credited with introducing both the fork and the custom of tea-drinking to the UK. Suddenly, everything Portuguese became the height of fashion, and the cookery books of the time, and for decades afterwards, contained recipes for various Portuguese dishes, including these little cakes.

These are ideal petit-four-sized cakes, packed with fruits and nuts and with a generous dash of alcohol. I like the unusual flavour and colour the candied citron brings, but you can use any mixture of candied peel you prefer. Serve with coffee for something a bit different to finish off a meal.

**MAKES 24 SMALL CAKES**

*150g plain flour*
*95g caster sugar, plus extra for glazing*
*95g butter*
*1 tsp ground cinnamon*
*½ tsp ground mace*
*1 tsp ground nutmeg*
*80g candied citron peel, thinly shredded*
*1 tsp caraway seeds*

*112g currants*
*16g slivered almonds*
*1 egg*
*1 egg yolk*
*2 tbsp brandy*
*1–2 tbsp milk, to mix, plus extra for glazing*

*1 x 24-hole mini-muffin tin*
*paper cases*

Preheat the oven to 170°C/150°C fan/gas 3. Line the mini-muffin tin with the paper cases.

Put the flour, sugar, butter and spices into the bowl of a food processor and blitz until the mixture resembles breadcrumbs. Tip the mixture into another bowl and stir in the citron peel, caraway seeds, currants and almonds.

Whisk the egg and yolk with the brandy and stir into the mix. If the mixture looks a little dry, add 1–2 tablespoons of milk. Spoon the mixture into the cases, filling them no more than two-thirds full.

Bake for 15–18 minutes until risen and golden brown.

Brush lightly with milk and sprinkle with caster sugar. Transfer to a wire rack to cool.

# SCONES
*19th century*

Properly made, scones have a unique texture and flavour, richer than bread, but not so rich as a cake. To my mind, scones are best enjoyed straight from the oven, their thin, crisp crust embracing a light and soft interior. This lightness is often lacking in scones not made at home, which can be dense and, dare one say it, claggy. A scone should not be a hockey puck, it should be a light, delicate and delicious treat, every time.

The best thing about scones is the speed with which they can be made. Once the oven is hot you can have scones mixed and baking in less than 10 minutes. There are three secrets to a light and airy scone. Firstly, keep the time between mixing in the liquid and getting the scones into the oven as short as possible. The liquid reacts with the baking powder to produce the aeration needed for feather-light scones. The longer you delay after adding the liquid, the less fluffy your scones will be. Secondly, the more the dough is handled, the heavier and stodgier your scones will be. You want to be handling the scone mix as little as possible: think of it as being red hot and touch it with your fingertips only.

Thirdly: rolling out of the dough. Don't. Again, it's delaying getting your scones into the oven and rolling and re-rolling the dough just squashes out the air the raising agent is trying to put in, leaving the finished scones tough and heavy. Simply pat the dough into a circle and cut it into 6 wedges. Separate the scones slightly, brush them with milk and into the oven they go. In 15 minutes they're done.

Possibly the best thing about scones is their versatility. While most of us think of scones as a teatime treat, they can be so much more. With a little flavouring they can be transformed into breakfast, lunch or a snack, without ever becoming soggy like sandwiches are wont to do. With a good basic recipe, and some imagination for variety, the possibilities are almost endless.

# MRS MCNAB'S SCONES

This scone recipe is attributed to Mrs McNab, a farmer's wife, who lived near Ballater, Aberdeenshire in the 19th century. Her deftness and lightness of touch with her baking was so famous that many visiting dignitaries to nearby Balmoral Castle, including the King of Prussia, used to call on her for tea just to sample her famous scones.

**MAKES 12 SCONES**

*450g plain flour, plus extra for*
 *dusting*
*60g butter*
*1 tsp salt*
*1 tsp bicarbonate of soda*
*2 tsp cream of tartar*

*1 egg*
*150ml natural yoghurt*
*150ml milk, plus extra for glazing*

Preheat the oven to 220°C/200°C fan/gas 7. Line a baking sheet with baking parchment.

Put the flour, butter, salt, bicarbonate of soda, cream of tartar and egg into the bowl of a food processor and blitz until the mixture resembles breadcrumbs. Tip the mixture into a large bowl.

Mix the yoghurt and 150ml milk together thoroughly. Gradually stir into the flour and egg mixture with a knife until the dough comes together into a ball.

Tip the dough on to a floured surface and divide into 2 even pieces. Pat and shape these into circles about 4cm thick and cut each circle into 6 wedges. Put the wedges on to the lined baking sheet, brush with milk and bake for 15 minutes until risen and golden. Turn the baking sheet around 180 degrees after 10 minutes to ensure even baking. Transfer to a wire rack to cool.

# MASTER SCONE MIX

While Mrs McNab's recipe makes a delicious scone, a dozen is a rather large batch for the average household, no matter how many scone-lovers it contains; ideal if you have company, but a little awkward for spontaneous scone-baking. My master scone recipe is a little less rich (it contains no egg) and makes a smaller batch of just 6 scone wedges; perfect for those moments when you find the bread crock empty, the bread in it blue and fuzzy, or when you are the recipient of unexpected guests. A speedy alternative breakfast or a comforting teatime treat, the possibilities are endless.

On its own, the recipe makes a delicious light, sweet scone, but it can also easily be adapted to other sweet or savoury flavours. A savoury scone makes a meal of a bowl of soup, and a sweet one can round out a packed lunch perfectly. Keep a batch of the dry mixture in the fridge for super-speedy scone-making; just heat the oven, add the milk, and bake.

MAKES 6 SCONES

*225g plain flour, plus extra for*
*  dusting*
*2 tsp baking powder*
*½ tsp salt*

*60g butter*
*30g caster sugar*
*milk, to mix and for glazing*

Preheat the oven to 220°C/200°C fan/gas 7. Line a baking sheet with baking parchment.

Put the flour, baking powder, salt, butter and sugar into the bowl of a food processor and blitz until the mixture resembles breadcrumbs. Tip the mixture into a large bowl.

Using a round-ended knife, gradually stir in enough milk until the mixture comes together into a soft dough. Tip the dough on to a floured surface and pat into a circle about 4cm thick. Cut the circle into 6 wedges.

Put the wedges on to the lined baking sheet, brush with milk and bake for 12–15 minutes until risen and golden. Transfer to a wire rack to cool.


## VARIATIONS

To ring the changes on your scone repertoire, simply follow the recipe as above and add your choice of flavourings to the bowl, just before adding the milk. Cooking time remains the same. Here are some examples to get you started.

SWEET:
*Orange and Sultana*
Add 40g sultanas and 15g chopped candied orange peel.

*Lemon and Blueberry*
Add 40g fresh blueberries and 15g chopped candied lemon peel.

*Date and Walnut*
Use half wholemeal, half white flour (both plain), and add 40g chopped dates and 15g walnut pieces.

*Date and Lemon*
Use half wholemeal, half white flour (both plain), and add 40g chopped dates and 15g chopped candied lemon peel.

*Orange and Cranberry*
Add 40g fresh cranberries and 15g chopped candied orange peel.

*Ginger and Lemon*
Add 40g chopped candied ginger and 15g chopped candied lemon peel.

*Apple and Cinnamon*
Add 50g chopped fresh apple and 1 teaspoon ground cinnamon.

SAVOURY:
Omit the sugar, then add one of the following flavour combinations for a great snack, lunch or soup accompaniment.

*Cheese and Herb*
Add 40g cubed strong Cheddar and 1 tablespoon chopped fresh rosemary.

*Breakfast Scones*
Add 50g chopped cooked sausage and 25g cubed vintage Red Leicester.

*Cheese and Pesto*
Add 40g cubed strong Cheddar and 4 tablespoons basil pesto.

*Chorizo and Pesto*
Add 40g cubed or sliced cooked chorizo and 4 tablespoons sun-dried tomato pesto.

*Cheese and Spring Onion*
Add 40g cubed strong Cheddar and 2 chopped spring onions.

*Cheese and Apple*
Add 50g chopped sharp apple and 30g cubed strong Cheddar.

*Apple, Bacon and Cheese*
Add 50g chopped sharp apple, 30g cubed, strong Cheddar and 20g cooked bacon.

# 7

# YEAST

Historically, due to the high heat needed to bake bread and the relatively low prevalence of expensive ovens, in many communities bread was baked in a communal oven by the local baker. Ingenious use of bread dough enriched and sweetened with additional ingredients, inspired a delicious tradition and range of bread-cakes. Home baking with yeast was restricted to cooking on a griddle or bakestone over a fire, but years of skill and ingenuity with this method led to the creation of some truly memorable traditional bakes from around the country, which, for many, are now only seen on the supermarket shelves.

# APPLE BREAD

*1820s*

This recipe was copied into the manuscript book of a Norfolk household from the *Ipswich Journal* in the early 19th century. Its simplicity appealed to me. It has just three ingredients—flour, yeast and apples—which together create an open-textured bread with a chew similar to that of sourdough, but with an underlying sweetness which, when toasted, tastes almost like honey.

I later found this same recipe reprinted word for word in my 1950 copy of *Farmhouse Fare*, which was created from recipes sent in to and collected by *Farmers Weekly* magazine. This means that at least one other person must have copied the same recipe from the *Ipswich Journal* and kept it alive in their family for 150 years, to be revived in 1950. So perhaps we could call this its 200-year re-revival!

Try this bread toasted, unbuttered, with some strong Cheddar and a crisp apple.

**MAKES 1 LARGE LOAF, OR 2 REGULAR LOAVES**

*4 Bramley apples*
*500g strong white flour*
*1 sachet (7g) fast-action yeast*
*butter or cooking spray or oil, for greasing*

*1 x 2kg/28cm loaf tin, or 2 x 1kg/23cm loaf tins, or similar capacity*

Put the unpeeled apples in a pan and cover with water. Bring to the boil, turn down the heat and simmer for 15–20 minutes until the apples are soft and cooked. The skins might split, but as long as the water is just simmering, the apples should hold together—fast boiling water will just give you apple soup.

Lift the apples from the water (keep the water—you might need some later). Remove the skins and scrape the cooked apple flesh into a bowl. Sieve the cooked apple to make a smooth purée.

Grease your loaf tin or tins.

Put the flour and yeast into a bowl and stir to combine. Add the apple purée gradually and stir to combine into a soft dough. You should need between 250g and 300g of apple purée. If you need more liquid, use some of the water the apples were cooked in.

If you have a mixer with a dough hook, work the dough for 10 minutes on medium speed. Otherwise work it by hand, but be careful not to add too much extra flour in the kneading—you want to keep the dough nice and soft.

Put the dough in a bowl, cover and leave the mixture in a warm place to double in size—this could be anything from 3–8 hours.

When sufficiently risen, tip the dough out of the bowl and knock it back.

Shape into 1 large loaf, or 2 smaller loaves and put into the greased loaf tin or tins. Cover lightly with a clean cloth and leave to rise for a further 30–45 minutes.

Preheat the oven to 200°C/180°C fan/gas 6.

Bake for 30–40 minutes until golden brown and the base sounds hollow when tapped. If the bread appears cooked, but is not sounding hollow, remove from the tin and return to the oven for 5–10 minutes to crisp up.

Cool completely on a wire rack before slicing.

# *BATH BUNS*
*1700*

Just as Chelsea Buns were hugely popular in London, so Bath
Buns were the regional bun of choice in the West Country. Some
sources link them to Dr William Oliver, founder of Bath General
Hospital, who is alleged to have invented them for his patients.
When his buns proved so popular with his patients that they put on
weight at his spa instead of losing it, he is supposed to have created
the Bath Oliver Biscuit to replace it. Colourful as this anecdote is,
this version of events is unlikely on two counts. Firstly, Bath buns
were known many years before the arrival in the city of Dr Oliver
and, secondly, that a doctor might be genuinely surprised to find
his patients gaining weight on a diet of buns enriched with vast
quantities of sugar, butter and eggs, is extremely unlikely.

A far more likely version might be that the good doctor improved
upon an existing recipe, or even purloined it for himself. Equally
possible is the notion that Dr Oliver had no connection with the
Bath Bun at all, and has merely earned it through his associated
biscuit success.

Bath buns are very much the peacocks of the bun world: golden,
gaudy with fruits and peel, dazzling with their crowns of nibbed
sugar. I've chosen an ostentatious version of these wonderfully rich
buns, which will make them stars of any occasion against even the
most heavily primped of cakes.

MAKES 12–16 BUNS

500g strong white flour, plus extra
 for dusting
1 sachet (7g) fast-action yeast
¼ tsp salt
60g caster sugar
90g butter
1 egg
150ml boiling water
150ml whole milk

60g candied peel, finely chopped
60g crimson raisins
50g lump sugar, to decorate
juice of 2 lemons

_For the glaze_
1 egg, beaten
nibbed sugar, to decorate

Line a baking sheet with baking parchment.

Put the flour, yeast, salt, caster sugar, butter and egg into the bowl of a food processor and blitz until the mixture resembles breadcrumbs. Tip the mixture into a heatproof bowl.

Pour the boiling water into the milk and gradually add to the bowl while mixing. The moisture in the butter and the egg will affect how much additional liquid will be required, so you might not need to add all of it. Stir and bring the mixture together in a soft dough.

Knead for 10 minutes then cover and leave to rise in a warm place until doubled in size. The richness of the dough means the yeast will take longer than, for example, bread dough to rise, between 1 and 2 hours.

Tip the risen dough on to a lightly floured surface and pat down. Sprinkle over the chopped peel and raisins and knead them into the dough, then divide the dough into 50g pieces and shape into buns.

Divide each lump of sugar in half and press a small piece into the base of each bun. Spoon a little lemon juice over the sugar then place the buns on the lined baking sheet. Make sure the buns are sufficiently spaced so that they won't touch when risen.

Cover and set aside to rise in a warm place for 30 minutes.

Preheat the oven to 180°C/160°C fan/gas 4.

Brush the risen buns with the beaten egg and sprinkle with nibbed sugar. Bake for 13–15 minutes until risen and golden then transfer to a wire rack to cool.

# BOSTON CAKE

*18th century*

I love finding a recipe named after a geographical place because
it gives me a focus when hunting for background information.
Although there is a possibility that the Boston referred to is the
city in Massachusetts, given the recipe's date and location in an
old family manuscript from Hainton, Lincolnshire, the more likely
candidate is the English town. As far as I am able to ascertain, there
is no modern tradition there of a fruit-dough cake.

What I did find, however, were fruit-dough cake recipes for Boston
Cake in the US, and a sprinkling of recipes for Bostonkaka, or
Bostonkakku, in regions around the Baltic Sea, which rather raised
an eyebrow. I was keen to try to find a link between these disparate
pockets of baking and to explain how variations of a similar recipe
got to be so widespread.

Back in the 13th century, the town of Boston in the UK was an
important port and a member of the trade-based Hanseatic League,
which stretched from the North Sea to the Baltic. It's not difficult
to imagine merchants and sailors taking back descriptions, or even
samples, of food to their home ports. Some of the future passengers
of the *Mayflower* also passed through Boston—perhaps they also
took the recipe for Boston Cake with them.

The modern American/Baltic recipe is for a cake made up of
spirals of filled dough, rather like a large cake made up of Chelsea
buns, whereas the original Boston cake is a large, fruited teacake.
Although very different now, these modern recipes might well be
descended from a recipe like the one in the manuscript. A lot can
happen in 700 years.

This cake is delicious to eat either on its own or spread with butter.
Being dough-based, it can also be toasted when past its initial
freshness, and makes a wonderful addition to the afternoon tea table.

MAKES 1 REGULAR LOAF

*90g butter, plus 25g*
*320g strong white flour*
*1 sachet (7g) fast-action yeast*
*2 tsp sugar*
*1 tsp ground cinnamon*
*¼ tsp ground cloves*
*½ tsp ground mace*
*120ml double cream*
*2 tbsp sweet or cream sherry*

*1 egg*
*180g currants*
*50g raisins*
*butter or cooking spray or oil, for*
*  greasing*

*1 x 1kg/23cm loaf tin (or similar*
*  capacity), or 1 x 24cm round cake*
*  tin*

Grease the loaf or cake tin.

Put the 90g butter and the flour into the bowl of a food processor and blitz until the mixture resembles breadcrumbs. Tip the mixture into a large bowl and add the yeast, sugar and spices.

In a pan over a low heat, warm the remaining 25g butter in the cream until melted. Remove from the heat, whisk in the sherry and egg and pour into the dry ingredients.

Knead together for 10 minutes until a smooth dough is formed then knead in the dried fruit and shape into a smooth loaf.

Put the dough into the prepared tin, cover and leave to rise in a warm place for 30 minutes.

Preheat the oven to 170°C/150°C fan/gas 3.

When the dough has risen, bake for 40–45 minutes until risen and golden. Transfer to a wire rack to cool.

# BUTTER BUNS
*Traditional*

These unusual buns are a great example of how the simplest
of ingredients can create something truly delicious. They are a
speciality of Shropshire and I buy some every time I'm there, but
I decided I needed to be able to make them for myself, because
they're that good.

The ingredients couldn't be more simple: a plain bun dough plus
sugar, butter and vanilla. However, put them together and they
really do make something special. The sugar, butter and vanilla are
creamed together and then folded inside circles of dough. As the
buns cook, the sweet butter mixture melts and seeps through each
whole bun while the sugar oozes out and caramelises around its
bottom edges. Once baked, they are brushed with milk, dusted with
icing sugar and covered with a cloth to cool. They emerge pillow-
soft, sweet, sticky and crunchy on the bottom and rarely last long
enough to cool down before people are diving into them.

MAKES 12–15 BUNS

500g strong white flour, plus extra
 for dusting
1 sachet (7g) fast-action yeast
¼ tsp salt
210g caster sugar
190g butter, softened
1 egg
150ml boiling water
150ml whole milk

1 tsp vanilla extract
butter or cooking spray or oil, for
 greasing

*To finish*
milk, for glazing
icing sugar, for dusting

Put the flour, yeast, salt, 60g of the sugar, 90g of the butter and the egg into the bowl of a food processor and blitz until the mixture resembles breadcrumbs. Tip the mixture into a large bowl.

Pour the boiling water into the milk and gradually add to the bowl while mixing. The moisture in the butter and the egg will affect how much additional liquid will be required, so you might not need to use all of it. Stir and bring the mixture together in a soft dough.

Knead for 10 minutes then cover and leave to rise in a warm place until doubled in size. The richness of the dough will mean the yeast will take longer than, for example bread dough, to rise, between 1 and 2 hours.

Once the dough has doubled in size, tip it out on to a lightly floured surface and pat down. Divide the dough into 80g portions and roll into balls. A little more or less won't matter too much, as long as they are all the same size, as this will ensure they cook evenly.

Beat the remaining 100g butter until soft and creamy then add the remaining 150g caster sugar and beat again until light and fluffy. Add the vanilla extract and stir to combine.

Grease and line 2 baking sheets with baking parchment.

*Prepare the buns as follows:*
Take one ball of dough and roll it out to a circle on a lightly floured surface.

Take 1 teaspoon of the whipped butter mixture and put it in the middle of the dough circle. Fold one side of the dough over the other, to make a semi-circle. With the edge of your hand, press the dough down firmly either side of the butter mixture.

Add another teaspoon of the butter mixture to the middle of the dough semi-circle, and fold again. Once again, with the edge of your hand, press the dough down firmly either side of the butter mixture. The dough should now be folded into the shape of a quarter circle. Place the finished bun on a prepared baking sheet. Repeat until all the buns are filled then cover and leave them to rise for about 20 minutes.

Preheat the oven to 180°C/160°C fan/gas 4.

Bake the buns for 12–15 minutes until risen, puffed and slightly browned.

Using a pastry brush, wash over the hot buns with milk and dust liberally with icing sugar. The milk will both soften the crust of the buns and give the icing sugar something to stick to.

Cover with a clean cloth to keep in the steam, and allow to cool.

# ROYAL CHELSEA BUNS

*17th century*

The Chelsea Bun is, arguably, the ultimate traditional bun. Certainly it is the most recognisable, with its spiral of dough baked into a distinctive square. It practically begs you to commit that most cardinal of table-side sins and play with your food.

In researching the history of Chelsea Buns, a fascinating tale emerged: that of a family business, their iconic premises and the famous buns beloved of royalty, rich and poor for over 300 years. Ultimately, there will be a recipe, so the impatient may wish to skip ahead, but the journey is enchanting.

## ORIGINS

These iconic buns originated in The Bun House of Chelsea. Or did they? As with many of the stories in this book, dig a little deeper and even a sentence as simple as this is riddled with inaccuracies.

For a start, there was no single bun house in Chelsea. Over the years there were at least four establishments specialising in buns, but only the last was ever in Chelsea itself. Admittedly, the others were very near—just a stone's throw from the eastern boundary of the borough (or village, as it was then) on Jew's Row—however, in an early instance of clever marketing, it was as obvious to the bakers then as it would be to us now that a 'Pimlico Bun' would not have the same aura of gentility that a 'Chelsea Bun' could command.

The longest-running and most famous bun house belonged to the Hand family, and it is with this establishment that most of the story lies.

The original bun house was once described as a stylish cottage with a well-kept garden,[23] and the fame of Chelsea Buns was already

well established when satirist Jonathan Swift first commented upon
them in 1711.

*'Pray, are not the fine buns sold here in our town; was it not
Rrrrrrrare Chelsea Buns? I bought one to-day in my walk; it cost me
a penny: it was stale, and I did not like it, as the man said, &c.'* [24]

An account of the area published in 1795 declared that the bun
house had, even then, been producing its famous wares for over a
century,[25] and when it finally closed its doors in 1839, it was said
that it had 'enjoyed the favour of the public for more than a century
and a half', pushing its origins back into the last years of the
17th century.

In 1730, the great draughtsman William Hogarth had recorded its
now very impressive frontage in an engraving. A covered walkway
supported by columns extended into the street, several feet above
street level. Cut into the edge of the walkway were steps, which
allowed the gentry to alight from their carriages directly on to the
walkway without risking their expensive footwear on the muddy
street. Patrons could either purchase their buns through the large,
low windows of the frontage, or enjoy them inside.

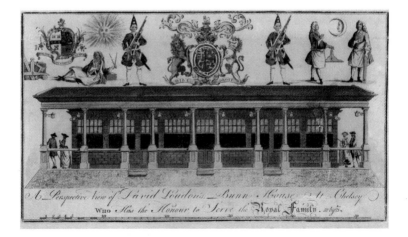

The interior was just as impressive and enjoyed a reputation as something of a Museum of Curiosities, displaying a variety of pictures, models, grotesque figures and modern antiques.[26] To the rear were laid out substantial gardens that included a grotto,[27] a particular and popular 18th-century fad that no doubt provided an additional source of income.

## POPULARITY

Several accounts of the life and times of the bun houses of Old Chelsea make much of the huge numbers of people that flocked to the area to sample the buns. Word of mouth alone would certainly have contributed to their popularity, but there were also other attractions in the area to draw the crowds. Maps of the day show Chelsea as a village, Pimlico a mere handful of houses and the area surrounding the bun houses a riot of pleasure gardens and wide open spaces.

Amongst the attractions for the rich were Strombolo House and Tea Gardens, Jenny's Whim house and gardens and Ranelagh Gardens with its avenues and breathtaking rotunda. For the poor there was The Five Fields, a vast open space that stretched north-east towards Buckingham Palace. On public holidays, the area was filled with entertainments, as well as less wholesome activities to draw in the crowds.

*'The Five Fields which stretched eastwards and northwards, and are now Belgravia, were a sort of Hampstead Heath of the eighteenth century, and were frequented by holiday makers in thousands, for whose delight drinking booths, swings, gingerbread stalls and various less reputable entertainments abounded, and fabulous stories are told of the number of buns sold on Good Friday.'* [28]

Holiday crowds flocked westward from the city both by boat and by land. The road from Buckingham Palace was notorious for highwaymen and footpads (a horseless highwayman), and this must have added a certain frisson of excitement to the prospect of 'going bunning' via this route. Nevertheless both King George II and King George III, and their wives and children, frequented the bun houses to sample their goods and delight the crowds. Their patronage soon led to the 'royal' titles of both the buns and bun house itself.

At the height of its fame in the late 18th century, the Old Original (and by now Royal) Bun House was rumoured to have taken over £250 on Good Fridays for their (Hot) Cross Buns. At a pre-decimal penny per bun, this sum would have come from the sale of around 60,000 buns.

For a family business begun in a cottage and baking in wood-fired brick ovens, this was an incredible feat. For purely practical reasons, preparations had to begin early; it was impossible to bake the quantity of buns demanded fresh on the day. More than three weeks prior to Good Friday, hundreds of yard-square black tins holding close to 150 spiced and fruited buns each, were filled, baked and then stored and kept moist before being reheated on the day itself. [29]

The combination of the holiday, pleasure gardens and funfair meant that the crowds on Good Friday were phenomenal. It was estimated that upwards of 50,000 people crammed into the area, sometimes as early as 4 a.m. The press of people, and the inevitable scuffles and arguments, alarmed residents so much than in 1793 Mrs Margaret Hand, matriarch and doyenne of the Bun House, was forced to issue a notice that 'she is determined, though much to her loss, not to sell *Cross Buns* on that day, to any person whatever; but Chelsea Buns as usual.' [30]

Despite the popularity of both Cross Buns and the regular Chelsea Buns, the closing of the pleasure gardens, especially Ranelagh in 1804, signalled the beginning of the end for the Bun Houses of Chelsea. In 1836, the last member of the Hand family died intestate and the property reverted to the Crown. It remained in business for a short while, and even took upwards of £100 for the sale of 24,000 buns[31] on Good Friday in 1839. However, less than a month later, the Museum of Curiosities was auctioned off and the building torn down to make way for 'improvements'. Although it was later rebuilt, its charm had been lost, and the final Bun House closed in the 1880s. As early as 1844, the changes to the community were being mourned:

> *'The Chelsea Meadows are now covered with bricks, either making, or drying, or built up into houses. The favourite Willow Walk, which led towards Chelsea from the Millbank near the penitentiary, has only one solitary dying willow left. The far-famed Chelsea Bun-houses have stepped back from the road where they formerly stood; they appear now as confectioners' shops in the line of houses forming the street, and the crowds who used to throng to them in Good Friday morning before the sun himself was up, are no longer to be seen there.'* [32]

## The Royal Bun House Family

By all accounts, the Royal Bun House was run by four generations of the Hand family. Contenders for the original proprietors of the Bun House are Robert Hand and Mary Gwinn, who married at Knightsbridge Chapel on 13th January 1667.[33] The Gwynne family were well established in Pimlico, running the Nell Gwynn tavern that stood just west of the Bun House.

While it is highly likely that the larger of the two Bun Houses did provide a good income for four generations of the Hand family, there is evidence that, for a time at least, their tenure there was interrupted. Firstly, there is the information contained in the business card of Richard Hand, which makes it very clear that, although originally of 'Ye Old Original Chelsey Bunn House', his subsequent location is at the King's Arms. Two additional pieces of information can be gleaned from this elaborate card. Firstly, the date of 1718 underneath the coat of arms, and secondly the engraver's name at the bottom: Wm Hogarth. William Hogarth did indeed begin his career engraving business cards while apprenticed to Ellis Gamble in not-too-distant Leicester Fields. And if they are one and the same, and the date on the card is that of its creation, then Richard Hand's business card might well be one of the first examples of the then 21-year-old Hogarth's exceptional talent. The second piece of evidence, coincidentally, also involving William Hogarth, lies in his 1730[34] engraving of the impressive frontage of the 'Bunn House at Chelsey', declaring it to be 'David Loudon's Bunn House'. If the Bun House did indeed remain in the same family for four generations, one explanation of this anomaly might be that David Loudon married a daughter of the Hand family and took over the running of the business, while Mr Hand Senior retired to The King's Arms.

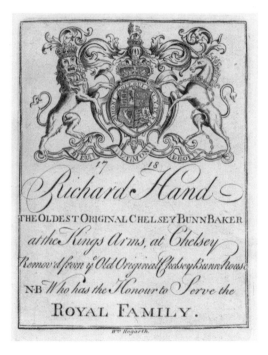

The third generation is represented by Richard Hand and his wife, Margaret. Richard Hand was an eccentric who called himself 'Captain Bun' and preferred to dress in a Turkish fez and a dressing gown. A 1773 engraving in the British Museum shows a Georgian gentleman elegantly dressed in coat, waistcoat, breeches, stockings and sporting a cocked hat putting a tray of buns into an oven.

The title of the engraving is 'Captain Bun Quixote attacking the oven' and might well be a reference to the eccentricities of Richard 'Captain Bun' Hand, although dated a full six years after his death, it is unlikely to be an accurate representation.

On the death of Richard Hand, the running of the Bun House was taken over by his widow, Margaret, and it is under her guidance that the Bun House was to enjoy its most successful era. The degree of her success can be demonstrated by the need to cancel the sale of Cross Buns at Easter 1793. Notice of Mrs Hand's death in July 1798 was given as: 'At Chelsea, Mrs. Margaret Hand, who for more than 60 years kept the Royal Bun-house there (so denominated by express permission).'[35]

Mrs Hand's tenure at the Bun House was succeeded by the younger of her two sons, Gideon Richard Hand. He too was described as:

*'An eccentric character, who dealt also largely in butter, which he carried round to his customers in a basket on his head; hot or cold, wet or dry, throughout the year, the punctual butterman made his appearance at the door, and gained the esteem of every one by his cheerful aspect and entertaining conversation: for he was rich in village anecdote, and could relate all the vicissitudes of the neighbourhood for more than half a century.'*[36]

Gideon Richard Hand died in 1821 at the age of 60 and his elder brother, the confusingly named Richard Gideon Hand, took over.

Richard Hand had made a career of soldiering, first in the 13th regiment of foot, where he rose to the rank of Lieutenant[37] and subsequently as a Lieutenant in the Staffordshire Militia.[38] At the time of his brother's death he was one of the Poor Knights of Windsor.[39] Despite being elderly himself, Richard continued to run the Bun House until his death in February 1836 at the grand old age of 84. His military career had left no time for family, and a search for any relatives[40] found none, and so his estate reverted to the Crown.

*Where was The Royal Bun House?*

Other than the tradition of the buns themselves, nothing now remains of this remarkable building and its colourful history. Although there are numerous engravings and etchings showing what a magnificent building it was, there's a great deal of vagueness regarding its actual location. A major difficulty is the evolution of streets as well as street names over the centuries: new ones have been created and old ones disappeared. Additionally, the area went from a hamlet of a few scattered houses to a heavily built-up metropolitan suburb.

But, using snippets of information from a multitude of sources, I have pieced together a reasonable idea of the Royal Bun House's location from the following:

• The larger Bun House had a frontage of 52 feet that extended into the street with a covered walkway.
• The other Bun House was built two doors further along, with a considerably smaller frontage, and also had a covered walkway extending into the street.
• 'The Chelsea Bun Houses—there were two of them—stood on the left side of the Pimlico Road, about 100 yards beyond the toll-gate by the "Nell Gwynn" tavern.' [41]
• 'Some houses built on the site of the bun house garden, at the back, are still called Bun-House Place.' [42]
• 'It was on the north side in that part of Jew's Row afterwards called Grosvenor Row, not really in Chelsea, being just across the rivulet which ran through the passage by the "Nell Gwynne". Its frontage commenced in Union Street.' [43]

The descriptions of the close proximity of the rival Bun Houses, together with the size of their frontages (one large, one small) that extended on to the street, meant that identifying them on a map turned out to be surprisingly straightforward. Both buildings are clearly marked on Richard Horwood's amazingly detailed 1792–9 map of London. The large garden and grotto behind the Royal Bun

House are also visible. Working backwards in time from this map, it is then easy to see the Bun House's original cottage and substantial garden in John Roque's 1746 map. John Greenwood's 1827 map of London is possibly one of the last to show the Bun Houses with their extensions over the street.

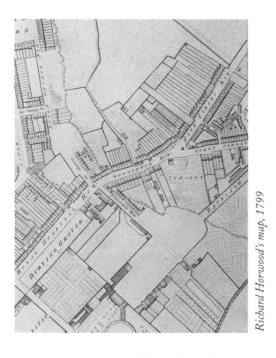

*Richard Horwood's map, 1799*

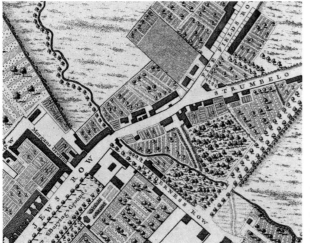

*John Roque's map, 1746*

Over the years, roads have changed both their course and their names. Jew's Row and Grosvenor Row are long gone. An echo of The Bun House's existence does, however, currently live on in the streets of 21st-century Pimlico: Bunhouse Place, originally built in the gardens of the Royal Bun House,[44] still exists, and provides the final clue to identifying where the Royal Bun House of Chelsea, stood.

The frontage of the larger of the two Bun Houses, the Royal Bun House, was described by authors writing years after they had been demolished[45] as commencing in Union Street. Union Street did not exist in the era of the Bun Houses, and there is no road of that name in today's Pimlico. It has been renamed Passmore Street, and runs north from Pimlico Road to Graham Terrace. Bun House Place runs east from this street, pinpointing the location of the Royal Bun House as being on the corner of Passmore Street and Pimlico Road. It was a little frustrating, after the painstaking piecing together of all the numerous sources and the scrutinising of maps, to find the following, almost casual, paragraph in an old book about Chelsea, but at least it confirms the location:

'Separated from "The old original Chelsea Bunhouse" by one house (a boys' school) was a more modern rival, which displayed its title on a board: "This is the old Oakley Bunhouse." No. 60, Pimlico Road, occupies the site of the former; No. 52, the latter.' [46]

The once magnificent Royal Bun House might be just a memory, but the place where it stood remains at 60 Pimlico Road. It is touching that in the 21st century, the site retains some of its royal connections. The premises is currently a showroom for Linley, a furniture company set up by David Armstrong-Jones, Viscount Linley, son of Princess Margaret and nephew to Queen Elizabeth II.

*Royal Chelsea Buns*

'To be good, it should be made with a good deal of butter, be very light and eat *hot*.' [47]

So what were they actually like, these buns that delighted both king and commoner?

Ask anyone today what a Chelsea Bun looks like and most will describe the immediately recognisable confection we know today—square spirals of sweet dough filled with currants, sugar and spice, their tops richly browned and shiny with glaze. However iconic the modern-day buns are, they bear little resemblance to the buns that drew the crowds in 18th-century Chelsea. The earliest printed recipe I have been able to find dates from 1854,[48] a good 15 years after the Royal Bun House was torn down. Although the recipe calls for the bun to be baked in the spiral we recognise today, it contains no fruit. All the snippets of information concerning the look and flavour of Royal Chelsea Buns I have managed to find point to a much simpler bun.

*'Before me appeared the shops so famed for Chelsea buns, which, for above thirty years, I have never passed without filling my pockets... These buns have afforded a competency, and even wealth, to four generations of the same family; and it is singular, that their delicate flavour, lightness and richness, have never been successfully imitated.'* [49]

*'The old Chelsea Buns were greatly in demand and were a superior kind to our common buns, more like Bath Buns. Old people say they were very rich and seemed full of butter. They were square in form and were made with eggs, with the kind of sugar, lemon and spice but without fruit.'* [50]

*'Note that the true Chelsea Bun of the Hands family was by no means the darksome and dismal lump which is now sold us as a hot cross bun. On the contrary, it was specially famous for its flaky lightness and delicate flavour.'* [51]

*'It was not round, but square in shape, and it came into the world in batches, the several individuals crammed as close together as the cells of a honeycomb ... Excellent they were—light, sweet, glistening as to their crowns in a sort of sugary varnish, and easy of digestion.'* [52]

To sum up, it would seem that the buns were square, baked close together in batches, were buttery, spiced, enriched with eggs, lemony sweet, light, flaky and with sugar-varnished tops. There was no fruit and no spiral. The square yard baking tins, described as holding 'close to 150' buns, would probably have held 12 rows of 12, giving 144 individual buns, 3 inches (7.5cm) square—a most substantial penny treat!

The recipe that follows is my interpretation of how Royal Chelsea Buns might well have tasted, based on my own personal experience of baking and taking on board all the qualities mentioned above. The buttery lightness and flakiness is achieved by treating the dough as flaky pastry, dotting additional butter and sugar over the surface and folding and re-rolling in a similar manner to various Lardy Cake recipes.

I don't believe Chelsea buns were originally spiralled, but can certainly believe that this approach was developed to try and speed up the manufacturing process. Compared side by side, the smooth-topped bun is altogether softer, lighter and more delicate, and although it requires a little extra effort, it thoroughly deserves its royal designation.

MAKES 22–24 SMALL BUNS

*500g strong white flour, plus extra*
*for dusting*
*1 sachet (7g) fast-action yeast*
*¼ tsp salt*
*90g caster sugar*
*115g butter*
*1 egg*
*2 tbsp Spice Mix (see page 326)*
*150ml boiling water*
*150ml whole milk*
*zest of 2 lemons*
*butter or cooking spray, for*
*greasing*

*For the glaze*
*80ml milk*
*4 tbsp sugar*

*1 x rectangular baking tin, at least*
*4cm deep (but no deeper,*
*otherwise the high sides will*
*prevent the heat getting to the*
*buns and they won't cook*
*properly)*

Grease your baking tin with butter or cooking spray.

Put the flour into the bowl of a food processor. Add the yeast, salt, 60g of the sugar, 90g of the butter, the egg and spices into the bowl of a food processor, and blitz until the mixture resembles breadcrumbs. Tip the mixture into a large bowl.

Pour the boiling water into the milk and gradually add to the bowl while mixing. Depending on the amount of moisture in the butter and the egg, you might not need all of this liquid. Stir and bring the mixture together in a soft dough.

Knead for 10 minutes then cover and leave to rise in a warm place until doubled in size. Due to the richness of the dough and the high sugar content, the yeast will take longer than, for example, bread dough, to rise—between 1 and 2 hours.

Once the dough has doubled in size, tip it out on to a lightly floured surface and pat down. Roll it out to a thickness of 1–2cm. Warm the remaining 25g butter until very soft, but not liquid. Using a pastry brush, spread a layer of butter over the dough.

Mix the lemon zest with the remaining 2 tablespoons of caster sugar and sprinkle this over the butter. Fold in the edges of the dough and knead gently to combine. If you'd prefer to make spiral buns, then instead of folding in the sides, roll the dough up from one long edge, cut into 3cm slices and arrange in your tin.

Divide the dough into even pieces (the exact number will depend on the size and shape of your tin). This amount will make 22–24 buns, each about 50g, which will rise to dainty, 5cm buns. Larger buns will require a longer cooking time.

Shape the buns into balls and set them in the tin, leaving a little space between each one to allow the dough to expand. Cover and set aside to rise a second time for about 30 minutes. The buns are ready when their sides are just touching.

Preheat the oven to 180°C/160°C fan/gas 4.

Bake the buns for 15–20 minutes, depending on their size, until golden brown.

While the buns are baking, mix the glaze by stirring the milk and sugar together in a small pan over a low heat until the sugar has dissolved.

Remove the cooked buns from the oven and brush them with the glaze. Set aside to cool slightly in the tin before turning out. These buns are best eaten warm.

# CRACKNELLS
## 1700

It's not unusual for there to exist several recipes with the same name that are actually altogether different. Such is the case with the Cracknell, which can be both a crisp biscuit and a yeast-raised bun made using a two-stage cooking process similar to that used to make bagels today. This is a recipe for the latter.

A brief hot water bath means that the Cracknells take on a beautiful chestnut colour and shine in the oven. I was particularly enchanted by descriptions of precisely when to fish the dough out of the simmering water: 'And lett it seeth tyll they doe swyme' (i.e. take them out when the Cracknells float).

Although they contain a little sugar, these Cracknells sit right on the fence between sweet and savoury, equally good dipped in a breakfast bowl of milky coffee or hot chocolate or nibbled alongside a glass of wine and some cheese.

These Cracknells have an extremely long shelf-life—weeks, as opposed to days, if you can make them last that long, that is.

MAKES 30–40 CRACKNELLS

*500g strong white flour, plus extra*
*for dusting*
*25g sugar*
*1 sachet (7g) fast-action yeast*
*2 tbsp aniseed*
*2 tbsp ground coriander*
*½ tsp salt*

*50g butter*
*1 egg*
*1 egg yolk (reserve the white)*
*warm water, to mix*
*cooking oil, for greasing*

*1 x 5cm plain round pastry cutter*

In a large bowl, mix the flour, sugar, yeast, spices and salt. Rub in the butter.

Whisk the egg and yolk, pour into the mixture and mix. Bring the mixture together in a dough with a little warm water, and knead until smooth, about 10 minutes. Cover and set aside to rise in a warm place for 1 hour.

Bring a large pot of water to a simmer. Oil a wire rack.

Tip out the dough on to a lightly floured surface and pat down gently. Roll the dough out like pastry until it is about 1cm thick. Using a plain 5cm pastry cutter, cut out circles of dough. It's better to work in small batches, so I suggest cutting out 5 to begin with, and make the next batch while the first ones are in the pot.

You can just cook the circles flat, but I think they look so pretty as folded triangles. Make the circles into little tricorns like this:

Place a circle in front of you.

Whisk the unused egg white and, using a pastry brush, paint the surface of the dough with egg white. This will help your discs stay stuck together while in the water.

Imagine the circle of dough is a clock face, and put the thumb and index finger of your left hand where the 6 and 10 would be. Put the index finger of your right hand where the 2 would be. Lift and push the edges of the dough towards the middle with all 3 fingers at once. Press firmly. Repeat with the rest of the batch.

Stir the water in the pot and, while it is still moving, gently drop the batch of shaped dough into the simmering water. Having the water moving will help prevent the dough from sticking to the bottom of the pan.

While they are cooking, cut and shape the next batch of dough.

Lift the dough out of the water when it is puffed and floating on the surface. Set aside on the oiled wire rack to dry. Repeat with the rest of the shaped dough.

When the last batch of dough has cooled and dried, preheat the oven to 180°C/160°C fan/gas 4. Line a baking sheet with baking parchment.

Arrange the Cracknells on the baking sheet and bake for 30–40 minutes until dark and shiny. Transfer to a wire rack to cool.

# *MUFFINS*
*18th century*

Ahhh muffins! Not the American kind, but the other sort—think bread-like, not cake-like. In fact, not just bready, but fluffy pillows of enriched bread dough that are a world apart from the beige hockey pucks wrapped in plastic that lurk on the supermarket shelf. Best of all—no oven required! Muffins are cooked on top of the stove on a flat griddle or heavy-based pan.

Bread muffins are quintessentially and traditionally British and have a very particular appearance—golden brown on their flat tops and bottoms, with a broad band of pale softness around the middle. Recipes can be found at least as far back as the mid 18th century, but there seems to be a lack of anything older. I suspect the reason for this is that muffins were traditionally made by bakers, and therefore unnecessary in domestic cookery books. Stories tell of the Muffin Man, who delivered muffins in towns and cities around the UK. Warm muffins always sold better than cold ones as it implied they were fresh. However, to be at their best, muffins need to be cooked a second time, toasted in front of the fire, so their temperature when purchased should have been largely immaterial.

Hannah Glasse's recipe for muffins always makes me chuckle. It is entitled 'To make muffins and oat cakes', but she gets so involved with enthusing about the proper way to make muffins, she wanders off at a tangent and gets so distracted that the oat cakes are never mentioned again. She even goes so far as to include instructions for building the cooking surface upon which you are supposed to cook your muffins. Despite her absent-minded tendency for distraction, when it came to the best way to enjoy muffins, Hannah was most specific on one particular point:

'*...don't touch them with a knife, either to spread or cut them open, if you do they will be as heavy as lead...*'

She claimed the correct method of preparation was to tear the toasted muffin apart gently, lay a thin slice of butter in the middle and then close it up again and keep it warm so that the butter melted, turning after a few minutes so that the melted butter might ooze gently through both halves: a simple yet effective idea I could really get behind, even if I haven't built my own griddle.

I found the tip about shaping with rice flour in Elizabeth David's book *English Bread and Yeast Cookery*. The rice flour dries the surface of the muffins without making them sticky or leaving clumps, so the excess is easy to brush off. If unavailable, substitute with cornflour or just use regular flour.

MAKES 12–15 MUFFINS

420ml whole milk
50g butter
1 tsp salt
2 tbsp granulated sugar
1 egg

450g strong white flour
1 sachet (7g) fast-action yeast
rice flour, for shaping and for
   dusting (optional)
semolina, for cooking

Pour the milk into a pan (or microwave-safe bowl). Cut the butter into small dice and add to the milk. Heat gently on the hob (or in the microwave) until the milk is warmed to body temperature (you can test it by dipping your finger into the milk; be careful that it's not too hot if you've heated it in the microwave) and the butter has melted.

Put the remaining ingredients, except the rice flour and semolina, into a bowl then slowly stir in the milk mixture to combine. It will form a rather wet dough.

When thoroughly mixed, knead for 10 minutes either with a dough hook or by hand until the dough appears stretchy and shiny. Cover and leave to rise in a warm place for 1 hour.

Tip out the dough and pat it down to deflate it. Divide the dough into 80–100g pieces and shape these into smooth balls, using rice flour as required; set out on a lightly dusted work surface, flattening each muffin slightly.

Heat a heavy-based or griddle pan over a low heat. Do not add any grease or oil. When the whole pan is of an even heat, scatter semolina over the base.

Use a fish slice/spatula to move the muffins into the pan. Depending on the size of your muffins and also your pan, you can probably cook several at a time, but first you might want to try a test-run on just one muffin, to check the heat of the pan and to see how long it takes to cook.

Cook gently until the undersides are nicely browned—between 5 and 8 minutes, depending on the size of your muffins—then turn them over.

Cook the second sides for a slightly shorter time. If you've made a test muffin, you can pull it apart to check the insides are fully cooked.

The semolina helps prevent the muffins from sticking to the pan, but it does get very browned, so wipe the pan clean after each batch of cooked muffins has been removed and add fresh semolina before you cook the next. Set the cooked muffins on to a wire rack to cool.

To serve: toast each side of each muffin under a preheated grill then pull apart and add a slice of butter. Put the two halves back together and allow the butter to melt.

# CRUMPETS

*18th century*

Another classic teatime treat, crumpets, like muffins, require a
second cooking, or toasting, to be enjoyed at their best. Both can
be made from the same list of ingredients, the only difference being
that crumpets are made with a batter as opposed to a dough.

If you like nice round crumpets then you will need a ring to cook
them in. You can find very stylish ones in cookshops, but if they're
only for occasional use, they're a rather expensive investment. A
more cost-effective solution is to search the canned foods section
in a supermarket for a suitably sized tin. The key is not to have the
sides too high, as it will make it difficult to work with. Buy however
many you think you might need; four is a nice even number and
probably the most that will fit in a frying pan at one time. When
you get home, take the tops off the tins, enjoy the contents, and
then take the bottom off the tins as well. Soak the tins in warm
water and remove the labels. You're left with a 'ring' of food-grade
quality for a fraction of the cost of a shop-bought baking ring. Best
of all, you're free to choose whatever size you like, from jumbo
down to mini. I've got two sets: mini ones from tins of processed
peas and large ones from tins of sponge pudding. I have also used
them to bake mini cakes, pies and tarts.

If you're less bothered about strict presentation you can just ladle
the batter into a lightly greased pan to cook. The resulting crumpets
won't be as thick, but they'll still be delicious once toasted and
buttered. Crumpets of this shape are called 'pikelets'.

**MAKES 15–20 CRUMPETS, DEPENDING ON SIZE**

*420ml whole milk*
*50g butter*
*1 tsp salt*
*2 tbsp granulated sugar*
*1 egg*
*450g strong white flour*
*1 sachet (7g) fast-action yeast*

*150ml warm water*
*½ tsp bicarbonate of soda*
*cooking spray, for greasing*

*3 or 4 baking rings (or clean, used tins)*

Mix the milk with 150ml cold water in a saucepan (or microwave-safe bowl). Cut the butter into small dice and add to the milk mixture. Heat gently on the hob (or in the microwave) until the liquid is warmed to body temperature (test by dipping your finger into it) and the butter is melted.

Put all the remaining ingredients, down to and including the yeast, into a bowl and stir vigorously to combine into a smooth batter. Cover and set aside to rise in a warm place for 1–2 hours.

When nicely bubbly and aerated, stir vigorously with a spoon.

Mix the warm water and the bicarbonate of soda together and add to the batter. Stir to combine then cover and set aside for another 30 minutes.

Grease a heavy-based frying pan and your baking rings. Put the rings into the pan over a medium heat (you'll need to cook the crumpets in batches of 3 or 4). If the rings are heated, they will cook the batter more quickly and help prevent it seeping under the edge of the rings.

Pour a little batter into the rings, to a depth of 2cm. At this point you might want to make a test crumpet, just to check that the batter is the correct consistency. If it's too thick then the signature holes won't form on the surface. If this is the case, add a little more warm water to thin the batter and try another test crumpet.

Cook gently until the tops have set and there is a honeycomb of holes over the surface of the crumpets then ease the crumpets free from the rings by running a knife around the inside edge. Lift off the rings (they will be hot, so wear protective gloves) and turn the crumpets over.

Cook for a further 2–3 minutes until lightly coloured. The crumpets will be toasted before eating, so you don't want the surfaces to get too dark while cooking. Set the cooked crumpets aside to cool on a wire rack while you cook the reaminder.

To serve, lightly toast both sides of the crumpets and spread with butter.

# *DOUGHNUTS*
*17th century*

This recipe had me puzzled for such a long time it makes me feel very foolish now. When I found a recipe 'To Make Do Nuts' written in a looped and cursive style of handwriting in a manuscript, I couldn't quite make out the first letter of the third word and I kept wondering to what kind of nut it referred. Could it be an early kind of ginger nut? Perhaps when cooked, the dish was shaped like a nut, but which one? I know that what I call a hazelnut is called both a filbert and a cob in other parts of the country, so might this be a colloquial name?

Of course the sensible thing would have been to stop and actually read the recipe, which took me an embarrassingly long time to do. Having done so, it soon became clear that this was a very early doughnut recipe. It was a real surprise to me to find a British recipe for something now so closely associated with the US. The only thing that had me momentarily stumped was the frying liquid. The recipe instructions said to 'boil them in *seam*', which I learned, thanks to food historian Ivan Day, was an obsolete Tudor word for lard. It is possible, then, that this recipe might be even older than the 17th century it is currently dated at.

These doughnuts differ from the type we know today, but they are so much better for it. For a start they are small, at no more than 3cm across, and therefore make perfect bite-sized treats. Their small size means they cook quickly and so the danger of soggy, uncooked dough in the middle is practically eliminated. Another difference is that they are made from an enriched and lightly spiced dough.

I have changed very little from the original recipe, merely suggesting specific quantities of sugar and spice where there were none and switching to oil for the cooking. They are delicious simply tossed in sugar after cooking, or for a more indulgent treat, serve with warm chocolate dipping sauce.

MAKES 20–30 BITE-SIZED DOUGHNUTS

*175g strong white flour, plus extra*
*for dusting*
*½ tsp fast-action yeast*
*1 egg*
*1 tbsp Spice Mix (see page 326)*
*25g caster sugar*
*15g butter*
*25ml double cream*
*60ml warm milk*

*oil, for deep-frying*
*caster or soft brown sugar, to*
*coat, or warm chocolate sauce for*
*dipping*
*1–2 tsp ground cinnamon*
*(optional)*

*cook's thermometer (optional)*

Sift the flour into a bowl and add the yeast, egg, spices and sugar. In a small pan over a low heat, warm the butter and cream until the butter is melted. Add this to the flour mixture. Gradually add the warm milk just until the mixture comes together in a soft dough (you might not need to use all of the milk). Knead for 10 minutes then cover and set aside to rise in a warm place for 1 hour or until doubled in size.

Tip the risen dough out on to a lightly floured surface and gently pat down. Divide the dough into 10g pieces and roll them between the palms of your hands until they are smooth and round.

Heat the oil to 170°C in a deep-fat fryer or saucepan. Test the oil temperature with a single doughnut first. It should sizzle gently when the doughnut hits the oil. Cook the doughnuts in batches of five or six. Larger batches will cool the oil too much and the dough will soak up the grease. They will take just 3–4 minutes to cook and should flip themselves over automatically when the bottom half is done (if they haven't flipped after 2 minutes, give them a little help).

Drain the cooked doughnuts in a wire sieve then toss them in sugar and cinnamon, if using, while hot. If you are serving them with dipping chocolate you won't need to coat them in sugar. Serve warm.

## VARIATIONS

You can flavour the dough with almost anything that takes your
fancy: orange or lemon zest, vanilla, rosewater, orange-flower water,
or other spices such as aniseed, mace, etc.

For a hidden treat, flavour the dough with vanilla then soak some
raisins in rum and put one or two in the middle of each doughnut,
making sure to carefully seal the dough around the fruit.

Flavour the dough with 2–3 tablespoons of cocoa powder and add
chopped candied orange or lemon peel to the middle, or a small
square of chocolate. Again, make sure you close the dough around
the filling carefully. When cooked, toss in a mixture of cocoa
powder and icing sugar. The chocolate ones are especially good,
as the chocolate forms a liquid centre inside the warm doughnut.

Toss the cooked doughnuts in coloured sugar to finish.

# GINGER ROLLS
*1857*

These little rolls come from *The English Bread Book* of the eminently thorough and sensible Eliza Acton. Ginger is wonderfully calming for digestive problems, so having a few of these rolls in the freezer is a great standby for those times when stomach upsets occur. The recipe is for a simple, soft roll with a generous helping of dried ginger to both soothe and settle a delicate stomach. Ms Acton also recommends these rolls for easing travel sickness, which, considering the relatively limited modes of transport available in 1857, is both far-thinking and extremely practical of her.

MAKES 8 ROLLS

*450g strong white flour, plus extra*
  *for dusting*
*1 sachet (7g) fast-action yeast*
*½ tsp salt*
*30g ground ginger*

*150ml hot water*
*150ml milk*
*butter, for greasing*

*8 mini-loaf tins*

Line a baking sheet with baking parchment or grease 8 mini-loaf tins.

Put all the dry ingredients into a bowl and stir thoroughly to combine.

Add the hot water to the milk and slowly stir into the dry ingredients until the mixture comes together into a soft dough. Knead for about 10 minutes until smooth then place in a bowl, cover, and set aside to rise in a warm place for 1 hour.

Tip the risen dough on to a lightly floured surface and pat down. Divide the dough into 8 even pieces and form them into rolls.

Arrange on the prepared baking sheet or shape them and put them into mini-loaf tins. Cover and set aside to rise in a warm place for 30 minutes.

Preheat the oven to 200°C/180°C fan/gas 6.

Dust the rolls lightly with flour then bake for 15–18 minutes until risen and golden. Remove from the baking sheet, or tins, if using, and transfer the loaves to a wire rack to cool. Cover with a clean cloth to keep the crusts soft.

# POTATO BREAD
*1837*

The addition of vegetables to bread flour dates back hundreds of years and probably began when an increase in the price of wheat caused the cost of bread to rise sharply. The expensive wheat flour was bulked out with cooked and puréed vegetables. I've tried several different vegetables, nearly all of which have added a delicious dimension to the loaf.

In addition to giving interesting flavour to loaves, this is also a great way to sneak more vegetables into your diet. Using pale, creamy potatoes avoids the need to explain any unusual colouration in the family loaf to children of a suspicious nature, thereby neatly heading off any potential objections.

Adding potato actually improves the quality of bread by keeping it moist and flavourful for several days longer than bread made with plain wheat flour. It also makes great toast, something that was noted as long ago as 1806,[53] although the chief benefit back then appears to have been how well it soaked up the butter.

As a general rule of thumb, one-third of your standard bread recipe can be replaced with warm mashed potatoes, and then mixed as usual.

**MAKES I LARGE LOAF**

*340g warm mashed potatoes*
*15g butter, plus extra*
 *for greasing*
*560g strong white flour*
*1 sachet (7g) fast-action yeast*
*1½ tsp salt*

*150ml milk*
*150ml hot water*

*1 x 2kg/28cm loaf tin, or similar*
 *capacity*

Put all the ingredients, except the milk and hot water, into a bowl and mix to combine.

In a separate bowl, mix the milk and hot water together and gradually add the liquid to the dry ingredients until the mixture comes together in a soft dough. Depending on the moisture in the potatoes, you might need a little more or less of the liquid. Knead for 10 minutes then cover and set aside to rise in a warm place.

Grease your loaf tin. When the dough has doubled in size (about 1 hour), tip it out on to a lightly floured surface and pat it down. Form the dough into a loaf shape and place in the greased loaf tin. Cover and set aside to rise a second time for 30 minutes.

Preheat the oven to 200°C/180°C fan/gas 6.

Bake the loaf for 40–45 minutes until risen and golden then remove it from the tin and return it to the oven for 5 minutes to crisp the crust. Transfer to a wire rack to cool.

# THE GRANT LOAF
*1930s*

If you're keen to bake your own bread and you're looking for a simple recipe to get you started, you could do worse than this one; it doesn't require kneading, it only needs a very short, single rise, and you can have a batch of three loaves cooling on a rack in an hour and a half. The recipe has been around for almost 80 years and is named after its creator, Doris Grant.

Tireless campaigner for healthy eating and unadulterated foods, Grant was a champion of fresh, natural ingredients and the minimum of food-processing. She maintained a running battle with major food companies in the UK for more than 60 years. Almost crippled with arthritis in her youth, Doris found relief from her symptoms by following the food-combining diet of the New York physician Dr William Hay. With her health restored, Dr Hay encouraged Doris to write her own book for the UK, and thus began a very successful publishing career. Alongside her many best-selling books, she is immortalised as the creator of the Grant Loaf.

The Grant Loaf was originally the result of a mistake. Doris began teaching herself to bake in the 1930s, and it was several months before she realised that she should have been kneading her bread dough. However, her no-knead method didn't seem to have made much difference to the quality of her loaves, and was a great deal easier and quicker than the traditional way, so she included her 'mistake' in her 1944 book, *Your Daily Bread*. Here, with only a few adjustments, is that original recipe.

The dough in this recipe ends up a lot wetter than traditional dough—so wet in fact, that kneading would be impossible if it weren't already unnecessary. The bread itself is firm without being brick-like, and has a wonderfully nutty flavour that makes great toast. I bake it in our house as our everyday bread, as well as using it for sandwiches and packed lunches.

This recipe makes three loaves for two reasons: one, it uses a whole bag of flour at once, so no messy half-bags to clutter up your cupboards and spill over everything; two, it makes sense, as well as efficient use of the oven, to cook more than one loaf at a time, and the additional loaves can be frozen for later use.

MAKES 3 REGULAR LOAVES

1.5kg (1 bag) stoneground wholemeal bread flour
28g dark muscovado sugar (or any brown sugar, or honey)
28g salt
1.3 litres warm water

2 sachets (14g) fast-action yeast
butter or cooking spray or oil, for greasing
3 x loaf tins (23 x 10 x 7.5cm, or similar capacity)

Preheat the oven to 110°C/90°C fan/gas ¼ (optional, see below).

Put the flour into a large bowl and place it in the oven to warm. It doesn't much matter if you don't warm it, but it does speed up the rising. Turn off the oven while you make your dough.

Put the sugar and salt into a large jug and add half the water. Stir to dissolve.

Grease the loaf tins, using butter, cooking spray or oil.

Mix the yeast into the warmed flour and pour in the sugar/salt mixture, then add the rest of the water.

Stir until the flour is fully mixed in. This is probably easiest to do using your hands, but using a utensil works well also. Personally, I use a large 2-pronged wooden fork from an otherwise unused set of salad servers, because the prongs can dig right to the bottom of the bowl and move more easily through the wet mix than a spoon. I regularly manage to whip up a batch of this bread without touching the mix with my hands at all! Remember: you're only mixing, not kneading—so as soon as all the flour is incorporated, you can stop. The dough will be much more moist than traditional bread dough—more like a fruit-cake mix or thick, badly-made porridge.

Spoon the dough into the loaf tins, making sure it's evenly divided —each tin should be approximately three-quarters full. If you want to measure by weight, it's approximately 900g dough per tin. Smooth the dough, making sure it is spread into the corners of the tin, then make a trough in the dough, down the length of the tin. This forces the dough to rise evenly. I find that if I don't do this, the loaves end up distinctly lopsided.

Set the tins somewhere warm to rise by about a third, until the dough is just above the top of the tins and nicely rounded. It should take no more than 30 minutes. If, like me, you're lucky enough to have a double oven, then put the 3 tins on to a baking sheet and then on the shelf in the top oven while the main oven heats up. NB: Don't put the tins on the floor of the top oven—even if they're on a baking sheet—as they will get too hot. Otherwise, anywhere warm and draught-free will do.

Preheat the oven to 200°C/180°C fan/gas 6. When the dough has risen, bake the loaves for 45 minutes then remove the tins from the oven and tip out the bread. Put the loaves back in the oven for 5–10 minutes to crisp up the crust, if necessary.

Transfer to a wire rack to cool.


VARIATION

This method can also be used with brown bread flour, for a slightly lighter loaf.

# CROSS BUNS
*17th century*

There is a belief in some parts of the UK that a Cross Bun baked on Good Friday would never spoil and would have protective, even curative properties. Hung in the kitchen, it would prevent fires; on a ship it would protect against shipwreck. Occasionally, small pieces would be broken off and eaten as a curative. These ideas descended from the belief in the power of the symbol of the cross, and may well date back to pre-Reformation days. The link with Catholicism could explain the somewhat bizarre edict issued in the last years of Elizabeth I:

*'That no baker or other person or persons shall at any time or times hereafter, make, utter or sell by retail within or without their houses, unto any the Queen's subjects, any spice cakes, buns, bisket or other spice bread (being bread out of size, and not by law allowed), except it be at burials, or upon the Friday before Easter, or at Christmas; upon pain of forfeiture of all such spice bread to the poor.'*

Imagine if this were published in modern times; you can almost picture the tabloid headlines screaming 'Queen Hates Buns!' In reality, it was much more likely to be part of a cunning plan by Elizabeth's advisors. The edict was signed, not by Elizabeth, but by her Privy Councillors, and was probably an attempt to distance the realm from the traits of Catholicism. Overtures were already being made to the Protestant King James VI of Scotland as being a suitable heir to the ageing Queen, so this edict banning the sale of spiced bread and buns, except at funerals, Good Friday and Christmas, might well have been more of a 'goodwill gesture' on behalf of the Council to reassure James of the country's faith .

I've been unable to find the date that this edict was repealed, but it set a precedent for the limited availability of such baked goods that echoed down the centuries to the heyday of The Royal Bun

House at Chelsea (see page 273). With no ovens at home to bake
their own buns, the general public would naturally have looked
forward to the two holidays in the year when spiced, fruited buns
would be available to buy, and so the crowds going 'a-bunning'
surged westwards from London towards the entertainments and the
famous Bun Houses around Chelsea.

You can read about the Bun Houses in the entry on Chelsea Buns
but, to cut a long story short, in 1793 the popularity of the cross
bun on Good Friday was so great as to lead to excessively boisterous
revelling on the surrounding streets. When the riotous behaviour of
the crowds became too much, Mrs Hand of the Royal Bun House
declared by public notice that 'she is determined, though much to
her loss, not to sell Cross Buns on that day, to any person whatever;
but Chelsea Buns as usual'. To have caused such riotous scenes, the
Cross Buns sold by the Royal Bun House were obviously as special
as their regular buns. Personally, I think that the buns they sold on
Good Friday were simply their regular cross buns with the addition
of fruit. It would make sense from a practical standpoint, not to
have to make two differing items, especially with the vast numbers
they were expecting, and why change what was obviously a winning
recipe? On the other hand perhaps, for this year, they just ran out
of fruit to add to the bun dough and Mrs Hand was covering up
this gaffe by trying to curry favour with her neighbours.

This recipe is based on the recipe for Royal Chelsea Buns (see page
279), with the addition of fruit and a little allspice if liked, to add
a little extra warmth. I quite like the dark speckles in the dough.

MAKES 20–24 BUNS

500g strong white flour, plus extra
  for dusting
1 sachet (7g) fast-action yeast
2 tbsp Spice Mix (see page 326)
½ tsp ground allspice (optional)
1 egg
¼ tsp salt
60g caster sugar
90g butter
150ml boiling water
150ml whole milk
30g candied orange peel, chopped
30g candied lemon peel, chopped
50g sultanas
50g raisins

100g almond paste (optional)
butter or cooking spray or oil, for
  greasing

*For the glaze*
4 tbsp milk
4 tbsp caster sugar

1 x rectangular baking tin, at least
  4cm deep (but no deeper,
  otherwise the high sides will
  prevent the heat getting to the
  buns and they won't cook
  properly)

Put the flour, yeast, spices, egg, salt, sugar and butter into the bowl of a food processor and blitz until the mixture resembles breadcrumbs. Tip the mixture into a large bowl.

Pour the boiling water into the milk and add to the bowl. Stir and bring the mixture together in a soft dough. Knead for 10 minutes then cover and leave to rise for 1 hour in a warm place, or until doubled in size.

Grease your tin with butter, cooking spray or oil. Alternatively, you can shape and bake the buns individually. Personally, I like the soft 'kissing crust' on the sides of the buns where they touch when baked close together.

Once the dough has doubled in size, tip it out on to a lightly floured surface and pat down. Knead in the candied peel, sultanas and raisins then divide the dough into even pieces. The exact number will depend on the size and shape of your bun tin. About 50–60g dough makes a small, neat bun when baked.

Set the buns in the prepared tin, making sure there is a little space between each to allow for expansion during the second rise.

Make a cross on each bun by either laying on strips of almond paste, or using a paste made from flour and water. Alternatively, cut the cross into each bun. The cut should be deep, but not reach the edges of the bun, as that will cause the buns to open out like soda bread.

Cover and set to rise a second time for about 30 minutes. The buns have risen enough when their sides are just touching. They will continue to rise in the oven, and so they will need a little space left to complete their rise.

Preheat the oven to 180°C/160°C fan/gas 4.

Bake the buns for 15–18 minutes, depending on the size of the buns, until golden brown.

Mix the glaze by stirring the milk and sugar over a low heat until the sugar has dissolved.

Remove the cooked buns from the oven, brush with the glaze and leave to cool slightly on a wire rack before enjoying.

These buns are best eaten warm. You can reheat cold buns in an oven preheated to 150°C/130°C fan/gas 2 for 5 minutes, or in the microwave for 15–20 seconds.

# LARDY CAKE

*Traditional*

Lardy Cake is a popular traditional bake, regularly seen in the bakeries in my home town, and one of my favourite treats as a child. So it came as something of a surprise to find that it was not universally known, and that the mere mention of the word 'lard' was once greeted with horrified looks. Having grown up with Lardy Cake, this reaction was a source of great puzzlement to me, because it is delicious.

The origins of Lardy Cake are in the countryside, where it was traditionally eaten as a mid-afternoon snack by the workers in the fields. Also known as 'fourses', this snack time was the afternoon equivalent of the morning's 'elevenses'. The calorie-heavy sweet dough, accompanied by a cool bottle of ale, was just the thing to keep energy levels up during the long days of harvest.

Lardy Cake is one of the simplest cakes to make, in that the main ingredient is bread dough. This is enriched by dotting lard over the rolled dough, sprinkling with sugar and dried fruit and then folding and re-rolling. The bakeries in my home town used to bake the cake as a giant slab, which was brought into the shop still in its tin, already cut into portions. During baking, the lard and sugar melt together to make a delicious chewy caramel that solidifies as it cools. This caramel used to concentrate at the edges of the tin, so for caramel fans, an edge piece was always preferable to a centre one. The centre squares of soft, pillowy sweet dough dotted with fruit had their fans also, but the real prize was a corner piece—the equivalent of two edge pieces rich with sticky caramel. Corner pieces of the Lardy Cake slab were much coveted.

I've tweaked this recipe a little in an attempt to spread the joy of corner pieces, without having to bake a mattress-sized slab of Lardy Cake, so that everyone can share. I've suggested crimson raisins, but you can use ordinary raisins or a mixture of sultanas and raisins.

MAKES I REGULAR LOAF CAKE

25g lard, diced
500g strong white flour, plus extra
  for dusting
1 sachet (7g) fast-action yeast
1 tbsp sugar
1 tsp salt
300ml warm water

*For the filling*
120g lard, diced
150g crimson raisins
120g caster sugar

1 x 1kg/23cm loaf tin, or similar
capacity

Grease your loaf tin. Cut a strip of baking parchment and lay it lengthways in the tin, so that the ends overhang the ends of the tin.

Put the 25g lard in a bowl with the flour, yeast, sugar and salt. Gradually add the warm water, mixing well, until the mixture comes together in a soft dough. Knead thoroughly until smooth, about 10 minutes. Cover and set aside to double in size, about 1 hour.

When the dough is fully risen, tip it out on to a lightly floured surface and pat down. With a floured rolling pin, roll the dough out to a large rectangle about 5mm thick.

Dot the 120g lard for the filling all over the surface of the dough. Sprinkle the raisins, then the sugar, over the top.

Cut the dough into strips as wide as your loaf tin and stack them on top of one another. Now cut through the strips vertically to make squares and stack these squares in the prepared tin with their cut sides uppermost. They will resemble bread slices in a loaf. Cover and leave to rise a second time for 30–45 minutes.

Preheat the oven to 200°C/180°C fan/gas 6.

Bake for 30–40 minutes until crisp and golden on top and cooked through. If the loaf seems to be browning too much, lay some baking parchment over the top until fully cooked. Cool in the tin.

# MARLE LOAF

*1736*

This is an unusual loaf from the first and foremost Scottish recipe book *Mrs McLintock's Receipts for Cookery and Pastry-Work*. Two different flavoured doughs are kneaded together to form a swirling blend of colours and flavours. This bread is delicious on its own, but especially tasty when toasted and enjoyed with cheese.

Almost nothing is known about Mrs McLintock, or even of the Glasgow printer that printed the book for her in 1736. Interestingly, just four years later, a similar book appeared in Edinburgh, entitled *Mrs Johnston's Receipts for Cookery and Pastry-Work* and consisting of all of the previous recipes in a reformatted layout. This detail caught my imagination. What was the back story? Was it a case of blatant plagiarism? Did Mrs McLintock quarrel with best friend Mrs Johnston, who then ran away to Edinburgh with a copy of the book to publish under her own name in revenge? Could the rivalry that exists between the two cities even to this day stem from a squabble between these two cooks? Or was Mrs McLintock swept off her feet by a dashingly handsome Mr Johnston, who married her and then whisked her away to the Athens of the North? We can only speculate.

It is interesting to note that, at a time when cookery books further south were being written by housekeepers and tavern proprietors with appropriately large quantities, Mrs McLintock's recipes are comfortingly unpretentious and domestic. Where English recipes were calling for a whole peck of flour (6.3kg), Mrs McLintock worked with forpets (a corruption of 'fourth of a peck'), which were a much more manageable quantity.

The word 'marle' is archaic, now sadly obsolete. It was used to describe the pattern of marble but somewhere along the line it became obvious that simply adding a 'd' to the end of 'marble' gave a perfectly adequate adjective. In the original recipe, each dough

was divided into four and arranged randomly in the tin, but I think
it better resembles the swirls in marble if you knead the doughs
together a little.

MAKES I LARGE LOAF

*For the white dough*
*350g strong white flour*
*30g white sugar*
*1 tsp ground ginger*
*1 tsp caraway seeds*
*½ nutmeg, grated*
*1 sachet (7g) fast-action yeast*
*30g butter*
*300ml warm milk, to mix*

*butter or cooking spray or oil, for*
*greasing*

*For the dark dough*
*350g rye flour*
*30g dark muscovado sugar*
*½ tsp grated nutmeg*
*1 tsp caraway seeds*
*½ tsp ground cloves*
*1 sachet (7g) fast-action yeast*
*30g butter*
*300ml warm water, to mix*

*1 x 2kg/28cm loaf tin, or similar*
*capacity*

Grease your loaf tin.

For each dough, put the dry ingredients and the butter into the
bowl of a food processor and blitz until the mixture resembles
breadcrumbs. (Alternatively, sift the flour and spices into a bowl,
rub in the butter by hand, and then stir in the yeast.)

Warm the liquid to body temperature (test by dipping your finger
into it) and gradually mix into the dry ingredients to form a
soft dough. Wetter is better with dough, so don't be afraid to be
generous with the liquid. A little extra flour is no trouble to add,
but trying to get more liquid into a dry, tough dough is extremely
difficult indeed.

Knead for about 10 minutes until the dough is smooth and elastic.

Put each dough into a separate oiled bowl, cover and leave to rise in a warm place for about 1 hour, until doubled in size.

When the doughs have risen, gently knock them back and divide each one into 4–6 pieces then mix all the dough pieces together and gently knead them on a lightly floured surface into one smooth dough. When you're happy with the marbling of the dough, shape it into a smooth loaf shape and place in the greased loaf tin. Cover and leave to rise for 30–40 minutes

Preheat the oven to 200°C/180°C fan/gas 6.

Bake the loaf for 40–45 minutes until risen and crisp on the outside, and the base sounds hollow when tapped. If the loaf seems cooked, but the bottom isn't crisp, remove the loaf from the tin and put it back into the oven for 5 minutes. Transfer to a wire rack to cool.

# *WIGGS*
## *1686*

Wiggs are slightly sweet, yeasted buns flavoured with spices and seeds. They are really quick to make, and take only 15–20 minutes to bake.

In the 17th century, together with some cheese and a mug of ale, Wiggs were a welcome supper for the working countryman returning from a long day in the fields. Gentleman farmer William Ellis wrote, at about the same time as Hannah Glasse, of a relatively simple sweetened dough flavoured with caraway. He claimed butter and eggs were too expensive an ingredient for enriching dough just for his farmhands. In contrast, older recipes appear to lack any such puritanical concerns; butter, eggs, cream, fortified wines, spices, seeds, rosewater and occasionally dried fruit and peel being generously employed in something akin to a frenzy of cupboard-cleaning, without so much as a backward glance at the budget.

Wiggs are also a bit of an enigma since their original shape is something of a mystery. Elizabeth David opened this little can of worms when she remarked, in her *English Bread and Yeast Cookery*, that no recipe she had come across ever mentioned the shape of Wiggs. They clearly did have an immediately recognisable shape because, in practically all the (50 plus) recipes I've read, the instruction is to 'make the dough up into Wiggs'.

Theories abound as to the original shape of these buns. Some, including Mrs David, favour something triangular, and suggest both shape and name derive from the Teutonic 'wigghe/wegghe', meaning 'wedge'. Others suggest these wedge shapes are formed by making the dough into round cakes and cutting a deep cross on the top, much like soda bread is today. Yet another theory suggests that the dough was baked in deliberately too-small circular tins, thereby causing it to rise up during baking and curl over the top in the manner of a periwig. While a most charming image, it doesn't really fit with the 'make the dough up into Wiggs' instruction that suggests the shape is formed before baking. Food historian Ivan Day notes that Wiggs were probably made in a variety of shapes, and personally favours the oval shape described by Randle Holme in 1688.

Now I love a mystery and, after hunting round some dusty corners of the internet, I've come up with a few more spanners to throw into the Wiggs works, plus a theory of my own. In consulting old dictionaries I found that Wiggs were thought by some to be a traditional Scottish bread, and that they were described both as 'a small oblong roll baked with butter and currants' (1808) and as 'a Chelsea Bun' (1782). The notes to the poem 'Lintoun Green' (1685) describe a Wigg as 'leavened wheaten bread, with thin crust, brown and round above, and white and flat below, gradually contracting to a point at each end'. An even older dictionary (1599) supports this by identifying 'wegghe' as fine wheaten bread, oblong and in the shape of the moon [*panis triticeus; libum oblongum, et libum lunatum*].

So altogether, the shape candidates now include wedge, round, round-and-quartered, oval, oblong, square-spiral (though possibly just square—see Royal Chelsea Buns, page 279), oblong-tapering and crescent-shaped. Personally I'm inclined towards the long roll, pointed at both ends, partly because of the Lintoun Green notes and partly because of Mrs Maria Rundell, whose 1827 edition of her wildly successful cookbook contained a recipe for 'Whigs' with instructions to 'form it into long pointed ovals or whigs'.

Just as an aside, the thought did cross my mind whether the Wigg might originally have got its name from one of its ingredients, because another meaning of wig/wyg/whig, is whey. Could this be the liquid with which they were originally mixed? Given the nose-to-tail eating and waste-not, want-not attitude of 400 years ago, together with the Jacobean penchant for using curd cheese in a number of dishes, both sweet and savoury, finding a recipe that could use the whey by-product isn't such an odd notion.

Of course, the fly in my Wigg ointment is the complete lack of any recipes, handwritten or printed, even hinting at the inclusion of whey. Undeterred, I decided to see whether using whey made any discernible difference by making two batches of Wiggs, one moistened with whey and one made with a mixture of milk and water. The result was two sets of wonderfully soft rolls, but the ones made with whey definitely had a lighter and softer texture. If you've made your own curd (see page 16) and have some whey to hand, I thoroughly recommend using it to make some Wiggs. Or you could make some specially, and use the curd for Maids of Honour (see page 157). Otherwise, the milk-and-water version gives a perfectly delightful soft crust and crumb.

**MAKES 12 ROLLS**

*450g strong white flour, plus extra*
*for dusting*
*1 sachet (7g) fast-action yeast*
*113g sugar*
*1 tsp caraway seeds or aniseed*
*¼ tsp ground cloves*
*½ tsp ground mace*
*⅓ nutmeg, grated*

*113g butter*
*about 300ml whey (or 150ml milk*
*plus 150ml cold water)*
*1 egg yolk and a little milk, for*
*glazing*

Put the flour, yeast, sugar, seeds and spices into a bowl and stir to mix. Warm the butter until it's soft enough to pour and add to the dry ingredients.

Add enough whey, or milk and water, to make a soft dough. The amount will vary depending on how much moisture is in the flour. Don't add all the liquid at once, and don't be afraid to add extra if need be. Knead briefly then cover and set aside to rise in a warm place for 30 minutes.

Line 2 baking sheets with baking parchment.

After 30 minutes, tip the dough on to a lightly floured surface and knock it back by gently pressing out the air.

Divide the dough into 12 pieces. Each piece should be about 75g. Make the dough up into wiggs. Just kidding. Make them into any shape you please.

Lay the buns on the lined baking sheets, well spaced out, just 6 buns on each sheet, because they rise quite dramatically during baking.

Preheat the oven to 180°C/160°C fan/gas 4. (I've deliberately put this instruction here instead of earlier, because wiggs require only a very short second rise, certainly no more than 15 minutes. If you switch your oven on only after the rolls have been shaped, by the time it is hot enough, the rolls will be ready to bake.)

Mix the yolk with a little milk and brush the rolls with the mixture.

Bake for 15–20 minutes until the wiggs are risen and golden brown.

Wrap the hot rolls in a clean cloth to keep the crusts soft as they cool.

# BITS & BOBS

There are some recipes that wouldn't fit comfortably in any of the previous chapters, but which I was reluctant to neglect, so I have included them here. Some will be useful for the recipes in the book, particularly if you want to ensure that your baking is completely home-made.

# CANDIED PEEL

*17th century*

A lot of recipes from the 17th century are concerned with the preservation of fruits and vegetables, in order that they can be enjoyed during the lean winter months. Even though sugar was expensive, jams, jellies, conserves and pickles were all carefully crafted and stored in the still room for later use. In addition, all manner of things were candied: angelica, cowslips, cherries, plums, apples, pears, eringo and elecampagne roots, currants, figs, gooseberries, thyme, grapes and roses. Today we're mostly limited to cherries, angelica and citrus peel on the supermarket shelf.

The difference in flavour between shop-bought and home-made candied peel is astonishing, and I have converted many a candied-peel-hater just by letting them taste some home-candied peel. Also, being able to create something so delicious from what is essentially a waste product, is fabulously eco-friendly. The beauty of making it yourself is that you can candy any citrus peel you like, and not be limited to just orange and lemon. It's not difficult or complicated, but I'll be honest with you, it is a bit repetitive. However, if you make a decent amount at one time, you won't have to repeat it for a good few months. Oh—and it'll make your house smell amazing!

*citrus fruit of choice*          *clean jars with lids*
*cold water*
*sugar*

Remove the skin from the fruit. Slice off the top and bottom (to make a flat surface to stand the fruit on) and then cut the peel from the sides of the fruit by slicing downwards. Keep as much of the pith as possible.

Scrape any flesh and membranes from the fruit rind. Don't worry if you can't get it all, it'll become easier after the peel has been boiled.

Leave the pith intact—it's the pith absorbing the sugar that keeps the rind juicy and helps prevent it becoming hard.

Place the rind into a pan large enough to hold it plus about 2.5cm of water. Add enough water to cover the peel. Bring the water to the boil and let it simmer for a minute or two, then drain.

Rinse the peel thoroughly, and also scrub the sides of the saucepan thoroughly as well. Why? The bitterness of the peel comes from the citrus oil in the skin of the fruit. Bringing the water to the boil helps release this oil, but it then floats on the top of the water, coats the rind when the water is poured off, and also congeals on to the sides of the pan. If you don't rinse the peel and scrub the pan well, you just end up boiling the peel in the bitter citrus oil, which rather defeats the whole purpose of this method.

Cover the peel with fresh water and bring to the boil again. Repeat until the peels are semi-translucent and very tender. To test whether the peels are soft enough, press a clove on to the peel—if it goes through the skin then the peels are done. How long this takes will greatly depend on the type and condition of the fruit itself, but as a rough guide, the number of changes of water are as follows: lemons = 4, oranges = 5, grapefruit = 6. Don't be tempted to rush this stage because the peels won't get any softer after the sugar is added. In fact, it'll just harden them further.

Leave in a colander to drain well.

While the peel is draining, make some sugar syrup: mix 1-part water to 2-parts sugar. Although 500ml water to 1kg sugar is straightforward, it might leave you with a lot of leftovers if you're not making much peel. Not very helpful I'm afraid, but to my mind, it is better to have a little extra syrup, than have to make more once you've added the peels because there isn't enough. I usually guesstimate by eye, and use non-standard measures (i.e. large mug or jug) and measure by volume.

In a large pan, heat the sugar and water slowly until the sugar is dissolved then bring to the boil and continue to heat until the mixture is clear.

Squeeze excess water from the peels by pressing them between several layers of kitchen paper—or I find that using a clean hand towel works best—they're surprisingly soggy peels!

Scrape off any remaining flesh and membranes, using the side of a teaspoon, and cut the peels into strips about 5mm wide.

Once the syrup is clear, drop in the drained peels. Make sure that there is enough syrup to allow all of the peels to be submerged.

Bring syrup and peel to the boil then cover and put on to the lowest heat. Let it stew gently, uncovered, until the rinds become translucent and jewel-like (almost like coloured glass). Stir occasionally. This takes about 1 hour. Don't be tempted to turn up the heat to speed things along, it'll just harden the peel.

While the syrup is stewing, sterilise your jars and lids, either by putting them through a hot dishwasher cycle or putting them into a cold oven and then turning the heat to 110°C/90°C fan/gas ¼ for 20–30 minutes. You can put the jars directly on to the oven shelf, or if you're using lots of small jars, set them all on a baking sheet so it's easier to remove them from the oven.

Transfer the candied peel to your sterilised jars, making sure the peel is completely covered by the syrup; this will keep it moist until required, and the high sugar content of the syrup will act as a preservative. When you need to use it in a recipe, rinse off the excess syrup and pat dry.

Seal the jars when hot and label when cold.

Any leftover syrup can be bottled and saved to drizzle over cakes or desserts. It will have a wonderful flavour.

# GUILT-FREE MINCEMEAT

*Hannah Glasse, 1784*

This recipe is actually an adaptation of Hannah Glasse's 'To Make Lent Mince Pies' recipe. Three things struck me when I read it:

- The mince pies were for Lent, which seems so unusual to us in this day and age, when they seem to be viewed as strictly a December treat, and of course this meant...
- No suet and no added sugar.
- The recipe was for both the filling and the pies themselves, so Hannah wasn't using stored mincemeat, but freshly made.

Nowadays we tend to make mincemeat far in advance of the festive season so that it can mature in flavour. Both the sugar and suet act as preservatives and so, when Christmas rolls around, you've got a jar of deliciously spicy sweetmeat and not a fizzing, fermenting jar of goo.

The downsides, of course, are having to be organised enough to remember to make it far enough in advance; making enough for those unexpected baking moments; and not making so much that you have problems storing it. Quite apart from it being unsuitable for both vegetarians and vegans.

Here, hopefully, is a solution. No suet means it's vegetarian and vegan. No added sugar means it is more suited to those who need to control their sugar intake (although there *is* sugar in the candied peel, so this isn't quite a sugar-free recipe). Best of all, it doesn't need maturing: it is literally mix and go.

The original recipe includes both hard-boiled eggs and chopped fresh apple. I've omitted both because (a) it involves hard-boiled egg, which is forever savoury in my head, and this recipe is for a sweet mince pie, and (b) the juice from the fresh apple might cause soggy pastry bottoms, plus it will shorten the keeping quality of the mincemeat. Feel free to experiment!

The mixture is gently warmed so that the fruits absorb the sherry, brandy and fruit juices. The finely chopped dates break down and bind everything together. The result is a mincemeat packed with flavour and with a much cleaner and fresher taste than traditional mincemeat. This mix makes just under 500g of ready-to-use mincemeat and it will keep for up to a week in an airtight container in the fridge, but no longer. Cooked in mince pies and frozen, it will keep for up to three months.

**MAKES JUST UNDER 500G**

*50g currants*
*50g raisins (crimson raisins look pretty)*
*50g sultanas*
*50g dates, finely chopped*
*35g dried cranberries*
*75g mixed candied peel, diced (see page 319)*
*pinch of ground ginger*
*grating of nutmeg*
*pinch of ground cinnamon*
*pinch of ground mixed spice*
*pinch of ground cloves*
*zest and juice of 1 orange*
*1 tbsp brandy*
*2 tbsp sherry*
*60–100ml apple juice*
*25g flaked almonds, chopped*

Put the dried fruits into a small pan with the candied peel and spices. If you're using home-made candied peel that has been stored in syrup, then there's no need to soften it in the pan—just stir it in with the nuts once the fruit has plumped.

Add the orange zest and juice, brandy, sherry and 60ml of apple juice. Stir gently to combine and set the pan over the lowest possible heat. Cover and let the mixture stew gently until all the liquid has been absorbed. If the fruit isn't as plumped and juicy as you would like, add a little more apple juice. The mixture should be moist, but with no liquid visible in the bottom. When you're happy with the consistency, stir through the chopped, flaked almonds. Use or store as required.

# *RASPBERRY SUGAR TO DRINK IN TEA*

*17th century*

I was enchanted by this recipe when I first saw it, because although not much of a tea drinker myself, I could absolutely imagine it being wonderfully refreshing. It's a simple idea, just raspberry juice and sugar, but the colour and aroma is fabulous. I imagine it best in tea without milk, but you can have fun experimenting.

This recipe dates from a time when tea drinking was just becoming fashionable. The Portuguese were great tea drinkers, and when the Portuguese princess, Catherine of Braganza married Charles II in 1662, she brought the custom of tea drinking with her.

Although tea had been introduced to London by Dutch traders a few years earlier, it was consumed mainly as a medicine. With the arrival of the young princess, suddenly everything Portuguese was fashionable, including the habit of drinking tea in the afternoon. It quickly became popular, with Catherine instructing the ladies of the court on the correct method of brewing to bring out the best flavour of the finest blends.

I gave some raspberry sugar to my mother, an avid tea drinker, but she actually prefers to enjoy a small lump after dinner instead of pudding.

*400g fresh raspberries*               *granulated sugar*

Line a baking sheet with baking parchment.

Place the raspberries in an ovenproof dish and put into a cold oven. Turn the heat on to 110°C/90°C fan/gas ¼ and leave the fruit to warm for 15 minutes. Remove the berries from the oven and press them through a sieve to extract the juice.

Pour some granulated sugar into a bowl and slowly add a little of the raspberry juice. Toss the sugar in the juice. You want it to be moist enough to clump together, but not so moist as to dissolve the sugar. Keep adding juice and sugar alternately until all the juice is used up.

Spread the moistened, and now delicately pink, sugar on the prepared baking sheet and leave to dry in a warm place. Stir once daily, breaking any large clusters into smaller pieces to help the drying process.

Depending on the humidity and the warmth of the weather, the sugar will take between 2 and 5 days to dry completely. Once it's thoroughly dry, store in an airtight container.

---

# SPICE MIX

This spice mix is different to any our 21st-century palates might have experienced in that it contains white pepper, but the flavour is definitely brighter and cleaner for it. While freshly ground spices will give the most intense flavours, if you're without the necessary equipment to achieve a fine result, ground spices can work very well.

*1 nutmeg*
*2 tsp white peppercorns*
*1 cinnamon stick*

*1 tsp dried ginger chips*
*1 x clean jar with lid*

Put all of the ingredients into a spice grinder and grind to a fine powder. Store in an airtight jar, away from sunlight. Label clearly.

Alternatively, mix together 2 teaspoons each of ground nutmeg, ground white pepper and ground cinnamon with 1 teaspoon of ground ginger.

# HOW TO CLARIFY BUTTER

Clarified butter is a great standby item to have in the fridge. Containing neither casein nor milk solids, there is nothing to burn or perish, so its shelf life, and that of recipes it is used in, is extended. I always make my citrus and fruit curds with clarified butter and they last much longer than those made with regular butter. I usually clarify 500g butter at a time and keep it handy in the fridge for this and other uses.

*500g butter*                              *1 x clean jar or plastic box with lid*

Put the butter into a small pan and set it on the lowest possible heat. Leave until completely melted and the milk solids have sunk to the bottom. Turn off the heat and let it cool for 30 minutes.

Skim and discard the debris from the surface, then either pour or spoon the clarified butter into a clean jar or a sealable plastic box. Don't let any of the milk solids become mixed with the clarified butter. Stop pouring when this looks like happening, but don't throw anything away.

Cover the clarified butter and leave it to cool in the fridge.

Pour the remaining butter and milk solids into a glass and leave it to solidify. Once it is set, cut around the solidified butter and remove the disc from the glass. Rinse in cold water, making sure all milk solids are removed. Add the disc of washed butter to the rest of the clarified butter, crumbling it to fit if necessary.

# APPLE JELLY
*1685*

Apple jelly is another great store-cupboard standby, because it has so many uses and is so straightforward to make. It can be used as a mild sweetener and to bind the fillings in Banbury or Currant Cakes; it's a fabulous glaze for fresh fruit tarts; it can be stirred into gravy or served with pork; and can even boost the pectin levels of jams without having to resort to cloudy commercial pectin.

The best apples to use are slightly under-ripe, but any firm green apple will do. I tend to use Bramley apples because they're readily available. Use small jars to store this jelly as, usually, just a small amount at a time is needed. Since the recipe is proportional, you can make as much or as little as you like.

**MAKES ABOUT 1KG, DEPENDING ON JUICINESS OF APPLES**

| | |
|---|---|
| *1–1.5kg green apples* | *clean jars with lids muslin* |
| *sugar* | *or cheesecloth* |
| *juice of 1 lemon* | *cook's thermometer (optional)* |

Sterilise your jars and lids either by putting them through a hot dishwasher cycle or by putting them into a cold oven and then turning the heat to 110°C/90°C fan/gas ¼ for 20–30 minutes.

Chop the apples into quarters or eighths and put them into a pan. Add enough cold water to cover and place the pan, covered, over a medium-low heat. Let the apples simmer gently for 25–30 minutes until softened.

Put a large sieve over a heatproof bowl and drain the cooking liquid from the apples. Discard the apple pulp.

Clean the sieve, put it over a large clean pan and line it with a piece of muslin or cheesecloth. Strain and measure the apple liquid through the cloth into the pan to remove any pieces of apple. For each 600ml of apple liquid, you will need 450g granulated sugar. Add the sugar and lemon juice to the liquid and stir over a low heat.

When the sugar has dissolved, turn the heat to high and boil until the liquid reaches a temperature of 105°C (the setting point for preserves). To test, put a small amount of liquid on a chilled side plate and chill in the freezer for 5 minutes. If the liquid wrinkles when a finger is pushed through it then it has reached setting point.

Turn off the heat and let the jelly cool for 5 minutes. Ladle into your hot jars. Seal while hot and label when cold.

# SEEDLESS RASPBERRY JAM

This is probably one of the easiest, and best, preserves to make. I never used to like raspberry jam because of all the seeds, but a few years ago I was given a huge bag of raspberries and decided to make jam because there were still lots left after we'd all eaten our fill of the fresh fruit. Since I was running low on jars, I thought I'd reduce the volume a little by sieving out the seeds and wow—what a difference it made. Without the distraction of the seeds it was just pure, unadulterated flavour. Astonishing! This is now my number-one favourite preserve. Raspberries are high in pectin, so the only additional ingredients are sugar and lemon juice.

MAKES 2KG

*1.2kg raspberries, slightly under-*     *selection of jars and lids*
  *ripe if possible*                    *1 x fine-meshed sieve*
*about 1kg granulated sugar*       *cook's thermometer*
*juice of 1 lemon*

Wash the jars and lids in hot, soapy water and arrange on a baking sheet. Put the raspberries into the ovenproof bowl.

Put the jars and the raspberries into a cold oven and turn the heat to 110°C/90°C fan/gas ¼ for 20-30 minutes. This will both sterilise the jars and encourage the juice in the fruit to run and make the next stage easier.

Remove the raspberries from the oven. Leave the jars in the oven to keep warm. Weigh your second bowl, make a note of the weight and put the fine-meshed sieve over the top of the bowl.

Pour the softened fruit and juice into the sieve and stir vigorously with a wooden spoon to extract as much juice and pulp as possible. It's probably best to do this a small quantity at a time. You need to keep stirring/pressing until there is nothing left in the sieve but a solid mass of seeds. I won't lie to you, this takes a while, but it's well worth it. Keep scraping the sieved pulp off the bottom of the sieve with the back of a knife. Don't use the spoon you're stirring with, as you might accidentally let some seeds fall into the pulp. Discard the seeds.

When done, weigh the bowl again and subtract the bowl's original weight to find the weight of the juice and pulp. Add this and an equal weight of sugar to a wide, deep pan. (Warming the sugar first will make it dissolve more easily.) Over a very low heat, stir gently until all the sugar has dissolved.

Add the lemon juice, and taste. Add more lemon juice, if you like a sharp jam.

Turn the heat to high and, using a cook's thermometer, heat rapidly to 105°C. This shouldn't take long at all. Even if it's not quite reached 105°C, remove from the heat after 10 minutes—prolonged boiling will ruin both flavour and colour.

Remove from the heat and pour into the warmed jars, leaving just a 5mm gap at the top. Seal immediately. As the jam and the air trapped in the jar cools, it will contract and eventually pull the 'safety button' on the lid back to its original position. After making a batch of jam I love sitting listening to the 'bink!' of the lids safely sealing in all that wonderful flavour.

# DEPRESSION-ERA BUTTERCREAM
*1920s*

If ever a recipe needed some serious spin-doctoring with its name, it's this one. Born in an era of economic hardship, this buttercream recipe manages to stretch expensive butter and sugar to go a little further but, more importantly, what you get is astonishingly good, and head and shoulders above a regular buttercream.

It's made by beating a thickened roux of flour and milk into butter and sugar. The mixture lightens and whitens to clouds of billowy softness.

Where normal buttercream can be a greasy, gritty, yellow lump, this buttercream is ethereally light, dazzling white, and silky smooth. It's also incredibly versatile in that you can add flavour and/or colour to the milk with no risk of spoiling the end result by accidentally adding too much liquid.

MAKES ENOUGH TO FILL AND ICE A FAMILY-SIZED CAKE OR TOP
A BATCH OF SMALL CAKES

*250ml milk*       *225g caster sugar*
*4 tbsp plain flour*      *1 tsp vanilla extract*
*225g butter, softened*

In a pan, gently heat the milk with the flour, stirring with a whisk until the mixture thickens.

Continue cooking and stirring for 1 minute. This extra bit of heating/stirring will 'cook out' the flour and ensure that the buttercream doesn't taste floury.

Pour the mixture on to a plate, cover with cling film, to prevent a skin forming, and cool. And by cool, I mean let it get absolutely cold. Rushing this step and adding warm roux to the buttercream will result in it becoming greasy and heavy.

Beat the butter and sugar together in a bowl for at least 10 minutes, until pale and fluffy. Do not skimp on the beating time. Obviously, a stand mixer would be ideal, but even with hand-held beaters you should still persevere for the full 10 minutes. This extended beating will get air into the mix, and the more air means a lighter, silkier buttercream. The mixture will become almost white in colour.

Add the thickened milk mixture and the vanilla extract. Continue mixing until fully incorporated, pale and thick, another 10 minutes.

Use immediately, as required. This buttercream will harden if stored in the fridge, and will become difficult to spread. However, a cake iced and kept in the fridge will retain the silky-smooth texture once it returns to room temperature.

## VARIATIONS

Don't be limited to vanilla as a flavouring; you can flavour and colour this buttercream just as you would any other. If you're concerned about a liquid flavouring making the mixture too loose, add it to the roux after it has 'cooked out' and before it has cooled.

*Coffee*
Add 2–3 tablespoons espresso coffee powder to the milk.

*Chocolate*
Add 2–3 heaped tbsp cocoa powder to the milk.

# CAKE DECORATING

I have quite strong views when it comes to cake decorating. I'm a firm believer in the food itself being the star of the show, and tend to shy away from sugar-paste decorations and the like. Of course, I also lack the patience and delicate fingers required for such artistic endeavours. So I was delighted to discover in some dusty Victorian baking books a couple of cake decorating ideas that satisfied both my personal preferences and my pointed lack of artistic ability.

Both these decorating ideas can be used to transform a simple sponge layer cake into something with real wow-factor. Bake and fill your favourite sponge cake according to taste, then choose one of the following to decorate it.

# LADYFINGER & RATAFIA BISCUIT DECORATION

*1890s*

Here, iced and decorated ladyfingers (Naples Biscuits/sponge fingers) are arranged upright around the edge of the cake, just like a Charlotte pudding. Ratafia biscuits are arranged over the top of the cake and painted with apricot glaze. Piped buttercream fills in any gaps between the biscuits.

Choose quantities appropriate to the size of your cake.

*egg white*
*icing sugar*
*2 contrasting food colours*
*Naples Biscuits (see page 101)*
*apricot glaze*
*Ratafias (see page 105)*
*Depression-era Buttercream (see page 331), flavoured to match your cake, or simply use chocolate*

*1 x length of ribbon, long enough to wrap around the sides of your cake*
*1 x piping bag fitted with a small star nozzle*

Mix the egg white with the icing sugar to a coating consistency. Divide into 2 portions and make each one a different colour. (Here, I've used orange and chocolate colourings.) Straighten the edges of the Naples Biscuits by trimming them with a serrated knife.

Decide on your biscuit pattern for the Naples Biscuits and trim them accordingly. You can have them all the same size, or have them in graduated lengths going from long to short. For a square cake, have the long biscuits in the middle of each side. For a round cake, place them at the 4 cardinal points (N, S, E, W) and arrange the other biscuits in-between. There should be 3 biscuits between each tall biscuit: 2 medium-sized biscuits and 1 short biscuit.

Dip the tall and short biscuits into the first icing, and the medium biscuits into the second icing. Allow to dry. Pipe a simple design in a contrasting colour on the top of each biscuit. Allow to dry.

Warm the apricot glaze and, using a pastry brush, paint the glaze on to the top and sides of the cake. Arrange the Ratafias over the top of the cake. You can also use any extra sponge fingers in the design. Cover with apricot glaze. Arrange the iced Naples Biscuits around the edge of the cake, pressing them gently into the apricot glaze.

Cut a length of ribbon and wrap around the sides of the cake to keep the Naples Biscuits in place. Fasten the ends of the ribbon with a pin.

Fill the piping bag with the flavoured buttercream. (I've used chocolate buttercream here.) Fill any spaces between the Ratafias with rosettes of buttercream and pipe a ribbon of buttercream along the top of the Naples Biscuits.

---

# MERINGUE ICING
*1890s*

This meringue icing is a twist on a technique traditionally used on a dessert we're all familiar with—Baked Alaska—repurposed for use on a cake. A quick bake in the oven gives the meringue a light crust while leaving it creamy underneath. Toasted coconut on the sides and swirls of piped meringue on top are filled with spoonfuls of sieved fruit jam that shine like jewels. Of course you can also use this to glam up your Baked Alaska, or to make an ice cream sandwich cake.

MAKES ENOUGH TO ICE THE TOP AND SIDES OF A FAMILY-SIZED CAKE, OR TOP A BATCH OF SMALL CAKES

*100g desiccated coconut*
*150ml egg whites*
*a few drops lemon juice*
*pinch of salt*
*1 sachet (7g) powdered egg white*
*100g caster sugar, plus extra for*
 *dusting*
*apricot glaze*

*selection of jams and jellies*

*2 x piping bags, one fitted with*
 *an 8mm plain nozzle, and one*
 *fitted with a 4mm plain nozzle*
 *(optional)*

Preheat the oven to 200°C/180°C fan/gas 6. Line a baking sheet with baking parchment and spread the coconut thinly over it. Toast the coconut in the oven for 4–5 minutes until lightly browned. Set aside to cool.

Put the egg whites, lemon juice and salt into a bowl and whisk to soft peaks.

Mix the powdered egg white with the caster sugar and gradually add to the mix, a spoonful at a time, pausing between each spoonful to allow the sugar to dissolve. Whisk until all the sugar is absorbed and the meringue stands in stiff peaks. Spread some of the meringue smoothly over the top and sides of the cake.

Decorate the sides of the cake with toasted coconut. The best way to do this is to put the cake on a wire rack over a rimmed baking sheet. When pressing the toasted coconut into the meringue, the excess will fall through the rack into the tin and can be gathered up and reused if required.

Fill the piping bag fitted with the 8mm plain nozzle with some meringue and pipe a design on top of your cake. The pattern can be as simple or as complicated as you like, just be sure to have some enclosed shapes to fill with jam and/or jelly. For additional detail, fill the piping bag fitted with the 4mm plain nozzle with some meringue and pipe over and around the initial design to give more depth to the design.

Dust the top with caster sugar then bake for 3 minutes. Turn the cake 180 degrees and bake for a further 3 minutes until lightly browned.

Warm the jams slightly and decorate the meringues by spooning them into the loops in the meringue pattern.

# HOW TO TEMPER CHOCOLATE

Tempered chocolate differs from chocolate that has just been melted and allowed to set in that it has both a shine and a snap to it, and it can be handled and not melt immediately so it's ideal if you're thinking of dipping some candied peel or Honeycomb Gingerbread (see page 113).

Professional chocolatiers have special machines which temper chocolate and keep it at the optimum temperature for their needs, but it's possible to temper chocolate at home with great success with the following equipment:

*1 x quantity of chocolate*       *1 x clean hand towel*
*1 x large, heatproof bowl*       *cook's thermometer*
*1 x pan of simmering water*

Chop the chocolate into small pieces and put two-thirds of it into the large, heatproof bowl. Put the bowl on top of the pan of simmering water, making sure the bottom of the bowl isn't touching the surface of the water underneath. Leave the chocolate until it is completely melted. Remove the bowl from the pan and wrap it in the hand towel to keep it warm.

Add the remaining third of the chocolate to the bowl and stir gently until it is completely melted. Continue stirring gently until the chocolate cools to the correct temperature for coating:

*Dark chocolate* 31–32°C
*Milk chocolate* 30–31°C
*White chocolate* 27–28°C

Should the chocolate become too thick, warm it gently over the pan of simmering water.

# *A LATTICE PASTRY TART COVER*
*1654*

This is more of a serving suggestion than a recipe, but I think it's a delightful idea, all the more so for being over 350 years old.

Preheat the oven to 200°C/180°C fan/gas 6.

When making a tart, treat yourself to a ready-rolled sheet of puff pastry and cut a circle slightly smaller than the diameter of the tart.

Lay the circle of pastry on a sheet of baking parchment and, with small pastry cutter shapes, cut a decorative lattice into the pastry, using either a repetition of a single shape or a combination of several different ones.

You have two options with baking. If you want the pastry to puff up high in a natural and uncontrolled way and have your lattice design become, for want of a better word, fuzzy, then brush it with beaten egg white and bake for 10–12 minutes until risen and golden. Transfer to a wire rack to cool.

A slightly different approach can result in a crisp, thin pastry and sharply defined lattice pattern: Cover the circle of latticed pastry with the base of a loose-bottomed cake tin. The slight weight will control the rising of the pastry and ensure that the outline of the latticework remains crisp and clean.

Bake for 10 minutes. Remove the base of the tin and brush the part-cooked pastry with beaten egg white. Bake for a further 2–3 minutes until golden brown.

Transfer to a wire rack to cool. Once cool, place the latticed tart cover on top of your baked tart.

# *NOTES*

## CHAPTER I

[1] Knight, Helen, *Lady Huntingdon And Her Friends*, 1853, retrieved from http://www.revival-library.org/catalogues/1725ff/knight.html 28/01/2013

[2] 'Om de beste slagh van pannekoechen te backen.' *De Verstandige Kock*, (1669), p19, by Marcus Doormick. Retrieved from http://www/ kookjistorie.nl/images/vk-scan/vk-c2r.jpg 11 March 2012.

## CHAPTER 2

[2] Simpson, J. P, P. M., and P. Z., *'The origin and history of an old masonic lodge, "The Caveac"*, No. 176'. Undated, circa 1905–1910, p. 31.

[3] *The Athenaeum*, vol. 13, April-October, 1823. Boston, p. 327.

[4] *Monthly magazine and British register*, vol. 55, 1823, p. 334.

[5] Callow, Edward, *Old London Taverns: historical, descriptive and reminiscent with some account of the coffee houses, clubs, etc.*, Downey & Co. Ltd, Covent Garden, 1889, pp. 32, 33.

[6] Evans, David Morier, *The City; or, The physiology of London business: with sketches on Change, and at the coffee houses*, Baily Brothers, 1845, pp.160–3.

[7] Chisholm, Caroline, *Female Immigration Considered In a Brief Account of the Sydney Immigrants' Home*, University of Sydney Library, Sydney, Australia, 2003.

[8] Simond, Louis, *Journal of a Tour and Residence in Great Britain during the years 1810 and 1811*, by a French Traveller, 1815, p. 27.

[9] Parkes, Mrs William, *Domestic duties; or, Instructions to young married ladies*, 1825, p. 87.

## CHAPTER 3

[10] Saunders and Otley, *The Vale of Glamorgan: scenes and tales among the Welsh*, 1839, p. 147.

# CHAPTER 4

[11] The other stanzas concerning the picture cards from the three other suits covering (somewhat alarmingly) marital infidelities and domestic violence, makes the purloining of a few pastries in this stanza positively mild by comparison.

[12] The current earliest known usage of the word 'jam' is in the 1681 manuscript book (published as *The Compleat Cook* in 1974) of Rebecca Price ('To make jam of damsons: Mrs Whitehead's Recipe'). Usage of the word might go back even further. A recipe in MS7113 of the Wellcome Library is also for a jam: 'Clear Jamm of Plums'.

[13] Hartley, Dorothy, *Food in England*, 1954.

[14] Heaton, Nell, *Traditional Recipes of the British Isles*, 1950, p. 77.

[15] www.richmond.gov.uk/home/leisure_and_culture/local_history_and_heritage/local_studies_collection/local_history_notes/richmond_maids_of_honour.htm retrieved 01/05/2012

[16] Ibid.

[17] Spicer, Dorothy Gladys, *From An English Oven*, 1948, p. 85.

[18] An advertisement in the Public Advertiser of Saturday, March 11, 1769, offered 'Almond and Lemon Cheesecakes, Maid of Honour, Sweetmeat Tarts'. Ayto, John, *The Glutton's Glossary: A Dictionary of Food and Drink Terms*, 1990.

[19] 'Daryols: Take Creme of Cowe mylke. oer of Almandes. do erto ayren with sugur, safroun, and salt, medle it yfere. do it in a coffyn. of II. Ynche depe. bake it wel and serue it forth'. Pegge, Samuel, *The Forme Of Cury, A Roll Of Ancient English Cookery. Compiled, about A.D. 1390, by the Master-Cooks of King RICHARD II*, 1780.

# CHAPTER 5

[20] http://www.british-history.ac.uk/report.aspx?compid=58878#s9

[21] Lady Ann Fanshawe's recipe does not mention salt, but other than this, her method is the same as the other two.

# CHAPTER 6

[22] Bright, Timothie, *A Treatise of Melancholie: Containing the Causes Thereof*, 1585, p. 27.

# CHAPTER 7

23 Burt, Isabella, *Historical notices of Chelsea, Kensington, Fulham, and Hammersmith. With some particulars of old families. Also an account of their antiquities and present state*, J. Saunders, Kensington, 1871.

24 *Journal to Stella, Letter XXII, entry for May 2, 1711.*

25 'The manufacture of Chelsea bunns should not be omitted, having been so long noted, and carried on upon the same spot for more than 100 years. The Bunn-house is situated in the parish of St. George, Hanover-square, which extends over a considerable part of the village.' Lysons, Daniel, *The Environs of London: Volume 2: County of Middlesex*, 1795. Retrieved from http://www.british-history.ac.uk/report.aspx?compid=45407 23 March 2013.

26 Bryan, George, *Chelsea, In The Olden & Present Times*, 1869, p. 202.

27 Blunt, R., *By Chelsea Reach: Some Riverside Records*, London, 1921, p. 56.

28 *The Gentleman's Magazine*, vol. 11, June 1839, p. 562.

29 Ibid.

30 King, Edmund Fillingham, *Ten Thousand Wonderful Things*, 1859, p. 151.

31 Frequently and erroneously reported as 240,000. The great wonder of the best Good Friday sales was upwards of £250. Quite apart from the sheer, logistical impossibility, given the facilities available, 240,000 would have generated £1000. It would appear that an initial typographical error of an extra zero has been perpetuated because 'nearly a quarter of a million buns' is much more memorable and impressive.

32 Chelsea Hospital, *The Penny Magazine of the Society for the Diffusion of Useful Knowledge*, vol. 13, C. Knight & Company, 1844, p. 298.

33 L'Estrange, Alfred Guy Kingan, *The Village of Palaces*, vol. II, 1880, p. 189.

34 Variously given as either 1730 or 1750, although the latter date is unlikely for what appears to be an exercise in perspective drawing.

35 *The Gentleman's Magazine*, vol. 84, 1798, p. 636.

36 Percy, Reuben, and Timbs, John, *The Mirror of literature, amusement, and instruction*, vol. 33, 1839, p. 210.

37 *The Scots Magazine*, vol. 38, 1773, p. 223.

38 *The London Gazette*, 9 February 1793, p. 120.

39 Ibid.

40 'NEXT OF KIN, IF the Relations or Next of Kin of Richard Gideon Hand, late of Grosvenor-Row, Chelsea, in the County of Middlesex, Gentleman, who died on or about the 21st day of February 1836, will apply, either

personally or by letter (post paid), to George Maule, Esq. Solicitor for the Affairs of His Majesty's Treasury, at the Treasury-Chambers, Whitehall, London, they may hear of something to their advantage.' *The London Gazette*, May 1836, p. 990.

[41] Ellenor, J. B., *Rambling Recollections of Chelsea and the surrounding District as a Village in the early part of the past century By an old inhabitant*, The Press Printers, London, 1901.

[42] L'Estrange, Alfred Guy Kingan, *The Village of Palaces*, vol. 2, 1880, p. 196.

[43] Ibid., p. 192.

[44] Ibid., p. 196.

[45] Ibid., p. 196.

[46] Beaver, Alfred, *Memorials of old Chelsea: A new history of the village of palaces*, 1892, p. 353.

[47] *The Gentleman's Magazine and Historical Chronicle*, vol. 11, 1839, p. 466.

[48] Read, George, *The Complete Biscuit And Gingerbread Baker's Assistant*, Dean and Son, 1854, p. 103.

[49] Phillips, Richard, *A Morning's Walk from London to Kew*, J. Adlard, London, 1817, p. 22.

[50] L'Estrange, Alfred Guy Kingan, *The Village of Palaces*, vol. 2, 1880, p. 191.

[51] Blunt, R., *By Chelsea Reach: Some Riverside Records*, London, 1921, p. 55.

[52] 'Some Savoury Reminiscences', *The People's Magazine*, May 4th, 1867, p. 331.

[53] Hunter, Alexander, Wilson, T., and Spence, R., *Culina Famulatrix Medicinæ: Or, Receipts in Modern Cookery, with a Medical Commentary*, 1806.

# *INDEX*

MARY-ANNE BOERMANS was a finalist in the 2011 series of
*The Great British Bake Off* and is now a successful food blogger.
Mary-Anne has been cooking and baking for more than 40 years.
She is passionate about home cooking and has amassed a library
of over 900 cookery books, with an emphasis on traditional, British
recipes. She lives in Worcestershire with her husband and daughter.
This is her first book.

# ACKNOWLEDGEMENTS

I have many people to thank in helping me to create this little taste
of history.
My husband Robert, and my daughter Sasha, for being there
through this sweet-toothed adventure; friends Carole Steele and
Ali Palmer for their unfailing enthusiasm and encouragement; my
family, in both the UK and The Netherlands; Pam Strange, Sheila
and David next door, Cath Lendon-Montrose and family, Rob
Horton and family, the staff at St Ambrose School, Neil, Tom and
the lads at Offmore Road Garage, and my husband's colleagues for
their willingness to taste-test and sample the many trial bakes and
experiments, and for offering constructive feedback; my friend Viv
Scholes for a huge effort proofreading this manuscript and making
so many thoughtful comments and suggestions; Yasmin and Sean
Limbert for the photograph of the lace meringues; Mr Ivan Day for
help in identifying ingredients; my editor, Caroline McArthur, for
weaving her magic, and the publishing team at Square Peg; my copy
editor, Jan Bowmer, and proofreader, Anne Sheasby, for thrashing
my recipes into order.